Twayne's Filmmakers Series

Warren French
EDITOR

Luchino Visconti

Luchino Visconti demonstrating how an orchestra conductor should function in a scene for Death in Venice. *(Courtesy of Museum of Modern Art/Film Stills Archive)*

Luchino Visconti

CLARETTA TONETTI

Boston University

BOSTON

Twayne Publishers

1983

Luchino Visconti

is first published in 1983 by Twayne Publishers,
A Division of G. K. Hall & Company

Copyright © 1983 by G. K. Hall & Company

Book production by John Amburg

Printed on permanent/durable acid-free paper and bound
in the United States of America

First Printing, April 1983

Library of Congress Cataloging in Publication Data

Tonetti, Claretta.
Luchino Visconti.

(Twayne's filmmakers series)
Bibliography: p. 202
Filmography: p. 205
Includes index.
1. Visconti, Luchino, 1906–1976.
I. Title.   II. Series.
PN1998.A3V5867   1983   791.43'0233'0924   82-21282
ISBN 0-8057-9289-9

Contents

About the Author

CLARETTA TONETTI was born and educated in Italy. She received her doctorate from the Catholic University of Milan. Now a resident of the United States, she teaches Italian language and literature in the Department of Modern Foreign Languages and Literatures at Boston University.

Editor's Foreword

ITALIAN CINEMA ACHIEVED its maximum impact on American audiences in 1960. Curiously, this was also the last great year of black-and-white film. The United States produced no classics that year except for Alfred Hitchcock's last great black-and-white shocker *Psycho*. Native output was overshadowed even by England's last great black-and-white "angry young men" films—Laurence Olivier in John Osborne's *The Entertainer* and the iconoclastic *I'm All Right, Jack*. But the really great sensations to come out of Italy that year were three black-and-white epics of the contemporary sensibility that marked the culmination of nearly two decades of devastating neorealistic filmmaking: Federico Fellini's *La dolce vita*, Michelangelo Antonioni's *L'avventura*, and Luchino Visconti's *Rocco and His Brothers* (in the shortened version for international release).

Fellini had already achieved a reputation among art-house patrons with *La strada*, but *La dolce vita* catapulted him out of this elitist ambience into reserved–seat performances at major theaters. Antonioni and Visconti had also been active filmmakers since World War II. The former was nearly fifty, and the latter well into his fifties, but they had not yet become household names even among American foreign film buffs (*La terra trema* was not seen in New York until 1965). They achieved celebrity, ironically, just at a time when their own careers were about to change direction, when the neorealistic techniques that they had helped to develop in the black-and-white cinema were about to give way in their own work to highly personal, introspective statements in some of the most glorious color films yet made.

The drastic change that was about to take place, not just in the career of these *auteurs* but in Italian cinema generally, was itself the subject of 8½, Fellini's first new film after an uncustomarily long layoff. There were also unusually long gaps at this point in the productive careers of the other two of this distinguished trio. (Antonioni's *La notte* and *L'eclisee* had been finished before his work became celebrated, but even these dissections of affluent decadence are a long way from *Paisan*.) The same year that 8½ brought a new narcissism to the screen, Visconti made his first new film in three years, *The Leopard*; the following year, also after a three–year absence from the screen, Antonioni released his first color film, *The Red Desert*.

Fellini's first color film and the most flamboyant of the lot, *Juliet of the Spirits*, closely followed them in 1965. The three films reflect a new preoccupation with the decadence and psychological malaise of the aristocratic and affluent classes, rather than a typically neorealistic concern with the struggles of an oppressed proletariat for liberation. The change was signalled in *La dolce vita* itself by Fellini's subtle shift from the initial neorealistic concern with prostitutes, celebrities, and the religiously exploited masses to the death-in-life of archaic aristocrats flitting through moldering palaces and the self-torture of intellectuals like Steiner, who shows the futility of any efforts to return to natural virtues.

Despite the similarities between the three directors' first great color epics, the films are strikingly different in their foreshadowings of the future courses of their creators. Fellini, in *Roma, Amarcord,* and *The Clowns*, becomes increasingly concerned with a dreamlike reincarnation of his own past and, in *Satyricon* and *Casanova*, with his highly personal concepts of decadent eras in the remote past. Antonioni abandons the Italian scene altogether and becomes the international explorer/exploiter of decadent cultures in England, the United States, Africa, and Spain. Visconti, on the other hand, turns back—as he had in the then–uncharacteristic but prophetic *Senso*—to the recent past, to the years between 1870 and 1940 in Italy and Germany.

The two nations had remarkably similar histories during this period. Long campaigns for national unity had resulted, finally, in the establishment of traditional monarchies in 1870. The countries became allies, and, although Italy was wise enough to withdraw from the triple entente in World War I and join the allies, both victorious Italy and defeated Germany were devastated by the conflict, which paved the way for the emergence in both nations of fascist dictatorships that remained allied to suffer common defeat in World War II.

Curiously, apart from the widely acclaimed *Rocco and His Brothers*, Visconti's most memorable work is not his films about his native Italy but his "German trilogy," *The Damned, Death in Venice,* and *Ludwig.* Like Fellini's three intensely personal films, *Juliet of the Spirits, Roma,* and *Amarcord,* the series moves backward through time rather than forward. *The Damned* relentlessly portrays Germany at the low point, the most depraved moment in its history. Then Visconti moves backward to dramatize his private theories about the causes of this national debasement as he traces the parallel tragedies of the artist-intellectual who tries to live without love in *Death in Venice* and of the royal dreamer who abandons reason and responsibility in *Ludwig.* The inheritors of this legacy of irrational passion and cold intellectualism are indeed "The Damned."

Visconti attempted to paint a similar picture of Italy's weakness for sentimental traditionalism and unfeeling materialism in *The Leopard* and *The Innocent,* but he never brought the strands together in a fable about Mussolini's "Balcony Empire" (nor is there any indication that he even pondered such a project, leaving it to Pasolini's generally unpalatable *Salò*). The problem seems surely to have been that Visconti himself was too deeply involved in the aristocratic traditions of Italy; as an outsider, he could look with more calculating objectivity on the *Götterdammerung* (an alternative Wagnerian title given to *The Damned*) in Germany.

In this book Claretta Tonetti ponders especially the unresolved tension in Visconti between his professed Marxism and his unsheddable aristocratic sympathies, pointing out how *The Leopard* did not, as intended, transcend Lampedusa's views, but turned instead into a sentimental tribute to a departed order. From the evidence she skillfully presents from Visconti's films, I think that the schism within him resulted from his perception that there must be a new order in Italy—and the world—that would liberate the long oppressed, but that this professed position was overwhelmed by an uncontrollable nostalgia for the elegant life of the *belle époque* he had known as a child. He knew that there must be a different future, but he longed for a vanished past. The irreconcilability of his Janus faces was vividly symbolized at the scene of his funeral, when his Marxist associates held a separate commemorative service outside the Cathedral where his traditional Roman Catholic burial rite was taking place. Even in death, he could not unite his two companies.

Trapped between a beguiling past that he intellectually disavowed and a future he foresaw with personal distaste, Visconti became more and more preoccupied with decadence. Moved beyond reason by a feeling that the world was going to hell, Visconti sought in literature and history those episodes that confirmed his vision and made them the basis of uniquely personal cinematic statements. Few filmmakers show such coherence over the whole course of their work, or such constant intensification of the images through which they communicate their visions.

Unfortunately, it has been difficult for American audiences to assess Visconti's achievement, for he has fared less well than many of his peers in the hands of American distributors. His first film, *Ossessione*, was long barred from this country because of the objections of the copyright holders of James M. Cain's novel *The Postman Always Rings Twice*, which Visconti drew upon without permission at a time when this country and Italy were at war. As Andrew Sarris has observed, our whole concept of neorealism would have been altered had we known of this 1942 film, which is the real fountainhead of the movement.

Of Visconti's other films, only the abridged version of *Rocco and His Brothers*, the German trilogy, and especially *The Leopard* have been widely distributed in this country (and the relatively quick disappearance here of the disconcerting *Ludwig* has prevented coherent evaluation of the trilogy). We are indeed in debt to Claretta Tonetti for filling in the details of the history of a remarkable corpus of artistic works that we have hitherto known only fragmentarily.

She is particularly well suited to making Visconti's work intelligible to the American public because she grew up in the same section of Northern Italy as Visconti before becoming a college instructor and resident of the United States. She is thus able to enlighten us about the significance of many details that he has worked with meticulous care into his film. We do not need to be Italian to perceive Visconti's principal concerns or to share his misgivings and nostalgia, but we do require an Italian's experience to draw from his films the subtleties in which he roots his speculations about central European history and psychology. Claretta Tonetti gives us a better sense of the richness of Visconti's (as well as Fellini's and Antonioni's) films than any number of careful re-viewings.

W. F.

Preface

I CHOSE TO write on Luchino Visconti because I find his films complex and rich and his personality intriguing. Attracted to controversy, Visconti always seemed to find a subtle pleasure in provoking gossip and criticism. His rebellious attitude animates films that entertain but seek above all to inform, to educate, and, sometimes, to shock.

Visconti's eclecticism, his fluctuations from one cinematic genre to another, and his unconventional life-style have provoked some critics to complain of ambiguity in his work. Indeed, Visconti is sometimes ambiguous, but ambiguity is not always a defect; if Visconti's work is at times inconclusive, at other times it provides a stimulating substratum on which the spectator can join the director in his creation and continue his labor. Thus the complexity of Visconti's work, in which the kaleidoscopic changes of color and shape maintain a unity through Visconti's intensity and daring.

Almost all of Visconti's films have been influenced by literary works, some of which were followed very closely, while others were abandoned at various stages to keep the intentions of the author and of the director clearly distinguished. Guido Aristarco, a film critic and a personal friend of Visconti, relates Visconti's estimation of the classics to a statement by Majakovskij. The Russian poet affirms his love for the classical works of literature but discourages people from venerating them acritically instead of considering them in the proper context of a past era and in their value for the present. And so, Aristarco says, Visconti's love for the great works of past literature is not blind: the director elaborates them and interprets them as a modern man who lives the problems of today.[1] Visconti did not always succeed in his cinematic renditions of literature; nevertheless, his films deserve attention for their expressive blending of sources with the director's personal interpretation and social concern.

After a brief introduction concerning important events in Visconti's life, I devote the chapters to the major films in the order of their release, first briefly summarizing the plot and then commenting upon the film. The quotations from the films are based on my notes, taken at screenings and translated from the original Italian. Interviews with Visconti, critical comments, and excerpts from literary works have also been translated by me (unless otherwise indicated) from Italian and, occasionally, from French, Spanish, and Latin. We have a saying in Italian: *Traduttore, Traditore* ("The translator is a traitor"). I carefully tried to avoid treason and hope I succeeded.

Claretta Tonetti

Boston University

Acknowledgments

I WANT TO express my thanks to Warren French for his inspiring and helpful suggestions. Since most of the material I used was collected in Italy, I also want to thank the people that have helped me in the search: my father, Teresio Micheletti, and Laura Raffo. My special thanks to my friends Irene Soriano and Robert Johnson for their encouragement. I am also very grateful to Andrea Effenson, of the Department of Modern Foreign Languages and Literatures at Boston University, who patiently and efficiently typed the manuscript.

Chronology

1906   Luchino Visconti born 2 November in Milan, Italy, the fourth child of a family of seven. His father, Giuseppe, Duke of Modrone, belongs to one of the most distinguished Italian aristocratic families. His mother, Carla Erba, comes from another distinguished family, owner of a pharmaceutical corporation.

1912   Starts his academic career, which proceeds with no success. He is a listless and disobedient student who runs away from boarding schools. In the Military Academy of Pinerolo he acquires a passion for horses.

1929   Starts his stable and successfully races his horses.

1936   During a sojourn in France he meets several artists, Jean Cocteau among them. Coco Chanel introduces him to Jean Renoir with whom, as an assistant, he works on *Une partie de campagne*; in Milan he produces, with the Company Città di Milano, two plays: G. Antona Traversi's *Carità mondana* and J. Mallory's *Il dolce aloe*.

1939   After his mother's death, Visconti is called to Rome by Renoir to be his assistant again for *La Tosca*, a work that was never completed by the French director because of the war.

1941   Wants to make a film out of Verga's story, "L'amante di Gramigna," but the project is censored by the Ministry of Culture.

1942   Directs his first film: *Ossessione*.

1945   Collaborates on a documentary called *Giorni di gloria* [Days of glory] and dedicates himself to the theater, producing Jean Cocteau's *Les parents terribles* and *La machine à écrire*, Ernest Hemingway's *The Fifth Column*, Jean Anouilh's *Antigone*, Jean-Paul Sartre's *Huis clos*, Marcel Achard's *Adamo*, and Caldwell's *Tobacco Road*.

1946　Continuing his theatrical activity, he produces Beaumarchais's *Le mariage de Figaro*, Dostoevsky's *Crime and Punishment*, Tennessee Williams's *The Glass Menagerie*, and Jean Anouilh's *Eurydice*.

1948　He directs *La terra trema*, his second major film, and returns to the theater with *As You Like It*.

1949–
1951　Continued intense theatrical productions, among which is Arthur Miller's *Death of a Salesman*.

1952　Directs Anna Magnani in the film *Bellissima* and in an episode of *Siamo donne* [We are women].

1954　Directs Maria Callas in *La Vestale* at La Scala; *Senso*, the most operatic of his films, is released.

1955　His cooperation with Callas continues in Bellini's *La Sonnambula*, with Leonard Bernstein as the conductor, and in Verdi's *La Traviata*.

1957　*White Nights* is presented at the Film Festival of Venice.

1958　Back to opera, he directs Maria Callas at La Scala in Donizetti's *Anna Bolena* and Gluck's *Iphigenie en Tauride*.

1960　*Rocco and His Brothers* (film) is successfully received by critics and public, but Visconti's production of *L'Arialda*, a play by Giovanni Testori, provokes problems with the censors.

1961　In Paris he directs Alain Delon and Romy Schneider in John Ford's *'Tis a Pity She's a Whore*.

1962　For producer Carlo Ponti he directs an episode called *Il lavoro* [The job] for the film *Boccaccio 70*.

1963　*The Leopard*.

1965　*Sandra*.

1967　Episode of *La strega bruciata viva*, first of three parts of *Le streghe* [The witches], produced by Dino de Laurentis. For the same producer he directs *The Stranger*, followed by *The Damned*, the first film of his German trilogy.

1971　*Death in Venice*.

1973　*Ludwig*.

1974   His direction of Harold Pinter's play *Old Times* provokes great controversy. He completes *Conversation Piece*.

1976   He finishes shooting *The Innocent*. Death arrives on 17 March, before he can edit his last film.

1

The First Thirty-Six Years and *Ossessione*

LUCHINO VISCONTI CAME to the cinema relatively late. Born on 2 November 1906 (". . . at eight o'clock in the evening. They told me that an hour later at La Scala [Milan's famous opera theater] they started another 'prima' in *La Traviata*"),[1] it was not until 1936, at the age of thirty, that he approached the medium that would be his most important and consequential activity for the rest of his life. There seems to be no connection between his early life and *Une partie de campagne*, but those thirty years were filled with formative experiences.

Interviews with Visconti give the impression that he enjoyed a privileged childhood with understanding and loving parents: "My father! A nobleman, but not a frivolous man—a cultured and sensitive person who loved theater and music. He helped us all to appreciate and to understand art. I grew up with the smell of the stage in my nostrils. And also with the smell of a pharmacy . . . because my mother's . . . relatives . . . started out selling medicinal products in the streets with a cart."[2] Eventually the cart became a successful business. When Carla Erba married Duke Giuseppe Visconti, she was one of the most admired young ladies of Milan, whose beauty matched her social activity: "Those great dancing parties," Visconti remembers, "those dinners had been lost in time. La crème of Milan came to our salons. And my mother was taking care of everything, but especially of the children. They trained us to grow up alive; I learned there to be rigorous."[3] But Luchino Visconti also learned to be a rebel who did not submit to regular studies and ran away from home twice during his adolescence. The first time, his father came to get him in Rome and, typically, took him immediately to see Michelangelo's Moses in San Pietro in Vincoli. "Since you are here, stay," Giuseppe Visconti told his son, "but at least get some education and go take a look at the monuments."[4]

19

Clara Calamai and Massimo Girotti as the doomed adulterers in
Ossessione. *(Courtesy of Museum of Modern Art/Film Stills Archive)*

Luchino Visconti always described himself as a terrible student, and his scholastic record bears him out. However, he was probably better educated than his peers due to his passion for books: "My father gave me *Du côté de chez Swann,* and it was like a fever. I stayed there with Proust, Stendhal, and Balzac."[5] At fourteen, he had read all of Shakespeare and used to present his father with huge bills from the best bookstores in Milan.

His family world was so intense that Visconti remained tied to it for his whole life: "I never felt the desire to create a family of my own. The rapport with my original family always fascinated me. I never left the world in which I grew up."[6] Of this world we can see the charm in photographs showing the family's splendid residences, Carla Erba's elegance and beauty (Visconti had her in mind when he chose Silvana Mangano as Tadzio's mother in *Death in Venice*), Duke Giuseppe's noble poise and, of course, the seven children at play. Among them Luchino distinguishes himself for his seriousness and for the "romantic" expression of his face, which becomes more and more serious and intense with the passing of the years.

In a photograph from 1927 we see him as a dashing young officer of the Military Academy of Pinerolo, where his interest in horses began. Even this experience, which may appear to be the frivolous pastime of a rich and pampered young man, turned out to be an important apprenticeship in methodology and rigor. Later on it greatly influenced his way of working on the set or on the stage: "I brought to the theater and to the set the same methods which I used to train horses," says Visconti, referring to his demanding schedules and his perfectionistic attention to detail.[7] "What are actors, after all?" he asks in another interview. "They are thoroughbreds. Nervous and sensitive. They have to be fondled or rebuked according to the occasion."[8] Visconti's encouragement and scolding of the actors, who sometimes gave the very best of themselves and other times broke into tears and refused to come out from their dressing rooms for hours, provoking more fury in the director, remain legendary. His habit of acting out the scenes for the actors ended only when his final illness forced him to limit himself, reluctantly, directing strictly from the chair: "I lost some vivaciousness, naturally," he says. "Yesterday Alain Delon came by and told me, 'Do you remember when you used to do every character in the film?' 'And now, my dear Alain,' I answered, 'I cannot do all those characters. I stay here saying, 'do this, do that.' "[9]

In 1936, a sojourn to France proved to be of paramount importance for Visconti, for there he acquired his interest in the cinema and became, for the first time, involved with politics: "I started to get close to the communists in 1936. . . . I did not know anything about communism and Marxism. I did not know anything about politics. But there was in France the Popular Front and all my friends were enlisted in the Communist Party. They clarified my ideas. At the beginning they looked at me with suspicion because they considered me a rich idiot, but later they changed their attitude."[10]

Back in Italy, Visconti tried out his newly discovered talent, producing two plays (*Carità mondana, Il dolce aloe*), and, after a trip to Hollywood, encountered the greatest sorrow of his life: his mother's death. "My mother . . . was the person whom I loved most. I was thinking: my life is finished, without her I do not care about living. But luckily Jean [Renoir] sent me a providential telegram."[11] The telegram from the French director invited Visconti to be an assistant for *Tosca*, a work that Renoir never completed because of the outbreak of war between France and Italy.

At the age of thirty-five, Luchino Visconti had very clear ideas about his professional future. He was ready to direct his first film, and he chose a short story by Giovanni Verga called "L'amante di Gramigna." Verga, born in Catania, Sicily, in 1840, is the most important exponent of the literary style called "verismo" (from *vero*, "true"), in which the writer is mainly concerned with expressing facts, often crude and tragic, without embellishment, in a form that reflects the language of the people. Verga intended to write a series of five novels that would have been the interlocking parts of a cycle called *I Vinti* [The defeated ones]. Anybody reading the two completed novels, *I Malavoglia* (translated in English as The House by the Medlar Tree) and *Mastro-don Gesualdo* can immediately perceive the reason for the series title: Verga's characters, in fact, are poor and defeated people, imprisoned in their wretched lives without possibility of escape.

These characters also populate Verga's eighty-four short stories, including the powerful and tragic "L'amante di Gramigna." Gramigna ("Crabgrass") is a ferocious brigand who terrorizes the Sicilian countryside along the Simeto. "Tired, hungry, burnt by thirst, in the immense plain, burnt under the sun of June," he constantly avoids the forces of law and order, which are desperately trying to capture him. His legendary ferociousness, coupled with his wolflike courage captures the imagination of Peppa, one of the most beautiful girls of Licodia, who breaks her enviable engagement to wealthy Finu and runs away to become the brigand's lover. Beaten and mistreated by Gramigna, Peppa burns with an irrational passion and remains with him until he is captured ("with foam at his mouth and his eyes as shiny as those of a wolf") and imprisoned for life.

After the death of her mother, Peppa, back at the house where she was born, abandons her son by Gramigna and at night reaches the prison, but Gramigna has been taken "on the other side of the sea." Peppa remains at the prison working as a cleaning woman and feeling a strange kind of "respectful tenderness" for the soldiers who have arrested her lover.

This dreadful subject chosen by Visconti was not approved by the censors, who were looking for more edifying stories to cheer wartime audiences and were opposed to representations that did not give an exemplary shine to Italian national life. But one year later Visconti, with the financial help of communist friends, filmed *Ossessione*, another tragic episode that created controversy and scandal. "At Salso, after the first showing," says the director, "an Archbishop came to bless the room."[12]

With the powerful *Ossessione* Visconti initiates both his cinematic career and also an ambiguity, or better, a discrepancy between his life and the themes of his work. It is, in fact, quite baffling to compare the director's life, which he has always been fond of describing as ideally full of vitality, understanding, and love, with the constant themes of solitude, tragedy, and the destructive power of sensuality in his films. Visconti never denied his interest in or experience of the dark side of life, but he proclaimed his faith in its positive aspects, especially when it came to personal experiences. He is difficult to understand, especially when a happy productive period yields a film in which tragedy and pessimism prevail. Visconti never really explained the deep reason for the coexistence of these two levels of his life so we will follow this fracture and switch from the memory of a happy childhood and a privileged youth to the drama of *Ossessione*.

Ossessione (1942): The Plot

The story of *Ossessione* occurs in the Delta Ferrarese, a marshy region in Northern Italy, right where the river Po pours into the Adriatic Sea. The events are very simple and revolve around the trio of almost every tragic love story: a dissatisfied wife (Giovanna), a vulgar husband (Bragana), and a charming stranger (Gino). Gino, a wanderer without a stable occupation, finds work at Bragana's inn and soon becomes Giovanna's lover. It appears to be increasingly difficult to keep the affair hidden from Bragana and the tension reaches a breaking point. Gino decides to resume his wandering life; Giovanna follows him, but, tired and dejected, she decides to turn back after having covered only a short distance.

Gino meets another wanderer, the ambiguous Spagnolo, and stays in his company until the day on which, by chance, he sees Giovanna again at a country fair. Rediscovering their passion for each other, the two lovers decide to eliminate Bragana. On their way home from the fair they murder him, simulating an automobile accident which the police find very suspicious.

A period of guilt and hostility between Gino and Giovanna follows the murder, but the news of Giovanna's pregnancy brings a short-lived peace. The two lovers decide to leave the place that reminds them of their crime in order to start a new life, but their dream is shattered by a real automobile accident in which Giovanna loses her life. The last scene of the film shows Gino being arrested while Giovanna's lifeless body lies on the street.

"I was way ahead of the school which is called *Italian Neorealism*"[13]

Anyone even vaguely familiar with the history of filmmaking would be surprised that *Ossessione* was made in 1942, at a time when the fashionable style in Italian cinema was still that of "white telephones," of chic modern gadgets adorning superficial, apolitical, drawing-room dramas about stylish people. Visconti, who based *Ossessione* on James Cain's novel *The Postman Always Rings Twice*, does not present a sanitized version of reality, but he interprets the story portraying a world where dirty dishes, wrinkled shirts, and powerful sexual desires, have taken the place of white telephones and insipid conversations.

The break with tradition and the beginning of neorealism is heralded by Giovanna at the beginning of *Ossessione*: "I am not a lady. I am a poor wretch." The quickness with which Giovanna and Gino become lovers, the woman's frankness in her disgust for Bragana ("when he touches me with those fat hands I would like to scream") and the sadness that follows their illicit love-making represent a turning point in the history of cinema. The idealization of reality is over in Italian films; the new trend, initiated by Visconti, will not suppress the dark side of life.

Visconti said that in *Ossessione* he wanted to represent the essential concerns of his work: social problems and poetry.[14] One can recognize this dual intent in the film's poetic interpretation of explosive social problems that are the building blocks of the film.

Giovanna, the "poor wretch," is a prisoner of her own womanhood. Her only escape is through the satisfaction of sexual desires outside of marriage, her one source of security. Even though, as it often happens in Visconti's work, the woman is the source of evil, the plotting, unfaithful, and instigating Giovanna is worthy of sympathy when, after a long day of hard and unrewarding work, she slouches dead tired on the chair. Her attachment to money is not greed but fear of poverty: "I was without a job," she says to Gino, "and I was accepting invitations to supper from passers-by. If you knew what it means to be broke in the middle of the street. . . . Do you know what it means to solicit invitations to supper?" At the end of *Ossessione*, a few minutes before Giovanna's death, Visconti shows us the pathetic image of a beautiful and frail little girl whose poverty compels her to work as a servant. The reference to Giovanna's life is evident: Elvira, the little girl, is a child-Giovanna, repeating the same life of hard work, fear of poverty, and repression of feelings and aspirations.

At the other extreme from Giovanna, representing total freedom from the demands of society and financial security is Spagnolo, the shady vagabond whose homosexuality Visconti presents as a political choice, a gesture of rebellion against a bourgeois society. Spagnolo's homosexuality is never openly declared, but indications of his particular affection toward Gino can be seen in the admiration with which he looks at Gino's features in the light of a match while the latter is asleep, and especially in the revealing words that he addresses to Gino when he tries to convince him to leave Giovanna: "I came by with the idea of taking you with me. If you were still the same I am sure that you would have accepted. I wanted to go to Sicily . . . it is a beautiful place. Have you ever been in Genoa? You can meet so many friends." But if Spagnolo's homosexuality is not overt, his misogyny is clear, since his main goal is to liberate Gino from the slavery of loving women: "If you stay with me I will teach you that one does not travel just to make love to women. You have to go as far away as possible. Listen to me, sail away . . . the sea air will clear your mind from all those ideas."

Spagnolo's political views are quite cautious and take the form of a personal, humanitarian socialism proclaiming that money must be spread to help other people: "Money has legs and must walk . . . if it stays in the pockets it gets moldy. You take a bite and then you give it to another who also can live." More than a Marxist, Spagnolo is a precursor of the beatniks and the hippies. He is a man who dropped out of a society he does not like and who loves the feeling of freedom that different streets and different people can give him. This figure of the vagabond, the antihero who criticizes a society in uniform, was not new in fascist Italy, for Cesare Pavese, in his novel *Paesi tuoi* (1941), had introduced the vagabond whose motivation is not a specific achievement but a strong desire to know places and people.

If *Ossessione* is an ambiguous film, Spagnolo is definitely the most ambiguous character. At times, with his nonconformism and his humanitarian ideas (even though he directs them only to men), he seems to become a symbol of freedom. However, an episode toward the end of the film, not fully explained by Visconti, casts a dark shadow on this character. This mysterious scene at the police station shows Spagnolo in front of the commissar. The sequence is very quick, and there is no dialogue indicating the reason why Spagnolo is at the police station; therefore we can assume that he was not arrested for vagrancy. Rather, he is there to accuse Gino of murder out of revenge for having been rejected by him. If so, his accusations must be at the level of suspicions since he has no proof of what happened and Gino never confided any secret to him. But the cryptic moment of this speedy episode comes in the greeting that Spagnolo receives from the commissar. The latter, a very unfriendly and standoffish person, greets Spagnolo with a very familiar "How is it going?" that introduces the suspicion that they perhaps knew each other before, possibly in a friendly way. Was the humanitarian Spagnolo already known by the police as a vagrant or as an informant? The familiarity of the greeting by the commissar suggests the second possibility. The character is left unexplained, and what appears in him as a glimmer of freedom becomes totally ambiguous, because his supposed rebellion against the system could be an act to masquerade his subjection to it. Several times Visconti said that in some of his movies he liked to develop his characters day by day, inventing them and changing them with the progression of the filming. Spagnolo first appears as a rebellious representative of a different way of life and ends up in the constricting atmosphere of a police station as a suspected informer.

Torn between the physical attraction for Giovanna and Spagnolo's dissenting voice is Gino, who hates Giovanna's static world but cannot renounce her for the love of freedom. Love of a man for a woman and love of a man for a man are two themes that develop on colliding trajectories in the film through the creation of a conflict centered on Gino. It is not difficult to discover where Visconti's allegiance lies. When Gino is with Spagnolo the feeling of contentment and freedom is expressed by the lightness of the horizon, the mysterious calm of the sea, and the relaxation of the two men sitting on a wall and sharing a cigarette. When Gino is with Giovanna the atmosphere is heavy and oppressive. This is particularly evident in an early scene in which, while the unwary husband gorges himself with food, the sexual tension between Gino and Giovanna, facing each other at the dinner table, reaches an almost unbearable point. Here, silence and glances are more eloquent than words, and the hot summer evening provides the most appropriate setting, with its sultry air, the rumbling storm, the wind, and the sound of mewing cats. When Bragana shoots some cats, the symbolism is evident: violence will occur with the inevitability of a Greek tragedy in which the main characters feel the closing-in of destiny and cannot do anything about it.

In almost all of his works, Visconti portrays the destructiveness of love. In *Ossessione* he examines this theme, particularly in the expression of heterosexual love. In fact, if it were not for the possibility of the betrayal perpetrated by Spagnolo out of jealousy and anger, the noxiousness of sexuality would be confined to the passion between Gino and Giovanna.

In an interview with *Cahiers du Cinéma*, Visconti calls Gino the symbol of revolution and freedom of thought.[15] This is indeed a peculiar definition, since it gives the attributes of the hero to a man who, if anything, is a typical modern antihero whose psychological traits are now common in many characters populating contemporary films and novels. Gino is a human being who neither conquers anything nor fights for what he believes in. Like Meursault in *The Stranger*, he confusedly struggles through an existence that he cannot comprehend. "Am I bad?," he asks a little girl. His thoughts are not free, and his "revolution" is nothing but a vague wanderlust that shows its frailty during his two breaks with Giovanna, when he follows the music of his own harmonica oblivious to the tiredness of his lover, and during his brief affair with Anita, a young prostitute whom he meets in Ferrara. Gino's fight against constriction is a mere impulse, an evaporating dream.

The elusiveness and the attractiveness of a totally free life is well portrayed in the acting of Massimo Girotti. Gino, the shallow revolutionary, stands in clear contrast to Clara Calamai, whose intense interpretation conveys the feelings of a woman who will fight forever at any cost to obtain her goal.

If in *Ossessione* we want to find a symbol of freedom of thought, we cannot limit ourselves to any specific character, but we must instead construct such a symbol with positive fragments taken from the various personalities and consequently see the image of freedom in Giovanna's strength, in Gino's dream, and in Spagnolo's unconventionality.

The Authentic Landscape of Provincial Italy

Ossessione's neorealism is not only in the story itself, but is also embedded in the texture of the whole film. It is said that at the first showing of *Ossessione* Vittorio Mussolini, the Duce's son, blurted out: "This is not Italy!" But it is Italy, the Italy of the northern countryside, also portrayed by Fellini in *La strada* and *Amarcord*. In this rustic setting, we see the development of the second theme that Visconti wanted to pursue—poetry. But just as *Ossessione* differs from the "white telephone" films, its poetry does not speak of epic adventure or idyllic scenery; rather it is drenched with the sometimes squalid essence of everyday life. Like the poetry of Cesare Pavese, it is made of solitude and silence, hard work and fatigue, morning fog and country fairs. Simple language, voices singing in the fields, flasks of wine and people turning hay in the slow winding of the hours with the same measured gestures—it is the life of simple people, of Bragana bicycling with the priest and telling him about quails and eels, of Giovanna toiling with dirty dishes in shadowy rooms decorated with images of saints and peacocks' feathers, of thirsty truck drivers and men playing *bocce.*

An exemplary scene portraying provincial life is the singing contest at the Caffè Amici Del Bel Canto. The hero of the evening is Bragana, who wins the singing contest with an aria from *La Traviata.* A strange pathos emanates from the voice of the fat man who, unaware, provides a swan song for the real-life tragedy that Gino and Giovanna are preparing that is both pathetic and grotesque because the singer is totally devoid of elegance. The music, a powerful tool that Visconti uses with flair, soars and stretches throughout *Ossessione*: from the alluring notes of the harmonica at the beginning to the operatic crescendo at the Caffè, where the tragedy is resolved, and finally to

the happy folk tunes of the *festa* at the inn, where the carefree notes
of the accordions emphasize the sadness and the guilt of Gino and
Giovanna. The dances and the happy voices cannot dissipate the
cloud of death hovering in the afternoon. When Gino bitterly says to
Giovanna: "It is not a pleasure guarding the house of a dead man," a
peasant woman dressed in black and carrying a billhook calls
Giovanna with a startlingly shrill voice, like a medieval call of death.

Tainted by the guilt of the murderers, the poetry of the simple life
turns into the poetry of despair: in the evening, empty bottles and
overthrown chairs are the only traces of a happy time in which the two
lovers could not participate. "I was in the mountains of Apuania a year
ago," says Gino, while Giovanna carries her solitude into a kitchen
loaded with dirty dishes and cooking utensils. What remains of their
lives is destined to be exactly what the party has been for them: a good
time from which they are excluded.

"Nothing is more bitter than the dawn of a day in which nothing
will happen. Nothing is more bitter than uselessness. Hanging tired
in the sky / a greenish star, is surprised by the dawn / . . . The
slowness of the hour / is pitiless for the one who is expecting nothingness."[16] This is the poetry of Cesare Pavese in *Lavorare Stanca*.
Published in 1936, Pavese's book obviously influenced Visconti's
poetry in *Ossessione*, as did other dissenting voices among the new
writers.

Giovanna and Gino savor their love briefly, as they lie in the sand of
the delta under a white sky stretching toward a horizon free of clouds.
Again Pavese's verses come to mind at the sight of the two bodies
resting on the sand and breathing the silence of the morning: "The
morning / will open up in a wide silence / softening every voice. . . .
It is worth being hungry or having been betrayed / by the sweetest
mouth, if you can come out into that sky / finding in the breathing the
softest memories."[17] But the lovers' feeling of peace is short-lived,
and their fate is leading them to the tragic ending of *Ossessione*.

Until the appearance of *Ossessione*, the ending of a film usually
supplied an answer to the problems developed in the plot. Only in
the 1960s did ambiguous endings become fashionable, bringing to the
screen the Pirandellian approach that was already accepted in the
theater. *Ossessione*'s epilogue is laden with questions, especially in
comparison with the 1946 American version of *The Postman Always
Rings Twice*. In *The Postman*, the odyssey of the murderer, who,

having escaped justice a first time, cannot avoid punishment for a crime he did not commit, bears out divine justice: God, like the postman, always rings a second time. The affirmation of God's wisdom and justice gives this American cinematic version of Cain's novel a reassuring resolution.

Theological implications do not play such an important role in Visconti's film. In *Ossessione,* religion is relegated to the words of a naive country priest who prays to Saint Lucy for good eyesight in hunting wild ducks, and who, unaware of the fact that Gino and Giovanna are guilty of murder, tries to bring some peace to them by suggesting a period of separation and then a marriage to put an end to gossip. Don Remigio, the priest, asks Gino and Giovanna to "remember God and our duties," but his words have no effect on the two lovers, who do feel the heaviness of guilt but are totally unconcerned with God and divine justice. Don Remigio's words represent to Gino and Giovanna nothing more than an echo of a tradition that is remote from their lives. Even in the brief moment of peace preceding Giovanna's death, the feeling of being forgiven does not come from God but from life itself: "We have stolen one life," says Giovanna, "but we have created another one. For this reason, I am not afraid anymore."

In the same fashion, punishment does not come from God but from life itself. God is not searching for Gino and Giovanna; only the contingencies of existence will complete the cycle of their lives. After the accident, an anguished Gino does not search for any explanation. There are no theological implications nor rational principles in what happened. It happened because it happened, absurdly because life is absurd. The fog, the wet asphalt, the carefree driving, the overturned truck and Giovanna's lifeless body are links of a chain that follows not the laws of causality, but the ones of casualty (if there are any), and create a proper ending for a film which developed under the sign of ambiguity, the mother of absurdity. These existential themes, pointing to a basic inability to understand life, are the undercurrent of almost all of Visconti's films.

In *Ossessione* we find not only the beginnings of *Neorealismo* but also some of the constant preoccupations in Visconti's work: poetry, ambiguity, and the director's delight in *épater le bourgeois.* Unfortunately, the film was denied release in the United States until the late 1970s because of the copyright holders' claim that Visconti had pirated Cain's story, so American audiences were long unaware of the films' prototypical importance both to the development of Visconti's work and to the emergence of *Neorealismo*.

The satisfaction that Visconti found in his defiance of middle–class thinking has always compensated for the disappointment derived from the often unfriendly reaction of the elegant audiences present at the openings of his films. It is not difficult to detect Visconti's pleasure in recollecting the disastrous reception of *Ossessione*: "I was standing in the back of the projection room, and I could see the scandalized reaction of all those fur-coated ladies: 'How disgusting,' they were saying. They did not imagine that in order to make that film I had to sell my mother's jewels."[18]

Visconti the rebel scorns the wealth of the class to which he belongs by selling a symbol of wealth and family, his mother's jewels, in order to make a shocking film. Moving thus from injury to insult must have given to the director not a small amount of pleasure since this episode has been described several times by Visconti himself during the course of different interviews. (Incidentally, Visconti's mother must have been very heavily bejeweled since her jewels were also used by her son to finance *La Terra Trema* [1948].)

The negative reaction of the first audience and, before that, the opposition of the censors were surmountable obstacles for the simple reason that *Ossessione* pleased Benito Mussolini—appropriately ambiguous acclaim for an ambiguous film. One is left to wonder if the dictator's approval soured the triumph. The cinematic career of Luchino Visconti thus begins with a controversial departure from the tradition of the "white telephones" and with a powerful drive toward a new style representing life, not as people would like it to be, but as it sometimes is.

2

The Italian Resistance and
La terra trema

THE YEARS BETWEEN *Ossessione* (1942) and *La terra trema* (1948) were tragic for Italians. Mussolini entered World War II with a shocking lack of preparation (the Italian army had ammunition only for about sixty days) but with the hope of a quick German victory. That hope turned sour for the Rome–Berlin axis. Of the 110,000 Italian soldiers sent to Russia, more than half perished—some killed in action, others by the freezing temperatures they were forced to endure. At home, Italian cities were subjected to relentless bombings. Calamitous events on all fronts gave rise to a movement of opposition to Mussolini which culminated on July 25, 1943. After a visit to King Victor Emmanuel III, who "accepted the resignations of the Duce," Mussolini was arrested on his way out and taken to a military barracks in Rome, then moved to the island of Ponza, then to the island of La Maddalena, and finally to Gran Sasso, in the Apennines, where he was to be liberated and taken to Germany by the SS Colonel Otto Skorzeny.

The events following the arrest of Mussolini were chaotic to say the least: Marshall Pietro Badoglio, nominated by the king as the new Head of State, announced on 8 September an armistice with the Allies, ordering Italian soldiers to cease hostilities with their former enemies and to react to "other provocations" presumably German. Mass confusion, total lack of leadership, uncertainty about who was the enemy and who was the friend, brought Italy close to civil war. Some remained loyal to Mussolini, who founded a new government in the north called Repubblica di Salò, and to the Germans. Others, the Partisans, initiated that period of Italian history called *Resistenza* ("Resistance") by fighting the Germans and collaborating with the advance of the Allies.

33

Alfio, Antonio and Vanni Valastro, three brothers of the princi- pal family of fishermen in La terra trema. *(Courtesy of Museum of Modern Art/Film Stills Archive)*

During the years of *Resistenza* Visconti was very active politically. When he could, he helped allied soldiers and hid Partisans. He was with them in the *Gruppo Azione Partigiana* ("Partisan Action Group") in the mountains of Abruzzi, a region in central Italy, and he continued his involvements in Rome, still governed by the Germans and the Fascists. Suspected of helping the Partisans, he was arrested: "I was arrested by the Fascists of the Koch group in an apartment in Rome—one of those apartments from which we would leave for clandestine actions. They caught me with the gun in my pocket. I was dragged to Pensione Jaccarino, their headquarters, and then thrown in jail. They told me, 'Give us the names or else,' They were also asking my friends for names. But we did not talk."[1] Visconti tells also of having been "almost shot."

These were difficult and dangerous times, and yet Visconti remembers them with fondness and with a certain nostalgia: "The *Resistenza* was the most interesting period of my life. We were alone with our thoughts and our dreams. Alone with the image . . . of our friends. . . . Some were intellectuals, some were workers. Their mothers waited for them to come back every evening."[2]

At the end of the war Visconti came back to his artistic profession with the frenzied outburst of vitality typical of people who have come back to health after a disease. He collaborated on a documentary on the *Resistenza* called *Giorni di gloria* [Days of glory], directed by Giuseppe de Santis and Mario Serandrei, and brought to the stage several works of foreign authors, among which were Cocteau's *Les parents terribles*, Jean-Paul Sartre's *Huis clos*, Caldwell's *Tobacco Road*, and Tennessee Williams's *The Glass Menagerie*. The theatrical activity of the late forties, successful but transient, served as a springboard for his second major film, *La terra trema*. In this film it is possible to discern the feeling of solidarity among the humble and destitute. Visconti, whose acquaintances before the war included mainly artists, intellectuals, and the wealthy, had shared in this feeling of solidarity as a result of the time he spent, during the *Resistenza*, in the mountains of Abruzzi with these people.

La terra trema (1948): The Plot

The film takes place in the Sicilian town of Aci Trezza, where the hard work of the fishermen is exploited by the wholesalers who dictate low prices for the fish caught night after night. Antonio Valastro, a young fisherman, is now the head of his family because of the death at sea of his father. With his grandfather and his brother Cola he struggles to feed the rest of his large family, including his mother, three sisters, Mara, Lucia and Lia, and three younger brothers, Vanni, Alfio and a baby still in his mother's arms.

Unable to force the wholesalers to raise the price of the fish, Antonio decides to work for himself and to sell directly to the fish market without the intervention of the dishonest intermediaries. In order to accomplish this he buys a boat by mortgaging the house.

After an initial success, a terrible storm ruins the boat and the Valastros are lucky to come back alive from the sea. Poverty and hunger are now besieging the family that loses the house right after the death of the grandfather and Cola's departure for another place where he hopes to find work.

There seems to be no end to the hardships of the Valastros: the people of Aci Trezza now scorn them, Antonio is abandoned by his girl friend Nadia, and Lucia succumbs to don Salvatore, a local policeman who lures her with little gifts.

All this happens while the wholesalers prosper and control the economy of the town by buying new boats and deciding on the distribution of work. At the end of the film, a defeated Antonio, accompanied by his two younger brothers, finds a job on the wholesalers' boats: his rebellion is over, but the Valastros will survive.

"The ground trembled . . ."

Having been coerced by fascist censorship to put aside a project involving Verga's story "L'amante di Gramigna," Visconti was attracted to Sicily in 1947 by an intense interest awakened before the filming of *Ossessione* (1942). The Sicily of Verga seemed to the northern Italian Visconti the "island of Ulysses, an island of adventures and strong passions." The world of the fishermen had the "imaginative and violent tone of epic poetry!"[3] A poetic and mythological vision characterizes these words written by Visconti in 1941. It was the Sicily of the volcanos and of the Ionian sea that Visconti's "Lombard eyes" were seeing while his heart was falling in love again with the works of Verga.

The epic aura of Sicilian life, however, did not conceal the hardship and the exploitation of the Sicilian people. Visconti observed sulphur miners, "sweating in the volcanic heat of the nearby Etna,"[4] and the frustration of landless peasants in a region where "immense domains" were left uncultivated by their rich owners.

Here in central Sicily, a film about the life of Sicilian workers took shape. Visconti explains: "Suddenly there came the sound of galloping horses. Hundreds of peasants galloped up from the horizon. The sound came closer, the ground trembled (whence the title of my film) under the feet of these battalions carrying red banners and tricolours. They were coming to occupy the uncultivated lands."[5] Unfortunately the occupation was brief, but Visconti planned to dedicate the final episode of a trilogy about fishermen, miners, and peasants to a victorious battle for the land.

The trilogy was never completed as Visconti originally conceived it. There is however a kind of Sicilian trilogy in *La terra trema* (1948), *Rocco and His Brothers* (1960), and *The Leopard* (1963). Rocco and his brothers are not Sicilians; they are from Lucania. The proximity of the regions and the similarities of the lives of the protagonists, however, provide a unifying thread. *The Leopard* returns to Sicily and jumps backward about one hundred years to a time when Italy was in the midst of an unfinished revolution that was always pushed back to the "old ways." The trials and tribulations of the fishermen of Aci Trezza start in the mentality of the nobles and of the new middle class in *The Leopard*, while *Rocco and His Brothers* portrays a drastic break with the past made by people similar to the Valastros in *La terra trema*.

In the original version, *La terra trema* is in Sicilian dialect with Italian subtitles because, we are told in the introduction of the film, the Italian language is not the language of the poor in Sicily. The linguistic contribution of the dialect, together with the use of villagers in place of professional actors, places *La terra trema* in the mainstream of *Neorealismo*, whose "real heart" is not necessarily the *Resistenza*, as Geoffrey Nowell-Smith says,[6] but is instead a gallant battle aginst the social injustices of life. Director Alberto Lattuada defined *Neorealismo* better than anybody else: "So we're in rags? Then let us show our rags to the world. So we're defeated? Then let us contemplate our disasters. So we owe them to the Mafia? To hypocrisy? To conformism? To irresponsibility? To faulty education? Then let us pay all our debts with a fierce love of honesty, and the world will be moved to participate in this great combat with truth."[7]

It is obvious that this combat to make known the truth demands a political involvement which, however, does not need to be chronologically limited to the *Resistenza*, but can travel freely across the barriers of time.

At this point in his career, Luchino Visconti was so conscious of the presence of *Neorealismo* that at the end of *La terra trema* he admitted to having tried, with this film, to give a style to Italian neorealism by seeking an intimate correspondence between form and content.[8] "The story grew from day to day, following the more or less logical order of a scenario that was more often than not suggested to me by the actors themselves," says Visconti.[9]

Antonio, the protagonist, was played by a fisherman, and Mara and Lucia, whom Visconti described as having the "grace of a portrait by Lenardo," were the daughters of a local innkeeper. Around them, the people of Aci Trezza provided episodes, organized by the director, by simply living and talking about their lives and aspirations: "The phrases were polished up and then rehearsed and recorded. In this way they provided me with every episode in the film, but without really understanding its overall meaning. When the two 'sisters' finally saw *La terra trema* in Venice, they were moved to tears by the fate of their 'brother.'"[10]

The whole town of Aci Trezza was involved in the filming of what began as a documentary that would have required the work of a week. The week lengthened into six months of filming. Francesco Rosi, introducing the script of *La terra trema*, informs us that the meager budget of the film was 6 million lire (about $10,000), which disappeared after a few days, due in part to Visconti's perfectionism.[11]

Two sequences, the return of the boats from a night at sea and the scuffle between fishermen and wholesalers, demanded one month of work. Luckily for the company, the people of Aci Trezza contributed to the constant improvisation that lack of technology and lack of funds required. In two successive trips to Rome and Milan, Visconti found more money, this time not from the Communist party, which had supplied the original sum, but from selling stock certificates and jewels. However, Visconti's salvation was producer Salvo D'Angelo, who provided the funds necessary to bring to a conclusion a film that had started with a staff of only two electricians and two cameramen.

Verghian Themes and Marxist Theories

Lino Miccichè calls *La terra trema* the only great Marxist film of *Neorealismo*, mainly because it presents a struggle that ends with no illusions of celestial solutions.[12] However, Antonio's first reaction to injustice is to join the system rather than to attempt to change it. Renzo Renzi, in a review written at a time when critics and public were still waiting for Visconti to finish the trilogy, rightly sees Antonio's individual rebellion as the first step of an awareness that

remains incomplete in *La terra trema* but that should be continued
and resolved in the other two episodes about the farmers and the
miners, in which the proletariat will not respond to injustice with
private rebellion but with a collective sense of social awareness.[13]

Because of its isolation as a part of a trilogy that was never completed, *La terra trema* presents peculiarities and contradictions typical of a work in progress. With an intriguing mixture of aesthetic and
Marxist theories, realism and mythical imagery, the film offers a
Sicilian reality in which the tension of a combat creates strife between
nature and people, people and people, people and ideas. The codifi-
cation of the conflict is in the images of beauty, in the angry voices,
and in the forces of nature that constitute the spine of the whole film.

From the very beginning, the "island of Ulysses" resounds with
angry voices of fishermen answering the yells of the wholesalers, and
in the din one can barely distinguish the haggling. The beach, swarming with people, is almost a battlefield where one group of fishermen
frantically tries to underbid another for the catch of the night.

The epopee here has its monsters, but not in the dead fish with
bulging eyes slammed on the scales, and not even in the slimness of
the tentacles of the octopus brandished by the angry fishermen. The
monstrosity here is not in the strange creatures that the immobile sea
is offering, but in that exploitation of men done by other men and
perpetrated with those scales that Antonio, later on, will throw into
the sea.

Directing the entire population of Aci Trezza in the long but
stunning opening scene proved to be a titanic struggle for Visconti
and his assistants, particularly Franco Zeffirelli and Francesco Rosi.
The latter remembers the comic but painful task of keeping a continuity in sequences that were filmed at considerable distances of
time because of changing meteorological conditions. Some fishermen
had shaved and changed their shirts at their wives' request, some
others insisted upon acting in their "real" boats, rather than in those
chosen by the director. Everything had to be recorded with the help
of sketches; since the invention of Polaroid cameras was still far in the
future. Careful attention to movements from the sea, formation of
boats, bells, voices calling from far away, voices responding from the
beach—everything contributed to a magic time that would last only a
few minutes.[14]

Throughout the film, Visconti develops the Marxist theme of the
alienation of man from work sold too cheaply to exploiters. It is hard

for Antonio to reach a clear awareness of the parasitic function of the wholesalers. At first he optimistically thinks that the situation can be changed for the better by having the young fishermen replace the old ones at the bargaining on the beach.

This is not a Marxist step, but it is nevertheless very significant because of a clear break with tradition. The old people in *La terra trema* are overtly Verghian characters taken right out of *I Malavoglia* for their resigned view of the destiny of life. "This is the sea that God gave us. . . . Since I have been in this world I have never seen young people doing things that old people must do," says grandfather Valastro. The young people are instead developing a consciousness totally foreign to the characters of Verga: they are respectfully challenging the old ways. But a more radical step must be taken. After a brief imprisonment for having started a riot, Antonio returns with a new determination.

He realizes that the wholesalers need the fishermen. This seems a very simple truth to comprehend, but it is quite an achievement for a young man whose education has been limited by a social system dedicated to the preservation of the status quo which has ingrained a feeling of low self-esteem in the working class. "How is it possible that someone needs us?" asks the younger brother Cola. "We are just working flesh like Jano's donkey." "Your father worked all the time and never complained," adds the grandfather. But Antonio is convincing: if they all agree, nobody will be able to "suck their blood" anymore. The members of his family, working for themselves, will set an example for everybody to follow.

But Aci Trezza, suddenly swept by the wind of new ideas, is nevertheless part of the perilous "island of Ulysses" and the Verghian themes, thrown for a while out of the window by Marxist theories, come back bursting the front door open.

A sea storm ruins Antonio's plans. Although the Valastros defy the exploitation of the wholesalers, they, like the doomed characters of Verga's stories, succumb to fate and the forces of nature.

Aesthetic Triumph

In the representation of the storm, *La terra trema* shows moments of great compositional beauty, especially in the departure of the men in their frail boat, shaken by a nasty wind that promises trouble. The gray heaviness of the sky lingers like a bad omen on the unquiet sea,

The fishing fleet against the awesome natural beauty of the Sicilian coast.
(Courtesy of Museum of Modern Art/Film Stills Archive)

while the wind intensifies and the bells of Aci Trezza start hammering in a mournful monotone. A leaden atmosphere wraps the women waiting for their men. Their fearful silence is broken only by the flapping of their shawls, which gives them the appearance of huge black birds unable to fly away from the treacherous rocks overlooking the sea.

In *La terra trema*, political concerns are expressed with an aesthetic care that at times distracts the viewer from the miseries of the people. We first admire tearful eyes and lonely expressions for their beauty and then notice the sadness of the situation.

However, I believe that in *La terra trema*, beautiful insights on painful matters are not to be inscribed to coldness or detachment on the part of the director, but should be seen as a tender gesture of sympathy and as a recognition of the beauty of unfortunate people. Poverty here is not undignified: it is sometimes exploitation, sometimes destiny, but the poor are victims that have not been degraded by their condition. Their nobility is expressed in their beautifully intense faces and passionate gestures. The crumbling walls of their homes and the meagerness of their food and resources are not dishonorable. Despite his sometimes criticized aestheticism, Visconti (the aristocrat) captured in *La terra trema* the nobility of the poor.

Until the storm brings about the collapse of the Valastros, the rising consciousness in the young people shows, at least in its first step, a Marxist inspiration. After the storm it is Verga's interpretation of Sicilian reality that dominates the narration, not only in the inevitability of fate but also in the influence of material possessions on the feelings of the people.

Verga's characters are obsessed by the idea of *la roba,* "property," which, for the people described, is essential to a code of honor. In "Cavalleria rusticana," a short story that became an opera with the music of Pietro Mascagni, Verga's dramatic and powerful narration illustrates the code of honor in a deadly duel that is as inevitable as the burning of the Sicilian sun. Alfio, the offended husband, and Turiddu, the seducer of Alfio's wife, silently obey the unwritten code that dictates the survival of only one of them.

While "Cavalleria rusticana" is Verga's most dramatic treatment of honor, "La roba," another short story by Verga, is the most vivid representation of an obsession with property. The protagonist here is Mazzarò, a man who has spent his life accumulating property "with his own hands and with his own head, by not sleeping at night and by catching malaria." He has no relatives or friends, but he has immense wealth. He does not drink or smoke, and he does not care about women. People say that "He was as rich as a pig, but his head was as brilliant as a diamond." When he becomes old and sick and is told that the time has come to leave his property, like a crazy man he runs out of his house and kills his animals with a stick, screaming "Come with me, my property [roba mia]."

In *La terra trema* this preoccupation with property does not reach the pinnacle of absurdity that it does in "La roba" but is nevertheless a swirling and powerful force that influences people to the point of overwhelming their feelings. Antonio, after the storm, loses Nadia's love and finds himself completely abandoned now that he is poor. Lucia, notwithstanding Mara's strong words about the importance of honor even in poverty, accepts the courting of don Salvatore in return for a necklace. Two shots show the viewer that for Lucia, who loves silk scarves and earrings and daydreams about her prince on a white horse, honor is now secondary to the little property a necklace represents. The first of the two shots is of Mara's reaction when Lucia comes home late. Mara, a quiet and sweet girl, loses her temper and slaps her sister with anger when she spots the necklace on Lucia. The other shot includes a basil plant on the windowsill during conversations between Lucia and don Salvatore. In Sicily the basil plant is a seasoning, but it also symbolizes sexual temptation and "evil" desires. In Verga's "Cavalleria rusticana," Lola, Alfio's wife, talks to Turiddu's with coquettish double entendre from behind the basil plant. In *The Leopard,* the book by Lampedusa from which Visconti derived one of his most famous films, the protagonist, Prince Fabrizio, visits a prostitute in an ill-famed section of the city of Palermo. The signal to the customers that a woman is available inside the house is a basil plant on the windowsill.

"One by one the branches of the tree dry up and fall," says the narrator, referring to Lucia's weakness and to Cola's decision to leave Aci Trezza. Cola, the second brother, unable to find a job in the town, makes the painful decision to look for work in another part of the world. While Antonio believes that since they are born in Trezza, they must fight in Trezza, Cola does not think that in every part of the world men are as mean as the ones that are now denying the brothers a job in order to punish their arrogance. "You know the world, Antonio," says Cola to his brother, "you have been in Taranto, Bari, even in La Spezia." "All over the world the water is salty; when we go farther than the rocks the current overtakes us," replies Antonio.

Antonio's words, showing his attachment to his family and to the town in which he was born, will be echoed by Rocco, in *Rocco and His Brothers* (1960). Antonio does not have Rocco's exceptional altruism, which is closer to sainthood than to humanity, but after moments of anger and desperation that bring him to seek some relief in the oblivion of drunkenness, Antonio develops a sensitivity to the community for which he feels, at the end of the film, a tenderness very similar to the one expressed by the sad eyes and simple words of Rocco.

Cola, not mellowed but exasperated by suffering, is lured away from his family by the mysterious presence in Aci Trezza of a foreigner who offers American cigarettes and recruits young men. Cola hopes to make a lot of money and to come back to Aci Trezza. We don't know what happens to him—*La terra trema* leaves this to the imagination of the viewer—but the mysterious stranger and the secretive escape of the young men from the town suggest an unhappy outcome.

The momentous seastorm is a turning point in the tempo of the film. The germination of ideas in the first half yields an intense crescendo with moments of beautiful significance: the first good catch of sardines gleaming in the nets like slivers of silver and the laughter and songs that burst spontaneously from the mouths of the people salting fish and mending nets on the beach.

In the second half of the film, after the seastorm, the rhythm of the narrative loses its intensity in an overlong account of the fall of the family. The only significant scene in the second half is the christening of the new boats of the wholesalers. This episode of *La terra trema* is a brief but graphic rendition of Gramsci's analysis of the "Southern problem." Antonio Gramsci, born in Ales, Sardinia, in 1891, was one of the founders of the Italian Communist Party and its best theorist at a time when Marxist ideas were not popular in Italy. Mussolini reportedly had said of Gramsci: "We have to prevent his brain from functioning." But Gramsci's brain never stopped working even under the harsh conditions during nine long years of imprisonment. Exceptional intelligence and courage allowed him to overcome the problems of his frail health and to produce his thirty-two *Prison Notebooks*, in which he expresses his Marxist ideas without using the forbidden word "Marxist," referring instead to a "philosophy of praxis."

Gramsci's analysis presents a society divided in strata: landowners, often aristocrats, that have no interest in the welfare of their workers, a middle class supported by intellectuals dedicated to the maintenance of the status quo, and, at the bottom, an uneducated mass of exploited peasants.

In the scene of the christening of the new boats we see fragments of this structured society. The guest of honor is an old baroness with sunglasses and a stole who is totally oblivious to what is happening around her apart from the pastries, which she consumes greedily, and the bottle of vermouth standing on the table. The priest, representing another part of the establishment in the south of Italy, blesses the new boats in front of the gleeful eyes of the middle-class wholesalers. In one short glimpse of the social structure of Aci Trezza, we see Antonio is a complete outsider: everybody is rejoicing with the wholesalers, and Nadia, Antonio's former girlfriend, is embracing Lorenzo, Antonio's personal enemy.

At its first showing in Venice in 1948, *La terra trema* drew a response from the public and from the critics that was far from flattering. Francesco Rosi explains the whistles and the insults as a reaction of the middle–class public against a "bourgeois" (Visconti) that had betrayed it. Rosi adds that even leftist critics disapproved of the "formalism of rags."[15] This disapproval is probably due to the difficulty of separating the documentary from the epic narration. Having started as a documentary, *La terra trema*, with its melodramatic twists and exaggerated situations, can be puzzling.

The cruel laughter of the wholesalers, at the defeated Valastros, covered by rags, is just too much for a documentary and legitimately poses a few questions about its truth. But if the documentary style is put aside and *La terra trema* is seen simply as a cinematic narration emphasizing the presence of injustice and cruelty, the overstatements should be accepted because art with a social message sensitizes the receptor about the often overlooked common injustice with the help of exceptional situations.

Antonio's rags, the beautifully tearful eyes of Alfio, and the half-naked babies express the Valastros' plight in spite of its exaggerated representation. Likewise, the cruelty is emphasized of some of the people of Aci Trezza who smirk at the Valastros' misfortune, especially the wholesalers who are capitalizing on the hunger of the family.

In the "bad" group Lorenzo certainly distinguishes himself for greed and cruelty, particularly in the scene in which he tries to buy, practically for nothing, the sardines caught and salted by the Valastros, claiming that their quality is inferior. In this scene where poverty and pride face cruelty and insensitivity the improvised actors surpass many of their professional colleagues. The viewer can see the anger rising in the faces of the Valastros, beaten by the circumstances but not deprived of their pride. Particularly in the eyes of the children, Vanni and Alfio, there is a readiness to fight at Antonio's side.

At the end of the film, the misfortune of the family and the cruelty of the wholesalers have a cathartic influence on Antonio, who, with his young brothers, goes back to work without bitterness but with the hope for a better world in which people will have finally learned "to love one another and to unite." The Verghian pessimism that has dominated the narration of the downfall of the family is abandoned here in favor of a more optimistic view of life.

Notwithstanding the difficult coalescence of opposed philosophies and the whimpering second half, *La terra trema* has the undoubted qualities of an aesthetically appealing film that takes a political stand and has a cultural perspective.

3

Working with Anna Magnani; *Bellissima*

AFTER *La terra trema*, Visconti returned to the theater, surprising those who expected him to continue in the vein of *Neorealismo* and in the treatment of contemporary Italian social issues. The eclectic Visconti directed Shakespeare's *As You Like It*, using scenery designed by Salvador Dalí. From the poor Sicilian world to Shakespeare, from documentary to surrealism, from Vittorio Alfieri's *Oreste* to Arthur Miller's *Death of a Salesman*, his eclecticism gave him the reputation of being an aristocratic dilettante who directed as a hobby.

Needless to say, Visconti did not appreciate this judgment and for practically all his life made every effort to disprove it by imposing on himself and on his actors a very heavy work schedule and an almost legendary perfectionism. It is quite paradoxical that his great culture, from which his eclecticism must stem, should have put him so often in a situation of not being taken seriously.

What many people could not forgive in Visconti was the fact that he was a nobleman, a very wealthy man, who professed a deep faith in communism. Indeed, for people believing that life-style and ideas should be consistent with each other Visconti's dedication to Marxism can be hard to understand. The conflict between Visconti's upper-class background and his Communist convictions, does, in fact, at times, cause the political intent to be overshadowed by aestheticism and personal concerns. After his theatrical parenthesis, Visconti returned to film in 1952 with *Bellissima* and a very contemporary subject: the development of the cinematic industry and the ambitions of those involved with it.

Bellissima (1952): The Plot

The Stella cinema company announces a competition to choose a beautiful girl who will act in the film *Oggi-domani-mai* [*Today–*

Gastone Renzelli, Tina Apicella and Anna Magnani as the troubled Cecconi family in Bellissima. *(Courtesy of Museum of Modern Art/Film Stills Archive)*

47

tomorrow–never], under the direction of Alessandro Blasetti. Hundreds of parents drag their children under the scorching sun of Rome, hoping that their girl will be the lucky new star. One of the mothers, interpreted by Anna Magnani, is Maddalena Cecconi, an aggressive working woman determined to win success for Maria, a cute but frail child in whom Maddalena wrongly sees immense acting talent. Even though Maria's performance at the first test is pitiful, the little girl is among those chosen for a more serious screen test. From this point on Maddalena works extra hard (her job consists of giving injections) to make enough money to pay for acting and dancing lessons, for a new dress, and for the hairdresser. Her enthusiasm is not shared by Spartaco, her husband, who is satisfied to lead a poor but dignified working–class life and who becomes increasingly worried about Maria's health.

The day of the first interview Maddalena meets by chance Alberto Annovazzi, a young man who works for Blasetti and who offers to help Maria. In order to send presents on Maddalena's behalf "to the producer, to the producer's wife, and to his girl friend," Annovazzi asks Maddalena for fifty thousand lire, which the woman can scrape together by using some of the money her husband has saved to buy a little house. Annovazzi uses the money to buy a motorcycle. Maddalena finds out but does not care since what she wants is the young man's help, even if the money has not been used in the way described by Annovazzi.

After Maria has done the screen test, Maddalena, anxious to find out about it, convinces a projectionist to let her hide in a place where she can observe Maria's performance and the reaction of the director and his assistants. To Maddalena's dismay, Maria fails badly, provoking cynical comments and laughter from the assistants, among whom sits Annovazzi. Indignant, Maddalena confronts the people who were laughing and leaves for home. Blasetti, however, the only one who did not laugh, chooses Maria, probably because she is not an actress but a normal little girl. Maddalena's experience has been traumantic enough to cure her of the cinema fever: she refuses the contract and gently puts the sleeping Maria into bed. From now on the little girl will be *bellissima* ("very beautiful") only for her parents.

"I made that film because I wanted to work with 'la Magnani.'"[1]

Nobody could have portrayed better than Anna Magnani the impetuous working–class woman who, with her nerve and aggressiveness, is determined to find for her daughter Maria the success that was denied her. Born in Alexandria but Roman to the core, this actress, who showed her dramatic bravura in her first great role in Rossellini's *Roma città aperta* [Open city] in 1945, was as fiery and temperamental as Visconti. "Anna had a difficult personality," says Visconti, "she was more pagan than Christian, she was vigorous and primitive and noisy. We had continuous disagreements, but not on the set."[2] Eventually, after *Bellissima* and for personal reasons never disclosed, Anna Magnani and Luchino Visconti did not speak to each other for several years, during which the director referred to Magnani as "a certain actress." The feud finally ended in a store where the two met by chance. Instinctively the actress embraced Visconti. "She was radiant," says the director. "Observing her face was like observing the expression of thousands of human beings."[3]

More than twenty years after *Bellissima* and after the premature death of the actress, whose funeral was attended by thousands of mourning Romans, Visconti had bitter words for those in the film industry who, "after her death were all there to acclaim her," but during her life preferred some "incredible idiots" to her.[4] Visconti chose Anna Magnani to represent a familiar character in his work: "the imperious and authoritarian mother," the character who, from *Bellissima* to *Rocco and His Brothers* to *The Damned* is "the mother hen who transfers her own enthusiasms, mistakes, problems, traumas, and aspirations to her children."[5]

Bellissima is a film about a film. A few years later, with *Otto e mezzo* [8½], Fellini will describe the struggle of a director torn between the contradictions of his own personal life, the expectations of the industry, and his own needs to say something relevant. With *Bellissima,* Visconti approaches the problem from a social point of view: the struggle is not within the soul of a pampered director but within the people who are touched by the rebirth of the Italian movie industry after the lacuna caused by World War II.

Pierre Leprohn in *The Italian Cinema* places the period of Neorealism between 1943 and 1950. When one deals with history, one deals with the necessity of imposing arbitrary chronological boundaries. Thus Leprohn's dates must be considered approximate, for they would exclude from *Neorealism Ossessione* (1942), which, if not typically neorealistic, is certainly a precursor of this style, and *Bellissima,* which also has distinct neorealistic characteristics. The best definition of this style was given by the director Lattuada, who called it "a great combat with truth." Visconti, the precursor, had initiated this combat by showing us an unpolished reality very different from that presented by the previous Italian cinema. Spontaneity, the use of nonprofessional actors taken off the streets, a spare journalistic approach to the facts, a social concern and denunciation of injustice, an attention to the "humble people," to those who never had anybody to celebrate them in their daily struggle to survive—all these are facets of *Neorealismo*, which represents a glorious period in the history of the Italian cinema, especially in the ability of its best directors to present the facts with a sublime mixture of harshness, cynicism, and, at the same time, a tender appreciation of life. Rossellini's *Open City* (1946), describing the time of the German occupation of Rome; De Santis's *Bitter Rice* (1948), a film concerned with the exploited life of the *mondine*, the girls in Piedmont who work in literally back-breaking conditions in order to clean the rice plant from the weeds in the rice paddies; De Sica's *Bicycle Thieves* (1948), with a script written by Cesare Zavattini, one of the greatest exponents of neorealism; and, of course, *La terra trema*, are the gems of this new and distinctive style.

Although *Bellissima* is not a classic of neorealism, it presents several concerns of that celebrated movement. Having presented the aspirations of the fishermen of Aci Trezza and their struggle to free themselves from the restrictions of an unjust system, Visconti is now concerned with the Roman working class, a segment of society certainly better off than the Sicilian fishermen but still needy. *Bellissima*, made and set in 1952, coincides with the economic rebirth of Italy after the disaster of World War II. Italy started to rebuild its industrial power in the late forties and continued this process for several years until the brief economic boom of the sixties, which saw the immigration of poor southerners to the affluent north. In the fifties, in fact, Cinecittà ("Cinema City"), the complex of movie studios built by Mussolini in 1935 not too far from Rome, flourished again after a period of total inactivity during the war, thanks to the new directors and to the worldwide success that Italian neorealistic films found.

The presence of Cinecittà, the popularity of its films, and the search for nonprofessional actors represented for many the possible fulfillment of fantastic aspirations. The veritable film fever that infects Maddalena Cecconi in *Bellissima* is spread at the very beginning of the film by a radio announcer: "Attention attention, fathers, mothers, and relatives! Stella Film is issuing a great competition. They are looking for a little girl six or eight years old. A pretty Italian little girl. It could be your and her fortune." In the next scene a crowd of adults dragging and carrying little girls presses against the entrance at Cinecittà, where a man with a loudspeaker is trying to bring order and silence so that the prospective actresses can be calmly interviewed by the director, Alessandro Blasetti. Blasetti, who plays himself in *Bellissima*, is described in the script written by Zavattini as "an emperor," and indeed in the middle of that vociferous and pleading crowd he has the assurance of a man of power, a man who could shape the destiny of the chosen one. This crowd is somewhat reminiscent of the one on the beach at Aci Trezza that tries to sell its catch of fish at the best price. In this case, however, the products on the market are the children, and this opening scene points to the subtle atmosphere of cynicism that pervades the film.

Certainly Maria could not have cared less about being a star; in fact, she gets lost in the crowd, and only after a frantic search does Maddalena find her playing near a small swimming pool, with her dress now all dirty.

Magnani takes charge of the film, displaying a sequence of emotions in a dazzling array of facial expressions and sparkling monologues. In the personality of this powerful actress there is no space for understatement—love, sorrow, anger, and hope are all expressed with unique and untranslatable intensity. From the start of the film to the end, Magnani speaks in *romanesco* (Roman dialect), which, with the exception of several slang expressions, can be understood by everybody in Italy. Visconti states in the introduction of *La terra trema*, that Sicilian is the language of the poor in Sicily. In Rome their language is *romanesco*.

Dialects in Italian Culture and Films

The function of dialect in expressing a social milieu is so important in Italian culture that a brief linguistic parenthesis is necessary. At the time of the Roman Empire, the official language of the Italian peninsula was Latin, which had spoken and written forms. There was, however, a certain uniformity of expression, which was fragmented after the fall of the Roman Empire into many different languages or dialects having Latin as a base but showing regional variation and foreign influence. In early medieval times Italy had several vulgar (spoken) dialects and one refined form of written expression: Latin.

But at the time of Dante Alighieri one of these vulgar dialects, Tuscan (that is, the language spoken by the people in Tuscany), predominated. This occurred mainly because of Dante, who recognized in the vulgar not an inferior language but a beautiful and rich means of expression even for serious written works. Before Dante, in fact, important literature was written in Latin and the vulgar dialects were limited to oral expression and a few written forms, such as songs and short poems.

Dante is called the father of the Italian language not because he invented it, but because he used the Tuscan dialect, which became the official Italian language, to write his *Divine Comedy*. Because of the works of Dante and, later on, of Petrarch and Boccaccio, the Tuscan dialect overtook the other dialects and soon became the Italian language, which even now is sometimes called Tuscan. The other dialects, languages in their own right with, in most cases, a literature, continue to be spoken, so that in a certain way it can be said that every Italian except the Tuscan is bilingual because he or she speaks Italian and a regional dialect. The dialects, however, are now relegated to an almost subcultural position. Thirty years ago, in grammar schools, words spoken in dialects by pupils were regarded by teachers as "mistakes." As the general level of education rises, dialects are slowly disappearing, which worries many people who do not want to lose a rich cultural heritage. Paradoxically, in the same schools in which dialects were forbidden thirty years ago, students are now offered courses in them.

Romanesco, the language of the less educated, was popularized in so many *Neorealismo* films that it became almost a fad in the sixties: people who were taught the "proper" Italian from the very beginning of their lives, started to express themselves in *romanesco*. The word "paparazzo," which refers to a photographer who chases jet-set personalities, is a *romanesco* name popularized by the film *La dolce vita*.

Magnani's language in *Bellissima* is a glittering *romanesco*, without which the film would lose its intensity and authenticity. To translate it into Italian or into a foreign language would be like pouring water into a vintage wine. *Bellissima* is untranslatable because of the intimate relation between Maddalena and her expression; without that language we would not have Maddalena, without Maddalena we would not have *Bellissima*. To translate the film would not be just a matter of diluting the picturesque, but of subtracting from Maddalena's moral character.

An Imperious Mother

In spite of her faults, Maddalena is an honest and faithful woman, faithful to her husband and faithful to herself. Surrounded at times by the mendacity of people who are trying very hard to impress the world by being what they are not, Maddalena never compromises her identity. She is a working–class woman from Prenestino, a working-class quarter of Rome, and even though she wants a better future for her daughter with every fiber of her body, we know that Maddalena will always be herself.

Maddalena's encounter with Tilde Sperlanzoni confronts her with a woman who, by trying to be what she is not, makes nothing of herself but a caricature, while Maddalena, even in her most irrational moments, always maintains her dignity. Tilde Sperlanzoni appears, uninvited, at Maddalena's house with the intention of giving acting lessons to Maria. She introduces herself as "Tilde Sperlanzoni, the actress," yet she takes advantage of a momentary absence of Maddalena, to gulp down the contents of two eggs after perforating their shells with a pin. The episode has its particular charm: Maddalena, who understands Sperlanzoni's problem, is trying to be complacent with a delightful irony, and Sperlanzoni continues to play the great actress by expressing herself in theatrical Italian. Maria, who is usually silent, holds the empty shell of the egg up to her mother, saying, "Mamma, the lady ate the egg."

That empty shell, symbol of her misery, does not deflate Sperlanzoni's ego. The actress, deaf to Maddalena's protests, brings Maria into the garden and, as a first acting lesson, tells the girl to pick imaginary strawberries under an imaginary oak tree. Maddalena follows the lesson from the window: "Who sent this crazy woman? What oak tree? You are turning my child into an idiot."

Even though Maddalena considers Sperlanzoni *una matta* ("a crazy woman"), she hires her because her determination to have Maria chosen overcomes her reason. Maddalena at this point perfectly fits the definition of women given by Visconti: "Women are marvelous and passionate creatures. But they lack rationality and they often provoke disorder and commotion."[6] Certainly not everyone would agree on the universality of this definition; in *Bellissima*, however, this is exactly what Maddalena-Magnani is: a passionate creature who creates commotion. Her passion is undoubtedly her daughter, whom she sees as *bellissima*, bright, and talented. At times she is a little worried, because Maria stammers and lisps and, at the dancing school, the little girl can hardly raise her leg to the bar. "Excuse me, madam" she says to the dance teacher, another Sperlanzoni-like creature, "but are you going to keep her all the time attached to the wall?" At the teacher's remark that Maria's legs are weak and that, after all, "one must dance with the brain also," Maddalena angrily answers that her daughter "was not born stupid," and that she should know because she is the mother. Because she is the mother Maddalena does not see that Maria is simply a quiet little girl who is being traumatized by the commotion and who does not seem to have any acting talent.

At the first interview with Blasetti, after which Maria is chosen along with many others for a screen test, Maddalena directs her like an orchestra maestro. Maria monotonously and almost incomprehensibly recites a poem. The choice is also infelicitous since the poem "Venice" tells of an enemy siege of the city, which is forced to capitulate because of lack of food and spreading pestilence. "Venice, your last hour has arrived—illustrious martyr you are lost," Maria recites pitifully under Maddalena's loving eyes. At first the scene is comic because Maria is the opposite of what a little actress should be, the funereal content of the poem is the opposite of what should have been chosen, and Maddalena's satisfaction with her daughter's performance outrageously contradicts an objective judgment. "She never recited it this well, not even at Christmas," Maddalena says, beaming. But hilarity is just the first impact of this scene, because when we reflect on it, all we feel is sadness for the little girl displayed as a product on the market and for Maddalena's passion, which does not permit her to see the ridiculous situation in which she has put herself and her daughter. The humor of the episode "seems smile, but it is pain," as Pirandello writes in his celebrated essay on humor which, willingly or not, Visconti could not have illustrated better.

Maddalena, who is usually very sharp in understanding people's intentions and feelings, does not understand the failure of Maria's performance. Spartaco, on the other hand, is very skeptical from the beginning. Visconti often said that Spartaco is the "positive" character, the one that will never be contaminated by bourgeois desires of success. Actually, this character does not have enough relevance in *Bellissima* to justify Visconti's judgment. His appearances are quite brief and, although he seems to be a loving father and a stable man, his actions or inactions, especially in relation to Maddalena, leave a lot to be desired. We first see him in the film when, aggravated by Maddalena's absence, he wonders whether or not to go to the soccer match. If in the 1950s his personality could have been seen in a positive light involving also his role as a husband, nowadays he sometimes appears rather brutish. "We'll talk about it tonight," he threateningly says to Maddalena and indeed, in a moment of anger, he pushes Maddalena around: "Here we are not eating anymore, we are not sleeping. . . . Watch it Maddalena, or I'll kill you."

Actually what Spartaco is doing is not uncommon in men who have been brought up with the idea that their wives must give them total obedience, and it is only the fact that Spartaco really loves Maddalena that prevents him from acting in a worse manner. Maddalena's vitality is too much for Spartaco, who is strictly tied to his family, ruled by a "hen" mother who puts extra pressure on her son. "Your wife is crazy. Tell her that she is crazy. You must demand respect," she says. "At least for once make her respect you," echoes Spartaco's brother Franco. Only if more space had been given to him, to express his essentially good values and his sincerity in opposition to the falsity represented by the hangers-on that Maddalena meets, could Spartaco have been the positive character that Visconti wanted; unfortunately his positiveness is one of noninvolvement. Spartaco is skeptical about Maria's chances for stardom because he does not try anything out of the solid but narrow values that he has received from his own mother.

Alberto Annovazzi also has a mother "hen." "She does nothing but say to me, 'Get busy, get busy, get busy,' and I get busy and she knows it; I don't let anything that comes close to me escape me, I don't have any illusions, but I don't want to have any regret," he tells Maddalena. Walter Chiari, who interprets Annovazzi, renders a very good portrait of the typical *cinematografaro*, a man who hangs around the movie set and helps wherever his help is needed. Among the *cinematografari*, Annovazzi is privileged because he sits with Blasetti's assistants. He is a master of opportunism. With boyish charm and mischievousness, Annovazzi takes fifty thousand lire from Maddalena, attends a dinner at the inn of Maddalena's mother-in-law, and later propositions Maddalena.

Here the *cinematografaro* is sincere and Maddalena, probably recognizing in his spunk some of her own, comes very close to accepting his proposal. Annovazzi's cynical but amusing spirit is, in fact, much more exciting than her husband's dull morality. "What a son of a good woman you are" (good woman in Roman slang means prostitute), says Maddalena, laughing at Annovazzi after he brushes off with levity the story of the motorcycle. "I know that you love your husband," he says to her, "but in this moment we feel good together. Listen Maddalena, have you ever tried to let yourself go sometimes . . . to do something absurd . . . like rich people do when they throw money away. . . ." A fiery woman like Maddalena cannot be insensitive to these words, and for a moment her eyes look suddenly tired and on her face appears a longing expression, but she quickly recovers from that "moment of weakness" and finds her sparkling Roman wit: "I have to go. You can stay here counting ants if you like. Do you want me to send you my mother-in-law. . . ?"

Maddalena remains faithful to her husband and to herself. Having overcome Spartaco's opposition and Annovazzi's courting, she single-mindedly pursues her goal. She drags Maria (how, by the way, did Visconti choose her?) like a doll, constantly talking to her, combing her hair, smoothing the wrinkles of her dress. She pushes through crowds and enters doors with the impact of a bulldozer. Maddalena has a fleeting premonition of what is about to happen when she recognizes an employee she saw in the film *Sotto il sole di Roma* [Under the sun of Rome]. "Are you working in the film with my child?" Maddalena asks the young woman. "No, I work at the assembling. I thought that I was so beautiful, so good and here I am; nobody called me any more." For the first time, Maddalena is assailed by doubts. Her expression turns from very pensive to very sad, and it seems that she is about to cry.

The next scene is marked by cruelty. *Bellissima*, in fact, is not only a film about the making of a film and about the ambition of an imperious mother; it is also about human cruelty, apparent at Maria's first interview and painfully evident at the screen test. Maria, pathetically awkward, appears on the screen with heavy makeup and a terrible haircut. She is so tiny (the part requires a seven– or eight–year–old girl, and Maria is only six and small for her age) and scared that she is unable to blow out the candles on a birthday cake. The assistants start to laugh at the little girl's failure, while Annovazzi, to protect his own job, denies having coached her. Maria, whose eyes are becoming more and more teary, starts the poem "Venice" and then bursts into tears. Her crying generates more laughter and cruel comments: "She stammers." "She is a dwarf." The only person who does not join the hilarity is director Blasetti, who is obviously irritated by such behavior and angrily fires Annovazzi.

Watching Magnani following her daughter's performance and the reaction of the small audience is an experience per se. Her face, especially her eyes, reflect in a dramatic way the combat in her soul: the hope, the unpleasant surprise, the disappointment, the sadness, the pain, and finally the anger succeed one another in a dramatic sequence that only a great actress could produce. At the first laughter Maddalena still has the spirit to hope, and with a forced smile she says to Maria, "They are enjoying themselves. Maybe you can make people laugh. Who knows?" She covers Maria's eyes with her hand to protect the child from the cruel mockery, but Maria has seen enough already. After the ordeal, Maria falls into a deep sleep, as if to say, "I've had enough. Now let me rest." Before she leaves, Maddalena confronts the laughing people: "Why do you laugh about this little girl? Why does she make you laugh so much? She is a little girl like the other little girls. Don't you have any respect for other people's feelings?"

The Squalor of the Cinematic World

Visconti's image of the cinematic world is certainly not flattering. With the exception of Blasetti, the members of the film company appear to be unfeeling and cynical *cinematografari*. Through the cinematic medium the director shows the falseness of the cinematic world; in a way, the cinema exposes itself. Its courage exposes its cowardice and this paradoxical situation is created by Visconti, the iconoclast, who, in the conflict between the world of dreams made of celluloid and the world of frustrated by honest reality, puts himself uncompromisingly on the side of the latter. Visconti's conviction did not change with the years: "If I should repeat that film," he said in 1974, "today I'll be much more pessimistic and much harder. There is so much presumption around, so much imitation, and since the ideas have been lost, the only way out is resorting to crass pornography and to disgusting violence to fill the absolute emptiness."[7] In *Bellissima*, the picture depicted by Visconti is not this dismal, but certainly the director has put in a world that seems to offer so much to Maddalena a great deal of cynicism and cruelty.

Cinecittà, however, is not the focus of Visconti's film. This world exists only to provide a setting for Maddalena's dream. *Bellissima*, as Visconti says, was mainly filmed so that he could work with Anna Magnani, who unquestionably is the great star of this film. Having kicked the *cinematografari* out of her house ("We are keeping our daughter. I did not put her into this world to make anybody laugh. For me and for her father she is so beautiful, so beautiful."), Maddalena apologizes to Spartaco for having created all that commotion and for having used the family's savings. She will go back to her work of giving injections and she will replace the money that she has lost, "even if I'll have to kill myself from work, even if I have to make all Rome come down with diabetes." Knowing Maddalena's determination, "all Rome" should start worrying.

A moving film, especially because of Anna Magnani's interpretation, *Bellissima* presents typical Viscontian touches like the aria "Quanto è bella quanto è cara" [How beautiful, how dear] from *Elisir d'amore*, by Donizetti, which opens and closes the film, and the abrasive intensity in the scenes of Maria's interview and screen test. Well–constructed, predictable, but entertaining, *Bellissima*, is one of Visconti's minor successes.

4

Operatic Melodrama *(Senso)* and a Dreamlike Vacation *(White Nights)*

VISCONTI CONTINUED his work with Anna Magnani, directing her in a short episode of *Siamo donne* [We are women], in which Roberto Rosselini also participated. Then, with a typical change of genre, he turned to opera, where he began his association with another star, Maria Callas. Directing the famous soprano, who in 1953 was about to reach the peak of her splendid career, was indeed a pleasure for Visconti, who always nourished a great love for music. He particularly enjoyed opera, which he had learned to appreciate very early in his life: "My mother's family was a family of musicians. I played the cello, my brother the violin and the piano. We had formed a quartet and my mother was directing us."[1] From 1953 to 1954, Visconti was at La Scala theater, a symbol of the cultural life of Milan, as the director of Maria Callas in Spontini's *La Vestale,* the first performance of which was attended and applauded by another giant, Arturo Toscanini.

Visconti would return to opera, but after his year at La Scala he was ready to return to the cinema. "Cinema, theater, opera—the problem of giving life to a representation is always the same. But there is more independence and freedom in cinema. Sometimes making a film I was dreaming about opera."[2] Cinema, theater, and opera—like clear streams these different genres converge in *Senso,* Visconti's fourth major film.

Senso (1954): The Plot

During a political demonstration in 1866 at La Fenice, Venice's opera theater, Franz Mahler, a lieutenant in the occupying Austrian army, sarcastically says that "Italians make wars with leaflets and

61

mandolins." Enraged by the remark, Roberto Ussoni, an Italian patriot and an organizer of the demonstration, challenges the Austrian to a duel.

Countess Livia Serpieri deeply admires her cousin, Roberto, with whom she shares the dream of a united Italy, free of foreign invaders. Roberto is condemned to one year of exile, but he continues to work with groups of patriots that are anxiously waiting for Italy to declare war on Austria. In the meantime, Livia meets Franz Mahler, and between the two "enemies" a love affair develops, submerging Livia in a passion that makes her forget the patriotic cause.

When the war starts, Franz, afraid of being killed or maimed, asks Livia for money to pay corrupt doctors that will provide a dispensation from the duties of war. Livia gives Franz the money raised by Italian patriots, and Franz leaves to buy his safety at the vigil of the battle of Custoza. Roberto Ussoni, on the other side, pleads with the Italian military establishment for a chance to fight, but the regular army refuses the help of the volunteer forces.

After the battle, won by the Austrians, Livia decides to meet her lover in Verona and finds Franz in a dirty rented room in the company of a prostitute. Made cruel by wine and remorse, the once charming lieutenant insults and humiliates Livia. Livia runs to the Austrian headquarters and denounces Franz, who is quickly executed as a deserter while Livia feverishly runs away through the dark streets of Verona.

"Long live VERDI also meant 'long live Giuseppe Verdi'"

Venice in 1866 was still occupied by Austrian soldiers, but the atmosphere of political restlessness was a prelude to the Third War of Independence, which united Venice and its territory to Italy in another of the fatiguing steps toward the complete unification accomplished in 1870 with the occupation of Rome.

This period of Italian history, which saw an end to small independent states and foreign occupation, is called *Risorgimento*. It officially started in 1848, with the First War of Independence, when the Italian forces of the Piedmontese army led by King Carl Albert attacked the Austrians that occupied Lombardy and Veneto, the territory around Venice. The Second War of Independence, fought in 1860, is known for the expedition of Garibaldi, the hero of the *Risorgimento*, who, with about a thousand volunteers, disembarked in Sicily and terminated the Bourbon domination of the Kingdom of the Two Sicilies, which included Naples.

While Garibaldi and his soldiers, the Red Shirts, were fighting in the south, King Victor Emmanuel of Piedmonte, who succeeded his father Carl Albert after defeating the Austrians in Lombardy with the help of Napoleon III, emperor of France, moved toward Garibaldi and met him at Teano, in southern Italy.

It was a friendly meeting during which Garibaldi, whose desire was to enter Rome, still a possession of the Pope, saluted Victor Emmanuel as first king of Italy. The year was 1860, the highlight of the *Risorgimento.* This patriotic movement had started unofficially years before, if not on the battlefield, at least in the hearts and in the minds of patriotic intellectuals who evaded the censorship of the occupying foreign power.

During the *Risorgimento,* art and politics were closely related. Artists expressed the people's yearning for independence and often started political demonstrations and riots, particularly through opera. Among the composers, the favorite was Giuseppe Verdi, whose emotionally rousing music told the story of oppressed people struggling for freedom and unity and provoked insurrections that started at La Scala and continued into the streets. The Austrian authorities could not prevent Verdi from writing music about the longing of the Jewish people for their land in *Nabucco,* because the musician could not be held responsible for the audience's interpretation. Any reference to oppression, any call to war and freedom stirred the audiences of that time.

Since open references to the unification of Italy were outlawed, and patriots were persecuted, the people found a meaningful but safe way to express themselves politically with the cry of *Viva Verdi* ("Long live Verdi"), mainly because the name Verdi is an acronym for *Vittorio Emanuele Re d'Italia* ("Victor Emmanuel, King of Italy"). Therefore, when people cried "Long live Verdi," they were not only expressing their enthusiasm for the composer, they were also saying, "Long live Victor Emmanuel, King of United Italy!"

In fact, the second meaning came to prevail over the evident one, which, perhaps because of its clarity, lost its impact in that time of conspiracy and ferment.

With *Senso,* Visconti tells us that "Viva Verdi" also meant "Viva Giuseppe Verdi," the musician. Opera, in fact, provides one of three streams (the others—a melodramatic love story and the background

of the Third War of Independence) that converge into the creation of
Senso, which, from the opening scene, shows its themes beautifully
intertwined. The golden opera theater of La Fenice in Venice
vibrates with the stirring music of Verdi's *Il Trovatore*; the opera stage
is stunning, and its vivid red and blue colors are repeated throughout
the film to emphasize the parallel between the melodramas on stage
and off the stage. Soon the political demonstration begins with the
throwing from the balconies of green, white, and red leaflets that fall
on the white uniforms of the impassive Austrian officers while the
music is interrupted by shouts of "Long live Verdi," "Long live Italy,"
and "Long live Lamarmora," the general who has mobilized his
troops to march against the Austrians and unite Venice with Italy.

Right after this demonstration the three main characters of *Senso*
are introduced: Countess Livia Serpieri, her cousin Roberto Ussoni,
and the Austrian Lieutenant Franz Mahler.

Visconti based *Senso* on a short story written by Camillo Boito, the
brother of Verdi's favorite librettist, Arrigo Boito. If we compare
Boito's story with Visconti's film, we immediately perceive the
greater depth attained by the director in presenting not only a story of
unfortunate sensuality but also the changing values reflected in the
many facets of the characters.

The most complex character is, without doubt, Livia. The
metamorphosis of Livia's personality from Boito's story to Visconti's
film is remarkable. In the short story she is a vain and selfish woman
whose main concern is her own beauty and the number of men
charmed by it. Her interest in Franz (Remigio in the story) is
awakened by his depravity: "I liked him because he was strong,
handsome, mean, and a coward."[4] Visconti's Livia is quite different.
Interpreted by the beautiful Alida Valli, she is an unhappily married
woman who lavishes her admiration on her cousin, Roberto, with
whom she shares patriotic ideals and aspirations. Defying her husband's sympathies for the Austrians and his counsel of prudence, she
does not hesitate to tell Franz after the performance of *Il Trovatore*
that, contrary to her husband, who advocates tolerating the Austrians, she, just like her cousin, is a real Italian. Her frankness and
pride call to memory the opening words of *Le confessioni d'un
Italiano* a novel written by Ippolito Nievo, a poet and a soldier who
joined Garibaldi in the expedition to Sicily and died in a shipwreck
during the return at the age of twenty nine. "I was born Venetian . . .
and I will die Italian for the grace of God," says Nievo's protagonist,

an eighty-year-old man who recalls in his memories the long struggle of *Risorgimento*.

Yet, when later on Livia denounces Franz to the Austrian general, she explains, "I came to do my duty as a faithful subject." "Are you an Austrian?," the general asks. "Venetian," is Livia's whispered reply. Her pride, her certainty, and her dignity have been swept away by her passion for Franz and by the humiliation he inflicted upon her.

In the rise and fall of Livia the title *Senso*, which in Italian can mean "sensuality," expresses not only the impact of a demeaning love affair, but also the baseness of unruly passions.

All of the titles that Visconti had in mind for this film ("The Defeated," "Custoza," "Summer Hurricane") carry the same imagery of loss and negativity and stress one more time the sensuality-defeat equation which pervades almost all of Visconti's works, from *Ossessione* (1942) to *The Innocent* (1976).

A ruinous presentiment insinuates itself into scenes of stunning beauty. The first one is the nocturnal chase in the streets of Venice, where we see Franz's white uniform pursuing the elusive red cape worn by Livia. The mystique of the city, of particular importance in Visconti's work, is rendered in beautiful visions of bridges, canals, water, liquid shadows, and light trembling on the wet stones that seem to hold the mystery of time. The discovery of the half-submerged body of a murdered Austrian soldier briefly interrupts the romantic sequence. Livia quickly recovers from the pity stirred in her by the sad event, while Franz sees it as the common occurrence that comes from the risk of being part of an occupying army. They both are too absorbed with their love affair to be jarred by the bad omen.

The next scene, also follows the same pattern of beautiful imagery stained with an ominous detail: Franz and Livia are sitting on the edge of a well whose tiles, lit by the moon, emanate a bluish light that reflects on the beautiful faces talking to each other on the edge of a mystery of which they can predict only the pleasure and not the danger. The second bad omen of the night, a broken mirror found by Franz, also reveals the personality of the Austrian lieutenant. "I like to look at myself," says Franz, "I never pass in front of a mirror without looking at myself. I like to look at myself to be sure that it's me. I am also sure to be me when I see a woman looking at me in the same way in which you are looking at me now." Livia is ready for a total commitment, but the handsome lieutenant collects love affairs as nonchalantly as he picks up pieces of a broken mirror. His pleasure is exclusively narcissistic; his desire for a woman is short–lived and selfish. Livia does not perceive Franz's smallness and falls hopelessly in love with him.

A few days later, on a luminous Venetian day, the sunlight follows Countess Serpieri, who climbs the steep and narrow stairs that lead to Franz's room. The Austrian lieutenant and the Venetian countess become lovers. In the bedroom scene, sensuality is suggested by the many shades of red, the fiery quality always present in the paintings of Titian, by whom Visconti is here definitely influenced. The imagery of the love scene contrasts with the banal conversation between the two lovers.

Similar contrasts appear in the other scenes involving Franz and Livia, especially in the surprising arrival of Franz at Livia's country villa. Here we witness a rather foolish dialogue between a woman who seems to represent the stereotype of the stupid lady in love and a craven man who has defected and wants a safe refuge. Franz has not been, as he says, dragged there by his love for Livia; he is simply looking for a place to hide. To overcome Livia's reluctance, he even makes the pathetic threat of "going out and being eaten by the dogs."

In *Senso*, a romantic film evoking a revolutionary time, in which the protagonists move as in an operatic scenario, melodrama is to be expected, as are its excesses of language. The weakness noted in some of the dialogue between the two lovers does not, therefore, refer to the melodramatic declarations, which are the logical expression of a film like *Senso*, but rather to some plain silliness on Franz's side and downright obtuseness on Livia's.

What we hear is quite insipid, but what we see is strikingly effective: the overdecorated nineteenth-century room, with its marble, its luxuriant carpets, and the soft light of the multishaped lamps that surround the kissing lovers, appears from above in a virtuoso camera shot. The atmosphere is heavier and darker than in the first bedroom scene in Venice with a prevailing purple hue, symbolizing Franz's shameless lies and Livia's guilt for giving hospitality and the money collected by Italian patriots to an enemy soldier. Livia forgets her love and admiration for her cousin, Roberto Ussoni, who is participating as a volunteer in the battle of Custoza, and forgets Italy at a moment of great importance for the new nation. Her "forgetfulness" calls to one's mind the dying words of Cavour, the diplomatic "weaver" who, throughout several years of tenacious political work, constructed the unity of Italy. "We made Italy," Cavour said, "now we have to make the Italians."

The theme of national political immaturity is presented through this love story, but even more through the unfortunate battle of Custoza, which was very much on Visconti's mind when he started *Senso*: "My original idea was concerned with the historical aspect. I even wanted to call it [*Senso*] *Custoza*, after the scene of a great Italian defeat. There was an outcry from Lux, the ministry, the censor. So the battle originally had much more importance. What I was interested in was the story of a bungled war, a war waged by a single class and ending in fiasco."[5]

Notwithstanding the prevalence of the operatic and love themes, the political tone is still very apparent in the final version of *Senso*, mainly in the representation of the battle of Custoza and in the figure of Roberto Ussoni, interpreted by Massimo Girotti (whom we also see as a minor character in *The Innocent* [1976] and as the protagonist in *Ossessione*). In Camillo Boito's *Senso*, the war is presented as merely an inconvenience for Livia, who cannot freely travel to meet her lover. The latter, equipped with a false medical dispensation that keeps him out of danger, shares Livia's outlook: "I will read the news of the war smoking; the more Italians and Austrians that go to hell the more I'll enjoy it."[6]

Much greater is the relevance given by Visconti to the battle of Custoza, where we see Roberto Ussoni, a character created by Visconti representing a typical *Risorgimento* idealist. He is, in fact, a man who not only says "Viva Verdi," but also lives up to all the implications of the slogan. Visconti develops the battle on two levels. He presents it first as a pure spectacle that builds up with a slow but dramatic crescendo in a green countryside, which at first looks very peaceful from the Serpieri villa. The lightness of the horizon, the carefully manicured flower beds, and the pale green of the trees convey a serenity that is illusory, because from another angle we see a movement of soldiers, carts, horses, cannons, and the first stretchers carrying the wounded. In a field dotted with orderly bundles of hay, the Italian army attacks: the blue lines of the soldiers advance slowly in a dusty light, in which the only vivid colors are the red, white, and green of the Italian flag. Were it not for the sight of blood and the cries of the wounded, this version of the battle of Custoza would belong for its melodramatic effects at the opera, set to the rousing music of Giuseppe Verdi.

Counterpointing the spectacle of the battle is the theme of the "bungled war," which Visconti develops through the emotions of Roberto Ussoni. Ussoni, who has risked imprisonment and has worked for several months to organize batallions of voluntary troops, sees his contribution rejected by the regular army, which, in the words of Captain Meucci, "will be enough for the country." The contribution of the voluntary troops could have been of great importance, considering the course of the battle in which the Italian army, after an initial success and a temporary retreatment, falls back in confusion mainly because of lack of coordination. The intervention of the volunteers could have given to the regular army enough time to regroup and possibly to win. This is very much in Ussoni's mind when we see him, wounded and sobbing, surrounded by the confusion of the Italian retreat—a very unfortunate debut for the new nation and an ominous presentiment of a much greater disaster that was to come during the First World War: the retreat of Caporetto. When Visconti talks about a bungled war waged by a single class, it is not difficult to see a reference to Italy's victory (but at what price for the nation!) in the First World War.

Custoza was, in fact, a relatively small battle—certainly recorded in all history books, but quite distant from the minds and the hearts of the average Italian, while the sufferings of the disastrous retreat of Caporetto is still a fresh memory. Its "official history" was published by the Ministry of Defense only in 1968.

In miniature Custoza presented the same causes of defeat: lack of coordination, improper command, and, in the refusal of the help offered by Ussoni, the military caste's rejection of forces of another class. In World War I, similar blunders led to a shocking waste of human lives and to the abuse of citizens whose political and civic education was minimal and neglected.

The political theme of defeat is also the insidious undercurrent of the relation between Livia and Franz. If the times were difficult for Italy, it has to be remembered that Austria was not in a better situation; while one nation was struggling to unify itself, the other was scrambling to stay together. Franz's words about the war reflect the tiredness of the Austro-Hungarian Empire: "We like elegant uniforms, the music, decorations. We are all ready to drink to the future victories but we don't want to pay the cost of it anymore—the loss of an arm, of a leg, a disfigured face or worse." Later, during Livia's visit to Verona, an ashamed and drunken Franz confesses: "I am a deserter because I am a coward . . . and I don't care. What do I care if my compatriots today have won a battle in a place called Custoza when I know that they will lose the war and not only the war?"

If the first part of *Senso* is mostly dedicated to passionate images and rousing music, and the second part is particularly concerned with the spectacle and the political implications of a battle, the third part presents a feeling of loss without remedy, which Visconti expressed poignantly in an alternate title for the film: "The Defeated." Gone are the beautiful music, the shimmering world of Venice, and the excitement of love. Franz's charm and Livia's beauty are replaced by the squalor of a rented room where one drunken deserter introduces a prostitute to another deserter, a Countess who has also betrayed the ideals in which she once proudly believed. The beautiful woman that once ran happily into the light of a Venetian morning now staggers through the stony streets of Verona among bawdy Austrian soldiers.

A somber blue permeates everything. The reds and the green of Titian and Veronese have given way to the dark tones of Van Gogh's *Starry Night* without the stars. In this darkness, Franz, betrayed by Livia, is dragged to his execution, a quick, routine affair carried through with indifferent efficiency.

A summer hurricane has swept away the lives of Roberto, Livia, and Franz in a tragic melodrama that has poured into their lives from the opera stage at the beginning of the film. "There are in life melodramatic people just as there are illiterate fishermen in Sicily."[7] With this statement Visconti intended to affirm a continuity in his work even if this meant baffling some critics who could not see how *Senso* could come after *La terra trema*, and disconcerting those among the public who consider melodrama passé.

"Melodrama has a bad reputation since it has been abandoned to schematic and conventional interpretation. In Italy this style meets a natural disposition in the people. . . . I love melodrama because it is at the border between life and theatre."[8] With these words, Visconti is saying "Viva Verdi"; most of all he is saying it with *Senso*, a film in which, during the tragic hurricane that ruins many lives, we have at least a winner: Verdi's music accompanied by the stunning colors of Titian and Veronese.

Considered by many to be Visconti's masterpiece, *Senso* quickly earned wide and enthusiastic acclaim. Positively received abroad, *Senso* was especially hailed in Italy where it met "a natural disposition in the people."

Visconti Becomes *Chiaccherato*

After *Senso*, Visconti returned to opera, again directing Maria Callas in Verdi's *La Traviata* and in Bellini's *La Sonnambula*, with Leonard Bernstein as the music director. In 1956 he ventured into another genre that he had never tried before: a ballet, *Mario and the Magician*, inspired by a short story by Thomas Mann. Luchino Visconti had become a very famous man in the Italian cultural scene. Successful, controversial, rebellious, he was also becoming what several years later Mino Guerrini would call "the most *chiaccherato* of all the Italian directors."[9] The literal translation of the adjective *chiaccherato* is "chatted," and people in fact chatted about Visconti: they did not gossip, but they chatted a lot. His eclecticism, his independent nature, which carried him constantly to the battle, his splendid life-style, so incongruous with his profession of Marxism, his sexual preferences, by then mostly directed toward men—all are facets of an enigmatic and extremely powerful personality.

In 1955, in an interview given by Visconti to Enrico Roda, an excellent journalist whose questions carefully avoid the cliché, the director unintentionally revealed himself. Asked: "Toward which faults, errors and human weaknesses are you more indulgent?" He answered: "Toward my own." Asked how much importance he gave to other people's opinions, he replied, "There are three or four persons who could make me change my mind with one word. But they do not know it. The others do not count." His suggestion for an eleventh commandment: "Always try to understand."[10]

Visconti's answers could inspire more "chatting," since although they do not explain anything, they do reveal a lot about the director's personality. Intelligence, arrogance mixed with tolerance ("always try to understand"), emotional secrecy ("Three or four people could make me change my mind with one word. But they do not know it"), exclusivity of feelings ("The others do not count") and an anarchist desire to break all the rules, transpire from this brief interview. Enrico Roda recognizes in Visconti a "very strong (*fortissima*) personality," and admits that he did not succeed in posing polite but embarrassing questions, because "Visconti's answers made me feel embarrassed. . . . They are not incoherent, nor insincere, nor contradictory; if there are contradictions they are intentional."[11] And so, always resisting an easier consistency, Visconti turns from the magnificence of *Senso* to the unpretentious *White Nights*.

White Nights (1957): The Plot

Mario, a young man who is new in town, spots a blonde young woman who is staring at the water of the canal from a bridge and who appears to be crying. At that moment two boys on a motorcycle invite

A violent moment in White Nights: *Mario (Marcello Mastroianni) is hit by the pimp.* *(Credit: Movie Star News)*

the girl for a ride and pass very close to her in order to scare her. This gives Mario the chance to display his chivalry by defending the young lady, with whom he soon starts a conversation.

The girl, Natalia, promises to be back the following night at the same time, which makes Mario very happy. He is greatly disappointed the next night, however, when he observes that the girl is trying to hide from him. Apologizing, Natalia explains that she is actually waiting for someone else and informs Mario about the troubles of her life: she lives with her blind grandmother and their poverty had forced them to take a lodger a year earlier. Soon a romance blossomed between the girl and the man, who, unfortunately, had to leave for another city but promised to be back in exactly one year. He had asked Natalia to wait for him at ten o'clock on the bridge where Mario saw her the night before. However, the lodger did not come to the rendezvous, and Natalia is particularly saddened because she has found out that the man is in town. Secretly hoping that the lodger has decided to end the relationship with the girl, Mario nevertheless advises her to write him a letter to find out about his intentions. Natalia has already done so and asks Mario to deliver the letter. The young man agrees but subsequently throws it away. The following night, Natalia accepts Mario's invitation to go dancing and enjoys herself greatly until she realizes that it is past ten o'clock and runs to the bridge despite Mario's protests. Later, after a fight with a pimp and the lodger, who happened to pass by, Mario finds himself face to face with Natalia, now humiliated and tearful. The lodger did not come, and she has decided to forget about him. When Mario confesses to having thrown away the letter, the girl is not upset because at this point she feels that the young man, by not having delivered the letter, has spared her another humiliation.

Happily, Mario now sees his chance to win Natalia's love, but when dawn comes, Natalia spots the dark figure of the lodger in the distance and runs to him, crying tears of joy. She then comes back to Mario, embraces him, and finally leaves him, walking away with the lodger.

"I gave myself a pause with *White Nights.*"[12]

Appearing after the splendor of *Senso* (1954) and before the powerful intensity of *Rocco and His Brothers* (1960), *White Nights* provided Visconti with a rest from his more demanding productions. If we compare this film to the previous ones and the ones to come, we can immediately perceive the relative simplicity of *White Nights,* which relies on a very small cast of experienced actors and is set in an unidentified city with water, canals, and bridges. Based on Dostoevsky's "White Nights," the film is largely faithful to the short story, with which it shares a dreamlike atmosphere and solitary, romantic main characters. But the oneiric and realistic elements are woven together by Visconti in a pattern that is different from the one created by Dostoevsky. Visconti's version takes place more than one hundred years after Dostoevsky's (written in 1848). The resulting anachronisms give the film a curious dream logic.

In the Dostoevsky story, a blind old woman, determined to control her granddaughter's every movement, pins the girl's dress to her own. In Visconti's film, the girl's behavior fluctuates from complete subservience to the old grandmother to staying out all night. Such peculiarities contribute to what Pierre Leprohn has called the film's "claustrophobic universe, which resembles less a prison or a camp than a mental hospital."[13]

The room in which we see Natalia and her grandmother in a flashback sequence is brightly illuminated and strewn with carpets that are there to be mended—a dreamy flash of light where a beautiful girl sits flanked by two old ladies in a setting that suggests an oriental fable.

In this setting Natalia sees the lodger for the first time. His background is as unknown as those of the other characters; it is indeed peculiar that Natalia, though completely in love with him, does not seem to know his name, his business or the reasons for his leaving. Then again, the girl does not even know her grandmother well. "My grandmother is a foreigner," she says to Mario. "I think she used to be rich."[14] Not much information indeed about the woman who raised her and keeps her pinned to her skirt. But all the characters in this film remain in a mysterious shadow, even Mario and Natalia, who talk about themselves almost all the time. We don't see them working and interacting with other people; we only observe them at night in a foggy world in which the feelings that they confide in each other seem to be shrouded in unreality. Like Dostoevsky, Visconti keeps his characters basically unexplained despite the long and introspective dialogues. As in the short story, the lodger, even when he is not present, is always in the background, eventually turning Mario's dream into a nightmare as his self-assurance mocks the young man's hopeless struggle to win the girl's heart.

The lodger's silent but powerful presence is well represented by Visconti in the scene at the opera, where we see only his knees and his hands but feel his magnetism from Natalia's expressions. In Dostoevsky's short story, the girl, called Nastenka, describes the lodger's behavior as very kind ("our lodger looked at me so nicely the whole evening, and he spoke so nicely to me."[15]), but Visconti introduces more sensuousness in this episode: we see the lodger's hands (he is sitting behind Natalia) move to her shoulders and provoke in the girl an obviously strong feeling that makes her turn and kiss the man's hand. Similarly, when Natalia finds out that the lodger is about to leave, her reaction compares in emotional intensity with the emotions described by Dostoevsky, achieving a physical impact which, because of the visual nature of the medium, conveys the spell that holds Natalia's mind and body.

The exhiliaration and the despair remembered by Natalia throughout the flashback are confided to Mario, the character who, in Dostoevsky's story, defines himself as "the dreamer." Interpreted in the film by Marcello Mastroianni, who gives the dreamer a familiar face, Mario appears as the most "normal" character, a realistic dreamer. In the dance hall where, in a rare moment, the couple is among other people, Mario tries to explain the relation between the two levels of dream and reality to Natalia, whom he sees dangerously captivated by the "unreal" world. "Everybody creates romantic dreams in their imagination," he says to the girl. "You don't desire anything more because you are creating your life, you're creating it according to your own whim."[16] But Mario also knows that dreams can sometimes completely overtake real life. "Fantasy is monotonous, it's the slave of shadow, of thought. Life, reality, is the happiness I feel now when I'm with you."[17] With these words Mario is trying to convince Natalia to free herself from the slavery of shadow, of one shadow in particular, and to accept the less exciting but real romance that he is offering. But Natalia suddenly remembers the rendezvous with the lodger and runs away while the young man explodes with anger. "You're crazy, that's what you are. Damn the moment I first met you." In frustration he picks up a prostitute. "If they're not whores, they're out of their minds," he says bitterly of women. "They belong in straightjackets."[18]

Mario's reaction, along with his impulsive decision to throw away the letter that Natalia had given him to take to the lodger, suggests that he is much less eccentric than Dostoevsky's dreamer. The latter, in fact, describes himself not as a person but as a character who lives "a mixture of something purely fantastic, something fervently ideal, and, at the same time, something frightfully prosaic and ordinary."[19] He calls himself a dreamer and identifies the dreamer as "not a man, but a sort of creature of the neuter gender."[19] Only such a person could at the same time be in love with a girl, deliver her letter to the man she loves, and experience her excitement vicariously. Visconti gives Mario a much more realistic personality. The day after he has failed to deliver the letter the young man clearly sees his strange situation: "I don't know what I was doing. I was dreaming. That's what I was doing. I was dreaming. Little lady, I am not playing your game. You've got the wrong boy."[20]

Although Mario likes to dream with Natalia during the "white nights," he is not a dreamer. He is simply a lonely young man in a strange town, where he tries to find some warmth and friendship. He is solitary by necessity and not by choice, as we see in the episode in which he enters a bar, not really to drink but to exchange a few words after returning from a weekend spent with the family of an acquaintance.

In both the film and the short story, the lodger maintains his mysterious allure, but the psychology of the main character differs in the film. Mario's feelings are unknown to the dreamer, and Natalia's strange behavior is magnified in the film, not only because of her grandmother's habits but also in relation to Mario. In the short story, her reliance on the dreamer can be understood in light of the man's sexual indifference. However, in the film Mario makes no mystery of his feelings for Natalia, who, older than the seventeen–year–old in the short story, is surprisingly insensitive to Mario's emotions. "You are looking at me like a man in love," she says to Mario right before giving him the letter. "You can't, after all I told you, fall in love. Anyway, you won't have time to."[21]

Mario continues his struggle to convince Natalia to abandon her futile hope to see the lodger again, and finally the girl seems resigned to accept his counsel. "I want to forget him. But I still love him. But I'll get over it, because now I have seen the truth."[22] Excited as a child, Mario takes Natalia for a boat ride while snow begins to fall, and the two playfully throw snowballs at each other in a deserted square overlooking the city. "Before, this city seemed so gloomy, so sad," says Mario. "It was my own fault, because all of a sudden everything's become so gay."[23] This happy episode, the only one in the film that is not tarnished by loneliness, delivers Mario and Natalia from the unhappy solitude that brought them together. With the coming of dawn Mario seems to have succeeded in taking Natalia away from her misty dream world. The sleepless nights consumed with tortuous wanderings of minds and hearts seem to give way to a bright dawn.

But this fable without magic is not meant to finish happily for Mario, who finds himself closed in again in the circle of his own solitude after the return of the lodger. Visconti replaces the philosophical reveries of Dostoevsky's main character with a visual oneiric quality represented by the night shots of the unidentified city, which at times appears as a labyrinth made of bridges, canals, narrow, dimly lit streets, and stairs that appear to lead nowhere.

White Nights won the second prize at the Festival of Venice in 1957, but it was not successful with the general public and is not considered an important work by critics. In fact, the beautiful photography is not enough to vitalize this film, which relies on the acting of a very small cast: Maria Schell, Marcello Mastroianni, Jean Marais—who, as the lodger, has a very small role—and Clara Calamai, the protagonist of *Ossessione* (1942), who plays the prostitute. As Visconti observed, *White Nights* represents a pause in which the director sets up a very small stage and, bringing some of the substance from Dostoevsky's short story, lets a dream world emerge from the night fog. In an interview with Giovanni Grazzini in *Il Corriere della Sera*, Visconti affirmed that a career cannot be limited to a succession of similar films. "In the career of an artisan (I don't consider myself more than this)," he says, "there can be summits and intermediate stages. Everybody has the right to a vacation."[24] *White Nights* is a working vacation, in which the director prepares for the artistic summits that he will soon reach with his next film.

5

"Anthropomorphic Cinema":
Rocco and His Brothers

BETWEEN *White Nights* and *Rocco and His Brothers*, Visconti worked again with Maria Callas at La Scala, directing Donizetti's *Anna Bolena* and Gluck's *Iphigénie en Tauride*. He also presented on the stage Arthur Miller's *A View from the Bridge*. In his work for the theater, faithful to his desire to take nothing for granted and to change old ways when change is needed, Visconti broke away from the traditional theatrical methodology. "More than a work of invention, ours was cleaning work. We had to put order on the stage, impose a new discipline on the actors, give to the representation an impression of truth. I eliminated the prompter, and I fought against the old vice of improvisation, I also imposed strict schedules on our latecomer audience. And so, the Italian theater of the nineteenth century came to an end."[1]

Notwithstanding his dedication to the theater, Visconti felt that drama presents a very quick and transient reward for a director who, after all, presents on the stage, and only for a very short time, the work of someone else. "Very little remains of the theater; it remains in the memory. Maybe it is better this way, it is better that it should be only a memory and the emotion of one evening."[2]

While directing Miller's *A View from the Bridge*, a powerful work about the lives of Italian immigrants in the United States, Visconti must have thought of a more permanent expression, his personal view of the same subject. His next cinematographical labor, *Rocco and His Brothers*, in fact concerns the lives of "immigrants" in their own country, Italy.

Rocco and His Brothers (1960): The Plot

A southern Italian family, composed of a mother, Rosaria, and five sons, Vincenzo, Simone, Rocco, Ciro, and Luca, move to Milan in

Spiros Focas as Vincenzo supports his brother Rocco (Alain Delon) after Simone beat him up. (Courtesy of Museum of Modern Art/Film Stills Archives)

search of better living conditions. The beginning is hard for everybody: the brothers start working at unsteady jobs; Simone tries
boxing, showing great promise by winning his first match.

Nadia, a prostitute, becomes Simone's lover, but it is soon apparent
that their involvement is different. Simone loves Nadia, but the girl
considers him one of the many. While Simone's boxing career disin-
tegrates because of his lack of discipline and seriousness, Nadia falls
in love with Rocco, who, almost as a joke, is also becoming a boxer.
The humiliation and the loss prove to be too much for Simone who,
instigated by "friends," rapes Nadia in Rocco's presence and subsequently inflicts a terrible beating on his brother, who refuses to
defend himself. After the violence, Rocco feels only compassion for
Simone and tries to persuade Nadia to go back to him; but Nadia is
also desperate: she loves Rocco, with whom she had hoped to share a
clean and normal life, and she hates Simone for the humiliation that
he has inflicted upon her. She refuses to go back to her former lover,
but she is unable to keep Rocco, who, unwillingly, is becoming a
successful boxer. Simone, now a derelict, finds Nadia at the Idroscalo, near Milan, where the girl is now making a living by soliciting
motorists. The young man is still in love with the girl and tries to win
her back, but Nadia insults him. Simone, now totally destroyed, stabs
and kills Nadia in an outburst of rage. Covered with her blood he
returns home where the family is celebrating a very important
victory won by Rocco.

Simone's arrival alarms everybody, and, after he confesses his
crime, the family is divided: Rocco wants to help him escape, but Ciro
believes that the only proper course of action is for Simone to give
himself up to the police. Rosaria slaps him, but Ciro, convinced that
he is doing the right thing, runs out to denounce his brother. In the
last scene of the film we see Ciro explaining to Luca, the youngest
brother, the reasons for his action. After the conversation, he enters
the Alfa Romeo factory where he is now a good technician. Luca
waves to him while Rocco's sad face looks on from the front page of a
sport magazine displayed in front of a kiosk.

"The anthropomorphic cinema."[3]

Probably the best example that Visconti ever gave of what he calls
the anthropomorphic cinema, *Rocco and His Brothers* is indeed a

story of "men alive in things."[4] The film, bursting with vitality, is like a crowded tapestry of human situations. The relatively simple plot is dense with emotions, while the lives of the protagonists interlock like the colored glasses of a kaleidoscope.

Completed in 1960 and presented at the Venice Exhibition while Luchino Visconti, with other Italian directors, stayed away, protesting the new management of the cultural event, *Rocco and His Brothers* did not win, but was considered the "moral winner." "At the projection there were three or four Christian Democrat ministers . . . who were saying, 'It's disgusting, it's a shame, this film cannot be given a prize.' And so they influenced the jury,"[5] says Visconti, to whom controversial reactions were certainly not new. What scandalized the ministers were the violent scenes, especially the rape and the killing of Nadia. Although *Rocco and His Brothers* did not win the *Leone d'oro*, the first prize at the Venice Exhibition, audiences were profoundly impressed by the high emotional charge of this film, and critics reacted favorably to it. In *Bianco e nero*, an Italian monthly review of cinema, ten critics gave an overall positive judgement of the film, praising its power, and its warmth. *Rocco and His Brothers* was also compared to a Greek tragedy for its dignity and solemnity.[6]

Rocco and His Brothers is, in fact, a tragedy, the tragedy of a southern Italian family whose struggle to adapt to new conditions of life in the North expresses a national problem. The film takes place in the late 1950s, a time of prosperity and industrial development in the North, during which the South remained in a seemingly endless lethargic state, depicted by many writers with pity and resignation and, more recently, with anger for years and years of bad government and exploitation.

This fracture between the "two Italies" was very much on Visconti's mind during the period of time in which *Rocco and His Brothers* was conceived. Visconti told Jean Slavik that "It's about a tragedy: the disintegration of a family from the South which is not able to adapt to the conditions of life in the North; a contemporary drama, because the inability of these two Italian regions to communicate continues in a disquieting way. I will insist on the inability to communicate between northern and southern Italians. We have our racism too."[7] With *Rocco and His Brothers*, Visconti touches a very sensitive nerve, which is exactly what he wants to do. "I heard of a journalist who, after the showing of *Rocco* to the critics, said, 'This film will bother 85 percent of Italians.' Great. It really pleased me."[8]

The Parondi family arrives in Milan from Lucania, the poorest of all Italian regions, a land of arid and fruitless mountains between Calabria and Puglia at the very end of the Italian Peninsula. This is the land described by Carlo Levi in his classic "Southern" book, *Christ Stopped at Eboli*. A physician, a writer and a painter, disliked by Mussolini's government because of his antifascist activity, Carlo Levi was sent, "in exile," from his native Turin where he resided, to the forsaken town of Gagliano in Lucania. Here Levi wrote a book that, in pages imbued with humanity, indignation, and admiration for the endurance of the people of Lucania, denounces their almost incredible poverty. Eboli is the name of the last town the train touches before entering Lucania; Eboli represents the last point of civilization before the desolation, the sorrow, and the toiling. Not even Christ visited Lucania, say the farmers; we are forgotten by everybody. Christ stopped at Eboli. This land is also described in very sensitive poems by Rocco Scotellaro, the former socialist mayor of Tricarico, a little town in Lucania. In homage to the memory of Rocco Scotellaro, who died in 1953 of tuberculosis at the age of thirty, Visconti chose the name Rocco for his protagonist.

Rocco Parondi is himself something of a poet. Celebrating a boxing victory, he says, after an ancient toast in Lucano dialect, "I want to come back to my land. And if it will be impossible for me, someone among us will go back." Then, turning to Luca with eyes full of tears, he adds, "Remember Luca, that is our land, the land of the olive trees, of the moon and of the rainbows." From the land of the rainbows, the Parondis move to the land of the rain, the fog, and the wet asphalt. Such is the first visual impression we get of the city of Milan, the busy metropolis whose big avenues, cars, and shops loaded with carefully displayed goods dazzle Simone, the one who will be swallowed by this new world, while Rocco, as if haunted by a premonition, looks at the new environment with pensive and sad eyes.

The impact of the change is also expressed by a linguistic dimension that can be appreciated only in the original Italian version. When the Parondis are "greeted" in the gym by men speaking *milanese*, they remain completely bewildered. Since one's language is probably the most important link with one's culture, it is interesting to note how well the assimilation of the fourth brother proceeds when Ciro, encouraged by Rocco to continue his victory toast in Lucano dialect, forgets the words and goes on in Italian. "Aren't you ashamed?" Vincenzo laughs. "You do not remember your language."

Verga's World Revived

Interwoven with the social phenomenon of emigration and its consequences is the ever-present literary influence in the background of Visconti's works. The director, in fact, sees *Rocco and His Brothers* as the second episode of *La terra trema* (1948) and links both films to G. Verga's book *I Malavoglia* [The House by the Medlar Tree]. The relation to *I Malavoglia* is certainly more evident in *La terra trema*, but there is no doubt that *Rocco* can be the logical continuation of *I Malavoglia*, since the film projects the aspirations and the frustrations presented in Verga's novels into a contemporary pseudo-solution, the promise of a new life in the North for an impoverished southern family. Visconti describes a world totally unknown to Verga, who published *I Malavoglia* in 1881, but the film echoes Verga's masterpiece not only in its themes but also in the unmistakable cadence of the dialogue, which is characteristically terse but replete with meaning.

In *Rocco*, every word counts because the characters are not very articulate. Every verbalization of feelings is a great effort, and because of this, sentences are short, linguistically primitive, and significant. For the Parondi Family, just as for the people in Verga's realistic work, language is not a sophisticated tool, a malleable form of expression; especially when spoken by Rocco, it leaves its mark like engravings in stones. When the trainer asks Rocco if he likes boxing, the "no" spoken by the young man, without any further explanation, says more to the viewer than a long dissertation on the evil of hitting another person. Similarly, after the rape, when Simone starts hitting Rocco, the latter does not react but simply murmurs, "You are my brother," which is a lapidary explanation for Rocco's behavior and mentality. These simple words betray in Rocco a complex inner world where the unity of the family is the supreme value that has to be preserved at any cost.

His rigidity in maintaining this supreme and ancient value is apparent in the scene in which, after Simone has publicly raped Nadia, he tries to convince the girl to go back to him. "Why must we not see each other any more? Instead of killing your brother you want to kill me. What have I done to you? Are you out of your mind?," asks Nadia, crying for the sorrow and the frustration of not being able to convince Rocco that his proposal is insane. "You convinced me that my life was wrong. You taught me to love you. And now, because of the bravado of a scoundrel, what was sacred and right before becomes wrong," continues Nadia, but her words have no effect on Rocco. He feels guilty because he took his brother's woman: "We are guilty Nadia. I more than you. You must go back to Simone. You are his woman." Nadia's love, his love for her, which was caring and tender only a few evenings before, are now secondary. By taking Nadia away from Simone, Rocco believes he has violated a sacred law. "I am a simple person, born and raised in the South. I betrayed my brother; I took his woman away." Rocco's simplicity, however, like the simplicity of Verga's characters is only apparent.

Ciro tells Luca in the final scene that "Rocco is a saint. But in the world in which we live, in the society that men have created, there is no place for saints like him. Their piety generates disaster." And indeed it does. Even Simone understands when he returns home with his clothes stained with Nadia's blood. Turning angrily to Rocco, who embraces him, he says: "So it is finished. Are you happy, champ? You wanted her to come back to me? You wanted this, didn't you?"

Rocco's goodness is a very positive factor in the first part of the film. His warmth saves Nadia from an empty life, but it becomes an almost inhuman force in the second part, when love and happiness are sacrificed in name of family and tradition, which have lost their reality in the new social structure. Rocco's insistence on sacrifice, his and Nadia's, only creates a chain reaction in which disaster involves not only the person whom he tries to rescue but Nadia and himself.

Rocco is like a man who desperately struggles to build a card castle in the wind, a prince Myskin who, carried away by the preaching of goodness, awkwardly knocks to the floor and breaks an expensive vase. The similarity between Rocco and Dostoevsky's Myskin does not end here. Rocco's goodness and his loving desire to understand and justify every human action, limits him to a position of impotent spectator. What does Rocco do in the face of the tragedy of Nadia and Simone, the Nastassya and Rogozhin of the film? Nothing. Rocco suffers, loves, and understands. In a world where the logic of love is often tarnished by the irrationality of passion, this is not enough. It will not save the lives of Nadia and Simone, both condemned; the former to death, in a quick, violent way, the latter to long years in prison.

Not only are Rocco's feelings socially useless, but they backfire in the hatred that the "loved" and "understood" people feel for him. Little communication remains between the members of the family whose private world has been shattered by the new environment. At the two ends of the spectrum we see the "very bad" Simone and the "very good" Rocco, both trapped in their own abrasiveness. This situation is similar to the one described by Italo Calvino in his surrealistic novel *Il visconte dimezzato* [The cloven viscount] written in 1952. The protagonist, viscount Medardo of Terralba, is split in half by a cannon ball, and the two halves, one bad and one good, come back home separately, the bad one going into a rampage of cruelty, the good one trying to mend the work of the bad one with self sacrifice and preaching. The interesting point is that both halves are equally irritating and troublesome to the people of the town, who are equally lost and confused in the face of inhuman badness and goodness.

In between Rocco and Simone are the other brothers: Vincenzo, not a very relevant character in the context of the family because he has now a family of his own; Ciro, who finds a job at the Alfa Romeo factory and becomes engaged to a Milanese girl; and Luca, the youngest one, who perhaps will go back to the South when things are better there. In the film we do not see much of Ciro, whom Visconti had intended to give a much greater role in the family. In an interview given to *Schermi*,[9] Visconti explains that in an original conception, later changed, Ciro had a much more significant part in *Rocco and His Brothers*. He should have had a business activity involving the transportation of olive oil from Lucania to Milan, creating a real bridge between the South and the North. This twist in the story, however, would have complicated and lengthened an already long film. Consequently Ciro's role was considerably reduced.

From Visconti's point of view Ciro is, in fact, the only positive character: Luca is still too young to count, Vincenzo conforms without asking himself any questions, Rocco and Simone are both tragic for opposite reasons. Ciro instead reaches an awareness and a maturity that allow him to understand the new world without losing sight of the old one. Ciro denounces Simone, but not out of cruelty. He does it because he knows that it must be done, even at the cost of being slapped and cursed by his mother. Crying and talking to Luca at the end of the film, Ciro explains, "When you grow up you will understand that you have been unfair to me; you all have been unfair. I loved Simone more than all of you did. He explained to me that we must defend our rights after we have learned our duties. Then Simone forgot all these things. I tried to learn my rights and my duties."

Visconti intended to make another film taking Ciro as the link for a continuation of *Rocco and His Brothers*. "I always think about a continuation. When I finished *La terra trema* I was thinking about a continuation. Now that *Rocco* is finished, I think about a continuation. For me, Ciro is the continuation. Probably Ciro . . . will become a little bourgeois, then maybe a rich bourgeois. And so I will conclude the cycle of *La terra trema*."[10] Unfortunately, the film about Ciro was never made.

The Parondi family pays a high price for a better economic situation. Celebrating his boxing victory, Rocco remembers an ancient Lucano custom: "Do you remember, Vincenzo," he says to his brother, "that the master bricklayer at the start of the construction of a new house throws a stone on the shadow of the first passer-by . . . because a sacrifice is necessary for the house to come up solid." Visconti liked this custom and decided to introduce it in the film at the risk of becoming too obvious and sentimental. "They told me about this Lucano usage, about this rite. So I put it in the film even if it becomes a little too symbolic. But in that moment I said: 'I'll do it, I don't care.'" They criticized me for it didn't they? They criticized me a little for Rocco's speech. Sometimes it became a little lyrical."[11] The lyricism, however, is absolutely coherent with Rocco's personality, his sadness, his useless and dangerous saintliness, and his homesickness for "the land of the rainbows."

Sorrow and sweetness punctuate Rocco's words, but it is not as easy to identify their intent: a sacrifice is required, but who is the victim? Rocco could be speaking about himself, trying so hard to keep the family together and becoming a champion in a sport that he abhors, or about Simone, whose career, so promising at the beginning, is now ruined.

Rocco and Simone are not the only two "victims." The whole family is victimized by the actions of Simone, from Rosaria, who would like to see her five sons all together "like the fingers of one hand," to Ciro, who finds himself alienated from the rest of the family when he refuses to help Simone escape justice, and finally to Luca, hurt by what is happening and unable to choose among his feelings of loyalty for each of his brothers.

The more obvious victim is Nadia, the center of two very violent scenes, shocking for their realism. In the rape scene we see Nadia surrounded by Simone and his friends, a terrified figure in the night fog who screams in vain for help. Rocco, shocked by his brother's fury, is unable to react, and it is Simone who yells, "Look at him

Nadia, look at your lover. Don't you see that he does not care about you. Why doesn't he help you? Why doesn't he jump on me to kill me?" Then, turning to Rocco, he yells with scorn, "Of what flesh did our mother make you?" Rocco moves only when Simone rips Nadia's underclothing and throws it at his face with more scornful words. Then, while Rocco is immobilized by his brother's friends ("Hold him tight, I want him to see well and to remember"), Simone rapes Nadia. A deep silence follows. While Rocco is crying, Nadia leaves slowly, her white silhouette stained with mud, her step heavy with pain and humiliation. Simone, whose thirst for revenge is never quenched, throws himself on Rocco and savagely beats him.

The darkness of the night, the cruel expectation of the spectators, the desperation of Nadia, Simone, and Rocco (wonderfully acted by Annie Girardot, Renato Salvatori, and Alain Delon) create a crescendo of emotions rarely seen. A magnetic force unifies Simone's violence, Rocco's tears, and Nadia's humiliation, like a knot that cannot be untangled but can only be severed by the icy blade of the following silence.

Visconti was obviously inspired by a story written by Giovanni Testori in a book entitled *Il ponte della Ghisolfa* [The bridge of Ghisolfa], which is also the location chosen for the filming of the rape. Published in 1958, *Il ponte della Ghisolfa*, the first book of a cycle entitled *I segreti di Milano* [The secrets of Milan], depicts the lives of lonely women, young prostitutes, aspiring singers, short-famed bicycle racers, and disillusioned boxers. In one of the episodes, entitled "What Are You Doing, Sinatra?" Dario, a young man nicknamed Sinatra because of his good singing voice, becomes the lover of Gina, a young prostitute who formerly "belonged" to Dario's brother Attilio. The latter, in the presence of some friends, having surprised Gina and Dario making love in the night near the bridge of Ghisolfa, rapes the girl and "teaches his brother a lesson," by hitting him. Testori's dialogue betwen the two brothers is strikingly similar to the words exchanged between Rocco and Simone, and the action seen on the screen closely follows the scene in the book.

Visconti's portrayal of a detestable act stemming from rivalry, jealousy, and self-destructiveness is, in this episode, close to perfection. Similarly effective but arguably self-indulgent is his depiction of the killing of Nadia. The setting was supposed to be the Idroscalo of Milan, a place where prostitutes had really been killed, but Visconti, tired of all the obstacles created by the censors, decided to film the episode at Lago di Fogliano, not too far from Rome.

Dirty and slovenly dressed, Simone is now a grotesque image of the handsome, promising champion who loved silk shirts and purple boxing shorts ("the color of the champions," Morini, his protector, used to say). Like a wolf looking for his prey, he slowly advances toward the car where Nadia is entertaining a customer. The latter, upon seeing Simone, flees, leaving Nadia alone with her former lover. Trying to conceal her fear Nadia asks: "Do you want money?" But Simone does not want money. He is trying for the last time to bring her back to him: "We together . . . if you want, we'll go away. Then it will be possible to start again, even for me." But in Nadia's eyes Simone is not only responsible for the rape but is also the cause of the loss of Rocco, her only love. Simone keeps pleading ("I'll pay you like everybody else"), then, overcome with anger, he beats her to the ground. Filled with remorse, he kisses her tenderly, but Nadia feels only hatred for him. "You are a coward, you are an animal, you are not a man. Everything that you touch becomes vulgar, dirty, lurid. You disgust me." Speechless, with a frozen look in his eyes, Simone advances toward Nadia and, covering her with his body, slowly sinks the knife in her side.

The scene has a questionable aesthetic violence, especially when the dark figure of Simone, projecting inescapable violence, hides the frail body of Nadia, who raises her arms in an evident reference to the cross formed by the two bodies; that of the victim and of the killer, a victim himself. The questionability of the shooting is in its aestheticism, which beautifies a repugnant act, and in the slowness of the stabbing which Simone, in his desperation, seems to savor as an act of love.

The Women in the Film and Other Themes

Rocco and His Brothers is a story about men in a men's world. The only two relevant women are two contrasting stereotypes: the mother and the prostitute, strangely united by their noxiousness, common denominator of their antagonistic roles. In an interview with Jean Slavik in *Cahiers du Cinéma*, [12] Visconti was asked about the destructive influence of women on men in his films. He reacted with ill-hidden irritation ("Don't you have more interesting questions?"), explaining that the presence of the degrading woman is simply an occasional requirement of the dramatic construction. He also called the emphasis given by the critics to the matter an unwarranted opinion.

Annie Girardot as Nadia assumes the position of a crucified person just before Simone (Renato Salvatori) murders her in Rocco and His Brothers. *(Courtesy of Museum of Modern Art/Film Stills Archives)*

Curiously enough, at the time of this conversation, which referred to *Ossessione*, Visconti was in the process of filming *Rocco*, where the negative influence of women is blatant. The boys, in effect, meet corruption because of Rosaria's ambition and Nadia's sexuality; their loss of innocence, with the consequential feeling of guilt that changes their lives, likens the modern situation to the biblical account of original sin. Nadia brings degradation with her seductiveness and the power of her femininity, and Rosaria, whose last words in the film are words of anger, ("Jesus Christ must feel remorse for what he did to us") is the tyrannical mother who "owns" her children and expects honor from them. To obtain it, she even encourages Simone and Rocco to try boxing, stimulated by Nadia's conversation about a champion with a car "from here to there."

Visconti chose a Greek actress, Katina Paxinou, to portray Rosaria Parondi, "She's a mother who wants to do everything. She is some kind of maternal authority who considers her children as objects, as forces to exploit. I needed a character like this. I looked for her in Italy and I did not find her, so Paxinou came to my mind; this Greek actress is so similar to our Southern mothers. I wanted her to be melodramatic, nervous, pushy."[13] Visconti said he intended to concentrate in Rosaria's character all the maternal, paternal, and domestic power and referred the interviewer to a photograph of the Parondis. In this portrait we see a proud and statuesque mother surrounded by five handsome and strong sons, while the father, in the background, hardly reaches Vincenzo's shoulders. "The father was not an indispensable element, he was insignificant. At a certain point he wore himself out. So they threw the little man in the sea and she remains the owner of the children, of these forces which she has unchained."[14]

From this point of view Rosaria is more than just a pushy mother; she is a mythological monster who uses her husband, discards him, and then uses her children. Naturally, she is not aware of what she is doing, and when problems occur she blames them on evil luck, on the bewitching power of Nadia, and ultimately on Jesus Christ. But there is a moment at which she comes close to the understanding of her responsibilities:

"Is it my fault? Is it my fault if I had the ambition of bringing my handsome and strong sons to the city so that they would become rich? Your father did not want to leave our town," she says to Ciro, "but I did not dream of anything else for the twenty-five years that we spent together. I wanted it for Vincenzo, for Simone, for Rocco. And for a while I thought I reached what I wanted. People were calling me 'signora.' In such a big city they called me 'signora,' for respect of my sons. But then what happened? Ciro, you must protect your mother's house! Do something. It is your duty."

Naturally, Rosaria's ambition is not the root of all evils; her decision to leave the poverty of her original town was a courageous break with a difficult past, and in spite of authoritarian, traditionalist narrow—mindedness, she cannot be blamed for the traumatic experiences encountered by the whole family in its struggle with the big city.

When Visconti speaks about the father, "the little man" whom they threw in the sea, he is not referring to any evil deed perpetrated by Rosaria (as Visconti's description of the woman might suggest), but to the natural death of the father, whose funeral in the Italian version of the film is at the very beginning and has the bier being carried by the sons and thrown into the sea. This scene, along with several others, including Rosaria's conversation with Ciro and part of the rape episode, are unfortunately absent from the American version, which, at two and one—half hours, is almost half an hour shorter than the original. Visconti, furthermore, wanted to film part of the lives of the Parondis in Lucania to develop the reasons for their move to Milan, but problems in the production made a second trip to Lucania impossible.

Boxing, another important theme of *Rocco and His Brothers* produces a dramatic and violent twist. Again referring to Verga, Visconti calls boxing the film's *carico dei lupini* ("cargo of lupines").[15] In Verga's *The House by the Medlar Tree,* the Malavoglias lose everything when their boat, loaded with lupines, is lost in a storm in which the father dies. The lupines represented their future, a possible improvement in their poor lives. In *Rocco and His Brothers,* the way out is the ring.

The realism of the fights is impressive: Renato Salvatori and Alain Delon, carefully instructed by professional boxers during the filming, developed such an effective skill that the face of their sparring partners sometimes did not need any make-up to look puffy. Visconti is very effective with dramatic black and white shots of the bloodied, pallid faces of the contenders, whose steps in the ring create a strangely graceful rhythm.

The gym and the ring scenes were also inspired by Testori's *Il ponte della Ghisolfa.* In *Rocco,* as in Testori's work, young men clad in loose—fitting uniforms are taught to use their bodies as punishing machines, which are eyed in the steaming showers by equivocal characters. During the fights of Simone, who is an instinctive and vulnerable character unable to deal with frustration, we are mostly aware of physical pain, especially when Simone begs for the throwing in of the towel. But during Rocco's fights we sense the emotional distress suffered by the young man who, after a victorious match, cries because for the first time in his life he felt hatred for another human being, his adversary. Even in the ring Rocco is, as Visconti said, "pure." He does not seem to feel physical pain, even when his adversary hits him with a vicious blow that opens up a cut over his eye. Later on, when Luca asks him if he was afraid and if he felt pain he answers: "No, I did not even see him in front of me. It was just like when I shadow-box, just like when I train." Even when he fights, Rocco keeps himself in the clouds. He has to give and receive punches because he must help his family with his hard trade, but his heart is not in the ring. There is no pain and no exaltation.

Visconti cleverly juxtaposes parts of Rocco's most important match with the killing of Nadia by shifting from the fog and the water of what is supposed to be the Idroscalo to the smoke of the closed arena, from Simone's switch-blade knife to Rocco's punches, from one form of violence to the other.

In *Rocco and His Brothers* Visconti sought to produce an "anthropomorphic" film by bringing out the human quality of the actor in order to obtain a unity between the "man-actor and the man-character."[16] Critics and public agree that this film is a very powerful work, a dramatic assault on the viewer's emotions. Like other Visconti films, even this successful work created controversies, especially with the censors, who considered the rape scene too explicit and the murder too violent. They did not allow the director to film the latter in the proper locality, but Visconti fought the restriction with his usual vigor and, in the end, succeeded in maintaining the integrity of the film by darkening some shots in the rape scene. Another difficulty, quickly surmounted, involved the name originally chosen by Visconti for the family. It was not Parondi, but Pafundi, a typical Lucano name that had to be changed because "real life Pafundis" protested against the use of their name for a family in which one of the members becomes a murderer and ends up in jail.

Apart from the self-indulgent melodrama of some scenes, *Rocco and His Brothers* is a great film, probably Visconti's best. It is an emotional and deeply felt work, a modern tragedy articulated on classic models with a carefully balanced mixture of contemporary Italian social problems, literary allusions, and well-studied psychological portraits.

6

Dream of a Dying World: *The Leopard*

RIGHT AFTER THE presentation to the public of *Rocco and His Brothers*, Visconti, showing his continued interest and admiration for the literary work of Giovanni Testori, decided to bring to the stage Testori's play, *L'Arialda*. Presented in Rome, *L'Arialda* whose protagonist is a sexually promiscuous girl whose language is very frank, received a hearty welcome, but in Milan two months later, in February of 1961, Visconti found himself again in conflict with the censors who, after the first performance, did not allow the production to continue. Visconti's battles with the censors over *Rocco and His Brothers* and *L'Arialda* are probably the reason for his "vacation" in France. In Paris he directed John Ford's English Renaissance drama *'Tis a Pity She's a Whore*, with Romy Schneider and Alain Delon.

Back in Italy, Visconti participated in the film *Boccaccio '70*, produced by Carlo Ponti. He directed an episode called *Il lavoro* [The job], with Romy Schneider, a young Cuban actor named Tomas Milian, and Romolo Valli, whom we will see in *The Leopard* and in *Death in Venice*. *Il lavoro* tells the story of a young, jaded aristocrat, Count Ottavio (Tomas Milian) and of his wife Pupe (Romy Schneider), who is just as jaded but more wealthy, thanks to her father's fortune. At the beginning of the film we are made aware of a scandal involving Count Ottavio, who, as headlines on the newspapers proclaim, has paid a call girl 700,000 lire (a little more than $1,000) for the entertainment she provided. The lawyer (Romolo Valli), worries about the possibility of retribution on the part of Pupe's father, who could ask his daughter to leave Ottavio and therefore take her wealth away from him as well.

Pupe, however, does not seem to be upset about her husband's call girl. Charging 400,000 lire every time (Ottavio will not have to pay

Visconti indulges his propensity for mirror scenes as Fabrizio Salina (Burt Lancaster) and Mariannina, the prostitute watch each other in The Leopard. *(Credit: Movie Star News)*

the in-between woman), she figures that soon she will be able to save 70 million lire, enough to open a boutique in the most elegant part of Milan. The film ends showing Ottavio paying his first check.

Just an episode, too short and flippant to be seriously considered, *Il lavoro* nevertheless criticizes the society that Fellini had depicted two years before in *La dolce vita*. The society without "guts" and "passions," as Fellini called it, is present here in *Il lavoro*, where boredom, loneliness, and absolute indifference are the controlling attitudes. Visconti, however, took only a glimpse at this world belonging to privileged, bored people of the sixties, because for a long time his mind was occupied by the thought of taking to the screen the tumultuous social changes occurring in Sicily one hundred years earlier.

Visconti's next major film, *The Leopard*, was based on Giuseppe Tomasi di Lampedusa's novel, which had been an unexpected bestseller in the United States. An expensive endeavor, produced by Goffredo Lombardo, the cast includes Burt Lancaster, Alain Delon, Claudia Cardinale, with Rina Morelli and Paolo Stoppa, who had already worked with Visconti in Miller's *A View from the Bridge* and in the unlucky *L'Arialda*.

The Leopard (1963): The Plot

The year is 1860 and the news of Garibaldi and his one thousand red-shirted soldiers disembarking in Sicily to put an end to the Bourbon kingdom and to unite the island to Italy has just reached the Salina family. Prince Fabrizio Salina sees in the event nothing more than a change of characters in a scene that remains the same, and he refuses to take any active role in the change. However, his nephew, Tancredi Falconeri, joins the Garibaldini and soon becomes an officer in the army of his majesty Victor Emmanuel, first king of Italy.

At Donnafugata, his summer residence, the prince witnesses the rapid ascent of don Calogero Sedara, an uneducated peasant who, by dint of hard work and by astutely making political connections, is now a very wealthy man and the mayor of Donnafugata. His daughter Angelica combines with her great beauty an education received in a boarding school in Florence and, naturally, a very rich dowry. All of these qualities capture the interest of Tancredi who, for the accomplishment of his ambitions, needs a lot of capital, since the only wealth remaining in the house of Falconeri is its noble title.

Prince Salina officially asks don Calogero for the hand of his daughter on Tancredi's behalf, and the young couple is officially introduced to the noble society of Palermo at a ball given by the Pantaleone family. Glad for the success of Tancredi and Angelica, the prince is also bitterly conscious of the end of his class and the end of his youth. The film ends showing his loneliness and isolation.

"If we want things to stay as they are, things will have to change."[1]

With *The Leopard* Visconti returns to that period of Italian history called *Risorgimento,* which he had already presented in *Senso* (1954). While in *Senso* the plot revolved around the Third War of Independence, the historical setting of *The Leopard* is the expedition of Garibaldi in Sicily. Leading about one thousand men, called the "Red Shirts" because of the color of the uniforms Garibaldi had chosen for his Italian Legion while fighting in South America for the independence of Uruguay from Argentina, Garibaldi disembarked in Marsala and with the help of local rebels defeated the army of Francis II, the Bourbon king. The South was eventually united to the North under Victor Emmanuel, king of Piedmont, who became the first king of Italy.

Visconti's projection on the screen of this epoch of social and political change is based upon the controversial best-seller, *The Leopard,* written by Giuseppe Tomasi di Lampedusa. This novel was published in 1958, a year after the death of its author, a Sicilian prince without a specific profession who for years had in mind the project of writing a novel concerning the political changes in Sicily at the time of the expedition of Garibaldi. The protagonist was to be the author's great-grandfather, Giulio di Lampedusa, recognizable in the novel as Prince Fabrizio Salina. A few months before his death, Giuseppe Tomasi feverishly started to write his novel, which, a year later and almost by chance, was read by Giorgio Bassani, the author of *The Garden of the Finzi-Contini.* Bassani immediately recognized the value of the novel which, published by Feltrinelli, became an immediate best-seller.

The Leopard is indeed an interesting book that deserves its fame for its vivid descriptions of stunning landscapes, for the sensuousness of its images, for the author's sensitive exploration of emotions, and for the well-described characters, especially the protagonist, Prince Salina, a bitter and proud man whose coat of arms shows a prancing leopard with whom the Prince metaphorically identifies. Yet the novel provoked many controversies. Aside from certain passages considered by some critics to be too ornate and decadent, the main controversy centered on the pessimistic political view of history presented throughout the book. Prince Salina is not only skeptical about the *Risorgimento*, but he also sees no possibility of improvement. Scornful of the present and nostalgic about the past, he retreats into the ivory tower of his nobility, contemplating death and refusing to help the new regime. Like any other social upheaval, the *Risorgimento*, called by many "the unfinished revolution," brought changes that were not all positive. The idealism and the heroism of some were at times painfully matched by the opportunism and the greed of others—Italy was united, but only geographically.

Lampedusa's skepticism, however, is pervasive. Personified by Fabrizio Salina, it gives to *The Leopard* a somber political overtone. In the prince's gloomy vision of life only one thing provides solace and peace: the contemplation of stars, pure and far away from the corrupt world.

A hopeless political outlook conflicts with the Marxist ideology that Visconti always professed, but the elegant charm of Fabrizio Salina overcame the objections the director might have had to the novel's political viewpoint. Although Visconti never discussed the conflict in these terms, his contradictory feelings are apparent in an interview with Antonello Trombadori. "Salina's pessimism," Visconti says, "makes him regret the fall of an order, which, for all its rigidity, was nevertheless an order, while our pessimism is charged with will, and instead of regretting the feudal and Bourbon order, strives to postulate a new one."[2] Visconti goes on to say that in his film he wanted to give a challenging charge to the conflict between the fall of the old order (that everything must change) and the establishment of the new (that everything remain the same). Asked if he shared Lampedusa's pessimistic conclusions about Sicily and the modern world, the director admitted that "As for me personally and as far as my film is concerned, I must say that those are not my conclusions; however, one must remember that the roads of hope are not straight and predictable but tortuous—they zigzag."[3]

In the film, however, nothing has been added by Visconti in terms of hope and of a more positive outlook for the future. Salina's views are taken directly from the book and manifest themselves in unequivocal terms during the colloquy between the Prince and

Cavaliere Aimone Chevalley di Monterzuolo, sent by the new government of Victor Emmanuel to offer the position of senator to Prince Salina.

A member of the small Piedmontese aristocracy, accustomed to the green hills of Piedmont covered with vineyards and to a modest but dignified existence, Chevalley is quite disturbed by the contrast between the squalor of the village of Donnafugata and the opulence of the Salina's palace. Alarmed by the hostile expressions of the villagers at his arrival, Chevalley finds reassurance in the courtesy of the prince, whose hospitality he enjoys while trying to push out of his mind the bloody stories about Sicilian brigands. Tancredi is more than willing to relate such tales in vivid detail, describing, for example, the kidnapped boy whose body was returned to his family in pieces and a priest who was poisoned with the Communion wine.

Chevalley survives Tancredi's horror stories and offers Fabrizio Salina the position of senator in the new kingdom of Italy. But to his dismay the prince refuses and suggests for the position don Calogero Sedara. Shaken by the prince's proposal, Chevalley pleads, "If honest people retreat, the door will be open for people without scruples, for the Sedaras; and everything will be as it was before. Listen to your conscience, Prince—help us." Salina responds by observing that "We are old Chevalley, very old. We have been a colony for two thousand and five hundred years. Now we are tired and empty. Sleep is what Sicilians want and they will hate those who want to wake them up." To Chevalley's objection that there are many active Sicilians in Turin, the prince impatiently qualifies his previous statements: "I said Sicilians. I should have said Sicily, the environment, the climate, the Sicilian landscape." Nothing can make the prince change his mind. His rigid view of history, his defeatism cannot be changed by the insistence of Chevalley. When the latter leaves for Turin the next day, Prince Salina concludes his political analysis of the night before by saying, "and then it will be different, but worse. We were the leopards, the lions; our place will be taken by the jackals and the sheep." We are left to wonder whether Prince Salina, having refused to help rescue the kingdom from the jackals, accepts any of the blame for this state of affairs. Nothing in the novel or the film lets us see a responsible participation; Salina's feelings and ideas are as oppressive as the long Sicilian summer that Lampedusa describes so well.

Salina's ideas cannot be appreciated by anybody who believes in political activism and responsibility. A Marxist like Visconti should not feel sympathy for don Fabrizio, who talks about himself as a leopard simply because he inherited a coat of arms. Nevertheless, Visconti was also a nobleman, and if he rebelled against his class by professing communism, he also maintained the expensive tastes, the elegance, and often the hauteur of his origin. His sympathy toward the character of Fabrizio Salina must stem from this.

Portrait of an Era

Like the novel on which it is based, *The Leopard* is not mainly concerned with a political message. It is most of all a portrait of a moribund epoch and of the end of a dynasty. Visconti's political ambiguity is balanced by the skill with which he handles this principal theme. The prince is painfully aware that his class is now defunct, but the other members of his family seem oblivious to this fact. In his book, Lampedusa vividly presents the "real" end of the Salina in two chapters, one concerning the death of the prince and the other concerning the empty existence of the Salina girls, Concetta, Carolina, and Caterina, all of them unmarried and leading secluded lives, totally involved with the veneration of false religious relics that clutter the family chapel. Visconti excluded the last part of the novel from his film, but on more than one occasion he powerfully depicts the dying order.

In the scene showing the arrival of the Salina family at Donnafugata Visconti devoted his celebrated attention to detail to the reconstruction of the main piazza of Donnafugata. A town called Ciminna was chosen because of its similarity to the description of Donnafugata given by Lampedusa. But since Ciminna did not have a palace, and its streets were anachronistically covered with asphalt, the facade of the Salina's palace was built in forty–five days in front of more modern buildings, and the asphalt was scraped from the streets, which were then covered with stones. The rocky streets leading to the town were also covered with dust, since Lampedusa stressed this detail.[4]

After a welcome from the mayor of Donnafugata, Calogero Sedara, the Salinas, followed by the townspeople, enter the Church for a Te Deum to thank God for the safe journey. A beautiful shot from the top of the altar shows their entrance under the indifferent and sad eyes of a multitude of statues. The deafening sound of the bells, the reds and the golds of the ecclesiastic robes, and the clouds of incense give the ceremony a frantic quality, while the Gregorian chants become a

Burt Lancaster as Prince Fabrizio in The Leopard *reads threatening tidings to his disturbed family. (Credit: Movie Star News)*

funeral wail. The camera focuses on the faces of the nobles, which express, in their ashen features, the death of their class and the end of an epoch: the houses of Salina and Falconeri are attending their own funeral.

Fabrizio, Stella, Concetta, Paolo, and all the others have the macabre and artificial look of corpses; even Tancredi, usually at ease in any circumstance, has a scared and bewildered look in his eyes. Always sensitive to pictorial compositions, Visconti has built here an impressive scene, which recalls, with its obsessive repetition of pallid faces of noble and suffering features, the paintings of El Greco. The international background of this painter, Greek by birth, Italian by artistic education, and Spanish by residence, aptly reflects the Sicilian nobility, whose heritage likewise involved the confluence of these three cultures.

Another telling representation of the decline of the nobility is the ball at the Panteleone palace. Visconti chose to end his film at this point, eliminating the last two chapters of the novel, which would have diminished the grandeur of the film. The ball heralds the transition from one class to the other: the old nobility, tired and empty, makes room for the ambition and the opportunism of the new wave of rulers. Everything is changing so that everything will remain the same. The importance given by Visconti to this event is evident: not only does the ball last for one-third of the whole film, but the care given to creating the *mise-en-scene* in the fourteen rooms in which the dance takes place is nothing short of marvellous. The curtains were authentically made of very expensive material, the costumes were painstaking reproductions of the originals, even in the number of petticoats worn under the gowns, and the search for authentic pieces of furniture lasted several months. Like Fellini who invited the Roman nobility to participate in the filming of *La dolce vita* (1960), Visconti invited members of the Sicilian nobility to be among the almost two hundred people participating in the ball. Tommaso M. Cimma describes the difficulties of daily providing the proper makeup and costumes for all of the actors perspiring in the oppressive heat and the fifty-five minutes it took to light the thousand candles illuminating the huge rooms in which the ball takes place. Cimma also mentions the enormous refrigerator and oven specifically built to keep the food at the proper temperature.[5] With this help from modern technology, Visconti could reproduce the magnificent buffet described with so much care by Lampedusa, whose colorful pen wrote about "coralline lobsters boiled alive," "waxy chaud-froids of veal," "pink foie-gras protected by cuirasses of gelatine" and "other cruel, colored delicacies."

Against a background of fleshy flowers, gold-rimmed mirrors, precious candelabras, palm trees, and polychromatic marble, an elegantly dressed multitude dances the hours away and unknowingly celebrates the passing of an era. The only person who is sadly aware of this transition is Prince Salina, who does not seem to notice the effervescent music, the grace of the dancing couples, and the gastronomic delicacies and sinks deeper into depression and disgust with the progression of the hours.

Lampedusa tells us that the prince felt "mildly nauseated" by the sight of young girls jumping on sofas and talking to each other in loud and squeaky voices. The sight of "the colony of those creatures" made him feel like the guardian of a zoo, and he expected to see them swinging from the chandeliers "exhibiting their rear ends." The mood of the prince deteriorates and permeates every aspect of his life with gloom: even the beauty of Angelica and Tancredi appears to the prince as sadly transitory as their love. To Fabrizio Salina the lovers are like actors reciting the parts of Romeo and Juliet, unaware of the presence of the hidden poison. Well directed by Visconti, Burt Lancaster[6] provides a convincing interpretation of Salina's feelings. Salina's expression becomes more and more melancholy, and his features acquire a spectral quality, especially during his contemplation of the "Death of the Just," a painting hanging from the wall of the Pantaleone library where the prince retreats to find some relief from the noise of the party. But the tired "leopard" finds enough energy to take his leave of the epoch with the elegance and dignity of a proud Sicilian noble. Invited by Angelica, the prince dances a waltz, finding again the dancing skills of his youth while the other couples stop dancing to admire Angelica's beauty and Fabrizio's aristocratic bearing. Only two of the spectators do not share the admiration: Stella, Fabrizio's wife, and Concetta, who, in love with Tancredi, must now observe Angelica's triumph, increased by Prince Salina himself. With this waltz, the nobleman not only pays homage to beauty and youth, but also officially and symbolically steps aside to make room for the bold new class represented by the Sedaras. This acquiescence does not disturb the pleasure the prince takes in the beauty and the freshness of Angelica. The gloomy thoughts that have been with him all night long leave his mind during the waltz, and for a while death was again "something that belongs to other people."

The waltz, which is the focal point of the ball is Salina's graceful swan song: his immobile political ideas keep him out of the new order, in which, perhaps, people like him could have made a change, but his elegance and charm allow him to step out with grace. This is not the first time in which the prince found himself face to face with the new power: in another circumstance that Visconti represents as well on the screen as Lampedusa did in writing, Salina steps aside without losing his dignity.

This occasion, not soothed by Angelica's beauty, is compared by the prince in Lampedusa's novel to eating a toad. The "toad" is the request for the hand of Angelica that Salina must make to her father, don Calogero Sedara, on behalf of his nephew, Tancredi. Paolo Stoppa, a well-known actor, shows his skills in portraying the inelegant and vulgar Sedara, whose clumsy social manners are offset by his cunning and indefatigable energy in pursuing wealth and political power. Bundled up in a badly tailored black suit, the gesticulating and perspiring Sedara arrives at the palace and sits in front of the prince, elegant as ever in his light lilac–colored frock coat. The prince makes the marriage proposal, which would have been unthinkable only a few years before, while the astute Sedara listens with feigned surprise. He informs the stunned prince, who did not believe that Sedara's wealth was so great, of the more than generous dowry with which Angelica will fortify the impoverished House of Falconeri. The prince's cool politeness and self–control in front of the excited Sedara disguise his humiliation in finding himself poorer than the mayor of his former fief and in having to inform Sedara of the poverty of Tancredi. The accord between the two men is sealed by an embrace, which the prince quickly performs by lifting the small Sedara from his chair, holding him for a moment against his own huge frame and putting him down again like a puppet. Lampedusa compares the comic sight to a Japanese floral painting in which a hairy black fly hangs from a huge iris. Yet the glorious House of Falconeri is not as impressive as the fields covered with wheat that are now the property of an ill-shaved don Calogero Sedara.

At the end of the meeting, an unexpected satisfaction turns the bitterness of the prince into a hearty laughter, which compensates at least in part for the swallowing of the toad. Don Calogero tells the prince with pathetic pomposity that heraldic researches were about to prove the nobility of the Sedara family and that Angelica could soon be called Baroness Sedara del Biscotto ("of the cookie"). Fabrizio Salina leaves the room laughing, while don Calogero is left to claim his nobility by himself.

The disintegration of the old structure and the building of a new one presenting the same characteristics even if the characters are different is also symbolized by the marriage of Tancredi and Angelica. Coming from very different backgrounds, the two are very similar in their ambition and opportunism. Angelica, educated in Florence thanks to don Calogero's farsightedness, is now ready to conquer the noble class that has scorned for centuries people whose origins were as humble as hers. With her beauty, wealth, and charm she is the rising star at the Pantaleone ball; from that point on, she will be Princess Falconeri. In return for the noble title she is giving Tancredi all the money that the young man needs to start his brilliant political career. Charming, witty, handsome, a hero in the Garibaldi campaign, Tancredi is no less of an opportunist than don Calogero Sedara.

Visconti recognized Tancredi's dubious character and asked himself if such a man could have supported, for his own personal ambition, the Fascist Party. Seeing the glimpse of an affirmative answer in Lampedusa's book, Visconti admits to having presented the character of Tancredi in "this disconcerting and contradictory light."[7]

Visconti does not elaborate on the contradiction, but we can assume that the director sees it in the presence of base traits in a nobleman heroic enough to fight and to be wounded in a revolution in the streets. But nobility and charm do not immunize people from vice: Tancredi's greed is more refined than that displayed by don Calogero, but it is just as despicable. It is the young man who observes that "Everything will have to change so that everything will be the same"; his articulate cynicism is as bad as don Calogero's clumsy cynicism. He is an opportunist, a charming and educated one, who is able to join the prestigious title of the Salinas–Falconeris with the wealth of the Sedaras. It is also interesting to observe how prejudiced the prince's views on human vices and virtues are. Salina, in fact, has nothing but scorn for the opportunism of the Sedaras, whom he contemptuously calls "jackals," while accepting the opportunism of his charming nephew with benign indulgence.

Money and power are not the only forces attracting Angelica and Tancredi to each other. An undeniable aura of sensuality envelops the two young people who are happy to chase each other in the enormous and unexplored rooms of the palace at Donnafugata. In scenes recalling the rendezvous in the granary between Livia and Franz in *Senso* (1954), the sun filtering through the closed shutters chases Angelica and Tancredi, who are kissing in the dark corners of winding staircases and mysterious rooms where silk whips with silver handles suggest erotic rites and self-inflicted punishment. Lampedusa describes this as the happiest time in the lives of Tancredi and Angelica because of the constant presence of a desire always alive because never quenched. Later, when they are "old and uselessly wise," their thoughts will turn to these days compared in the novel to "one of those overtures that survive a forgotten opera." What we see on the screen is a visual symphony of light and darkness, of sudden explosions of reds against backgrounds inundated by the sun, of spatial rhythms, as the camera moves from room to room.

Tancredi and Angelica certainly do not distinguish themselves for idealism and purity of feelings, but their elegance and beauty cannot be denied. Alain Delon and Claudia Cardinale skillfully interpret the two young socialites, always concerned with their appearance and with the desire to charm. At the Panteleone ball they simply conquer everybody with a cool and calculated self-control masqueraded as spontaneity and natural flair. A master at this art, Tancredi finds in Angelica an eager student. "I love you darling," he says to her. "You are beautiful, you are rich, you are ambitious. You'll quickly learn. You want to have a beautiful place in the noble world of Sicily. Together we can face any competition, any fight."

The Dream of Sicily

Prince Salina, don Calogero, Tancredi, and Angelica are not the only characters in *The Leopard*. Sicily, the ever-present background against which the characters are delineated, is itself a powerful personality in the film. At the beginning we see the luxuriant vegetation surrounding Palermo, the wildflowers and the orange groves in a triumph of green and purple and red slightly toned down by the blue of the faraway mountains. Then from Palermo the camera follows the voyage of the Salinas toward Donnafugata in the very heart of Sicily, and the political ambiguity of the island is reflected by its diverse geography. The swarming vegetation of the Palermitan gardens is replaced by a barren lunar landscape. On the yellow mountains punished by the sun, the horses dragging the coaches appear in a masterful long-distance camera shot as black insects struggling on piles of implacable dust. The strange "density" of nature of which Camus speaks is epitomized here in Sicily in these absurdly beautiful surroundings where, Lampedusa writes, death is not darkness but light.

The Sicilian landscape drenched with sun wraps the whole film in an oneiric aura as we view Angelica and Tancredi exploring the ancestral palace, the prince walking in the dusty streets of Donnafugata, the hunting scenes, and the dancing away of an era. Even the fighting of the red-shirted Garibaldini in the streets of Palermo presents a surrealistic imagery where dust, hysterical women taking revenge by murdering Bourbon soldier with knives, and the charge of the Garibaldini, weave a tapestry from almost unbelievable events. Visconti ended the scene of the fighting in the streets with an unusual detail: a young Sicilian boy places a chair on top of a barricade and daringly laughs at the Bourbon soldiers while waving an Italian flag, on which soon appears the date of the Garibaldi expedition, 1860. That year in Italian history was a dream in the minds of many idealists that disappeared at dawn with the less noble demands of reality.

Visconti's insistence on giving *The Leopard* the "presence" of Sicily was very costly. It would have made more sense from a financial point of view to film certain sequences in the theater with the help of good props rather than building anew a section of Palermo and the facade of the palace at Donnafugata, along with its streets. But the director's insistence was based on his usual perfectionism and most of all on the necessity of "being" in Sicily in order to create the oneiric atmosphere permeating the film.

The Leopard is a modern epic in which heroism is sometimes ambiguous and heroes are not virtuous, in which answers do not come easily, and virtues and vices share an elegant, beautiful, and often disconcerting background. Very favorably received by critics and public in Italy and abroad, *The Leopard* is also a film of conflicts: historical, geographic, amorous, psychological, and political. Sometimes struggling himself with contradictions, Visconti nevertheless produced a powerful work.

7

Dubious Ventures into Pirandelloism and Camus: *Sandra* and *The Stranger*

THE LEOPARD, A SUCCESS WITH the critics and the public, became a financial winner, establishing Visconti's fame not only in Italy but also in the rest of Europe and in the United States. Franco Cristaldi, the producer of *Sandra*, called Visconti one of the most courted European directors. "His films had been successful on all markets; his name and fame constituted a financial security. American producers . . . were making incredible offers to him."[1]

Afte: the spectacle of *The Leopard*, Visconti decided to direct a much more economical film, produced by Franco Cristaldi, the producer of *White Nights*. Calling Claudia Cardinale (the beautiful Angelica of *The Leopard*) for the part of the protagonist, he moved with his troupe to Volterra, an ancient Etruscan city located in Tuscany, to film his eighth major cinematic work, *Sandra*.

Sandra (1965): The Plot

Sandra, a young and beautiful woman, returns to Volterra, the place where she was born and spent her childhood and adolescence before leaving for New York, where she will live with her new American husband, Andrew. Sandra's father, a scientist, died in Auschwitz, and her mother, who remarried, is now in a clinic for mental diseases. Sandra believes that her own mother and Gilardini, the mother's second husband, had denounced her father to the Nazis and are responsible for his death.

Gianni, Sandra's brother, arrives from London to meet his sister's husband, and the suspicion soon arises that between brother and sister there existed a more than fraternal love. Gianni, apparently a spoiled young man who once faked suicide in order not to go to a boarding school, has written a book entitled *Vaghe stelle dell'Orsa*

109

Marcello Mastroianni as Meursault in a distraught moment after his arrest in The Stranger. *(Credit: Movie Star News)*

[Beautiful stars of the Ursa], in which he describes the incest of two adolescents, and he secretly threatens Sandra with his intention to publish it.

The uneasiness of the atmosphere culminates at the dinner table, when terrible accusations are exchanged by Gilardini and Sandra. Andrew, shaken by the possibility of an incestuous love involving his wife, demands an answer from Gianni. Receiving none, he hits Gianni and storms out to leave for New York.

Brother and sister reach a dramatic confrontation, after which Gianni kills himself. His body is found by a friend, Pietro, while Sandra is attending a ceremony for the unveiling of a bust in honor of her father.

"The anguish of not being. . ."[2]

What does Visconti mean with this phrase, which he uses to explain our participation in the drama of *Sandra*? He refers to the mystery of life, a mystery that is not clarified, but increasingly complicated, by explanations—a mystery that is present in every human being and that shows its baffling sides every time our existence tries to explain our essence.

In *Sandra* (the thoughtless translation of *Vaghe stelle dell'Orsa*) Visconti tentatively probes into the problem of ambiguity through a sordid family drama. Visconti compared filmmaking, particularly the making of *Sandra*, with ceramics—one never knows how the work will come out of the oven.[3]

Certainly Visconti kept the oven on for a long time. In fact, the script of *Sandra* was not a blueprint determined at the beginning and then fleshed out by the introductions of the characters in the proper slots, but it was a profound search by the director into the maze of human conscience and responsibility. For this reason we have two scripts of *Sandra*, the first of which was never filmed because it lacked the necessary ambiguity in its treatment of guilt, which is crucial to the problem of "not being."

In the first version, Gianni is a dissipated man who enjoys himself by stimulating passionate feelings in his sister. He is a coward who pretends to shoot himself and an egomaniac who is determined to publish his book. In the first version, Sandra's motives for revenge and her expectation of aid from her brother are too absolute—a problem that lingers even in the final version. For this reason Sandra has been called a modern Electra,[4] but the desire to avenge her father's death is less important to Sandra than her struggle with her relationship with her brother.

Also, when we consider the analogy between Sandra's desire for revenge and Electra's, we have to keep in mind that if Sandra is an Electra, she is a modern one, and this qualification makes an important difference. In Greek mythology there is a relentless Fate, and the roles of protagonist and antagonist are clear because the characters are *defined* as either guilty or innocent. Our era does not judge guilt with the rigor of ancient times, but this greater tolerance has not contributed to the elevation of the human being; on the contrary, it has left us in the tightening grip of doubt. Responsibility for the atrocious murder of Emmanuel Wald Luzzatti at Auschwitz, cannot be pinpointed. Even people directly touched by it, like Sandra and Gianni, confuse the issue of guilt with personal feelings.

Gianni, for instance, sees Sandra's pilgrimage to Auschwitz as a mortification for her sexual desires and an excuse to persecute her mother and Gilardini. "You have been in the concentration camps to reconstruct the agony of our father," he says to Sandra. "You hid your affection for me under a mask of sacrifice. You created for yourself a moral in order to persecute a poor sick woman and a rascal." In these confused times of "not being" even sorrow wears a mask. After seeing *Sandra* we know about guilt, we know about an oppressive curtain of smoke that nobody has the courage to cross but as Mario Verdone observes, at the end of the film we don't know more than we know at the beginning about the sins of the characters.[5]

By the end of the film, when the rabbi pronounces the funeral prayer in front of the marble bust of Emmanuel Wald Luzzatti, and Pietro, the doctor, is about to tell Sandra of the suicide of her brother, there remain more questions than answers: How could Sandra be so lighthearted as she leaves the house in the morning, after Gianni has threatened to commit suicide, "this time for real"? And what is the meaning of the fearful expression on the mother's face, half covered by a black glove, when the bust is unveiled? Is it remorse? Did she, together with Gilardini, denounce her late husband? Was there an incestuous passion between brother and sister? Does the mother claim this because she is mentally disturbed or did she become ill because of "the monstrosity" perpetrated in her house? Why is Sandra opposed to trying a new method of therapy, recommended by Pietro, on her mother?

The film avoids melodrama by concealing the innermost thoughts and motives of the characters. The result is a Pirandellian search for a truth that cannot be discovered because it may not exist. *Sandra* bears an obvious resemblance to Pirandello's *Right You Are*, in which family members struggle with the double edges of their relative truths, and to *Six Characters in Search of an Author*, where a family circles fearfully around sexual "impropriety."

Sandra also resembles Pirandello's plays in its use of an observer, in this case Andrew, the American husband. Andrew's observation of the developing drama expresses the search for conviction, always elusive in Pirandello's plays because of the insolubility of the situation, although his response is emotional rather than intellectual. Andrew's angry reaction to the confused reality is that of an honest, dull, but loving husband jarred by the possibilities of a past treason and of an incest.

While it is impossible to establish responsibility for the death of the father, it is relatively easy to assess the erotic games between brother and sister. On one hand we have the constant denial from Sandra; on the other, telling hints from Gianni. But the imagery that Visconti provides leaves little doubt. The first meeting between brother and sister occurs in the garden, amid trembling leaves shaken by the sudden rising of the wind. This scene recalls a poem by Federico García Lorca, in which the wind is a symbol of sexual desire:

> Déjame tranquila, hermano,
> son tus besos en mi espalda
> avispas y vientecillos

("Leave me alone, brother, your kisses on my shoulder are like wasps and wind ")

The effect of the wind on Sandra explains her irritation with Gianni when the latter takes off his shirt in front of her.

In another scene Sandra and Gianni meet at the bottom of a dry ancient Roman cistern. The rendezvous has the unambiguous quality of a secret meeting between two children playing a dangerous game. The spiral staircase, the shadowy silence of the place, the humidity reeking from the ancient walls, Gianni hiding playfully behind a column, and especially the wedding ring he takes from Sandra's finger to put on his own—such details bring us right to the brink of a concealed truth.

The heavily suggestive meetings between brother and sister are distinguished in three progressively menacing levels of expression: the first meeting is light and stimulating like the mischievous wind that fills the screen; the second, dark and sensuous inside the mossy walls of the Roman cistern where we come very close to a physical revelation; and the third, a scary walk along the abyss of truth. In yet another scene Gianni pleads for companionship and love, hinting at but never revealing the kind of affection he desires. "I burnt my book for you, Sandra," he says. "You are so young, so beautiful. Come back as you were."

The weight of the scene is all on Jean Sorel, who is able to give to Gianni the pathos of a man who is perhaps immoral, but who is "still capable of a great gesture." The great gesture, from Gianni's point of view, is the burning of the book, but even about this event we cannot be sure, because we have only his word and no proof. But we do have proof of Gianni's death, the "great gesture" which, in its macabre finality, gives the film its only resolution.

Rinaldo Ricci sees a parallel between the end of Gianni and that of Gregor Samsa in Kafka's *Metamorphosis*.[6] The similarity that Ricci sees is in the representation of Gianni dying on the floor and discerning out of the window the first light of dawn while the last breath of life flows from his nostrils. But this is not the only resemblance between Kafka's story and Sandra's.

In *The Metamorphosis*, Grete, who takes care of Gregor, is closer to him than the other members of the family, who are either terrified (the mother) or ashamed (the father). Gregor, who longs for his sister, expresses his feelings in a frighteningly sad episode in which he crawls toward Grete, who is playing the violin. "He was determined to force himself on until he reached his sister, to pluck at her skirt, and to let her know in this way that she should bring the violin into his room. . . . He would never again let her out of his room—at least not for as long as he lived."[7] But Grete also becomes terrified by Gregor's change, and eventually she is the one that pronounces his sentence: "It has to go."[8] And Gregor lets himself die.

Similarly Sandra, after a time of intense closeness, refuses to communicate with Gianni, whose nature alarms her. She finally pushes him out of her life. "If you go away, I'll kill myself," Gianni threatens. "If you leave me it will be the end of me." Gianni lowers himself to the state of an insect, an insect that pleads, yells, and cries, but Sandra is unmoved. "You are already dead for me, Gianni."

The passion of Gianni is unmistakable, but Sandra's stony answers
and her coldness seem to contradict her brother's admissions. Step by
step the viewer, provided with clues, is taken closer to the source of
the "mystery," but Sandra continues to deny everything. The
passionate tension between brother and sister, contrasting with the
calm rapport between Sandra and her husband, seems to support
Gianni, but to the very end, after we have established the existence of
feelings and desire, we don't know exactly what happened between
the two. Every character, Visconti said, with the exception of Andrew, is ambiguous, and it is impossible to give a logical explanation
to a world dominated by deep, contradictory, and unexplainable
passions.[9]

There is, however, a time when these passions are simply felt and
do not require explanations from the logical mind. This time is
childhood and early adolescence. Gianni refers to this "precivilized"
period in a conversation with Sandra. "Suddenly I remember everything, our silences, our conversations, my anxieties, the sleepless
nights. A feeling already felt when I was a child, in the age in which
one should not know passions." *Sandra* is also and especially a film
about longing for the past and a drama about growing up and out of
the cauldron of childhood.

The theme of lost youth is suggested by the original Italian title
Vaghe stelle dell'Orsa [Beautiful stars of the Ursa], which is also the
title of Gianni's book and a line from a poem by Giacomo Leopardi,
recited in part by Gianni:

> Vaghe stelle dell'Orsa, io non credea
> tornare ancor per uso a contemplarvi
> sul paterno giardino scintillanti
> e ragionar con voi dalle finestre
> di questo albergo ove abitai fanciullo
> e delle gioie mie vidi la fine

[Beautiful stars of the Ursa, I did not think that I would come back to
contemplate you, shining on the paternal garden, and to talk to you from this
place where I lived as a child and where I saw the end of my happiness.]

Beauty, memories, night, ancestral home—all these elements have
the tenderness and the sadness of a lost paradise, a garden of Eden
with the serpent lurking in the grass.

As a background for the lost paradise, Visconti could not have
chosen a better place than Volterra, rising and crumbling on the

remnants of an Etruscan necropolis. The mocking smiles of the Etruscan gods, seemingly addressed to those who want to discover the secrets of these mysterious people, express the laughter of truth. Unfortunately, the elusive and scornful grins of the Etruscan statues have not been utilized by Visconti, who emphasizes only the death images of sarcophagi and crumbling alabaster. But the Etruscan sensuousness that lingers at every site once inhabited by this race is a tangible presence in the heaviness of the nights, in the softness of the leaves, and in the slow decaying of palaces and churches.

Sandra is a nocturnal film, in which somber tones are representations of repressed sexuality. All the important scenes take place during the night, while the diurnal events are irrelevant and brief links between one night and the other. The tour of the city taken by Andrew with Gianni as a guide, was actually filmed in the middle of the day but was transformed into a night sequence with the help of modern technology supplying the camera with lenses that changed the sun into the moon, and the light of the day into darkness. We see Andrew, the logical one, more often in the daylight than Sandra, who shares the sun with Andrew at the beginning, during their trip to Italy, and then progressively slips further into the night by joining her brother, a real creature of shadow, who appears in the obscurity of the twilight, decides to put an end to his own life in the darkness, and dies right before the breaking of dawn. After her brother's death, Sandra reappears in the clearness of the morning at the dedication of her father's bust. The sordid calls of a forbidden sexuality are gone with the person who issued them.

It would seem at this point that a tearful Sandra, dressed in white mourning, has come home to bury her past and has succeeded, but it would not be the characteristic of the film to reach such an unequivocal conclusion. The rabbi's words hint at the mystery that remains: "The earth will give life back to the shadows." The shadows that Sandra is trying to bury, we are left to believe, will come back.

Definitely not a film for people looking for mere entertainment, *Sandra,* distinguished by good acting, is a well constructed and profound work. Even though the public and critics expected from Visconti another historical giant like *The Leopard, Sandra,* with its narrow psychological labyrinth depicted in black and white tones so different from the lively color of the preceding film, was liked and appreciated in Italy.

Satisfied with its success, Visconti returned to the theater with Chekhov's *The Cherry Orchard* and Arthur Miller's *After the Fall,* which he directed in Paris. Back in Italy in 1967, he accepted an offer to direct an episode of the film *Le streghe* [The witches], entitled "La strega bruciata viva" [The witch burned alive], which concerns the life of a movie star involved in publicizing a detergent.

  With this episode Visconti encountered great obstacles due to disagreements with producer Dino De Laurentiis, who considered the episode too long and wanted it cut, against the will of the director. Nor was this the last conflict that Visconti encountered that year. Having decided to film Camus's *The Stranger*, with De Laurentiis again as producer, Visconti hoped to work freely on his personal interpretation of this great literary work, but he found himself in an even more inhibiting situation.

The Stranger (1967): The Plot

  Meursault, a Frenchman living in Algiers, receives a telegram informing him that his mother has died at a home for aged persons. On a scorching afternoon, he attends the wake, accepting a *café au lait* from the housekeeper and subsequently following the funeral to the burial site. The day after, on the beach, Meursault meets Marie, a pretty young woman who, from that day, becomes his lover. He also becomes friendly with Raymond, a pimp, who has started a quarrel with an Arab, his girl friend's brother.

  During an afternoon spent on a secluded beach, Meursault, Raymond, and Raymond's friend Masson spot two Arabs that are slowly walking toward them. One of the two men is the Arab holding a grudge against Raymond. A violent fight, in which Meursault does not participate, ensues, leaving Raymond bleeding from a gash in the arm and from a lighter cut in the mouth produced by a knife which one of the Arabs has suddenly pulled out. After being taken to a doctor, Raymond, animated by a vindictive desire, returns with Meursault to the place of the fight, this time with a gun, but at the sight of the weapon the two Arabs quickly vanish and the two Frenchmen return to Masson's beach bungalow where Marie and Mrs. Masson are waiting. While Raymond steps inside, Meursault returns to the place of the incident for no apparent reason. Oppressed by the heat and by the sun, and with Raymond's revolver in his pocket, he comes to a standstill in front of one of the Arabs who is resting near the rocks. The two men silently stare at each other for a while; then the Arab pulls a knife out of his pocket and the sunlight, reflected by the blade, hits Meursault's forehead. The latter shoots once and then four more times in the inert body of the Arab.

A trial ensues, but it soon becomes clear that the death of the young Arab is now secondary: the issue is Meursault's behavior at his mother's funeral and his irreligiosity. The *café au lait* that he drank during the wake, the cigarette that he smoked, his friendship with a pimp, his liaison with Marie, which began the day after the death of his mother, and his disbelief in God are the evidence that brings the death penalty.

Meursault spends the last few days before his execution not in fear but in tender remembrance of life on the outside. When the chaplain, whom he has always refused to see, finally finds a way to get inside the cell and tries to extract a prayer from him, Meursault refuses and passionately reaffirms his belief in this life with all its futility and yet with all its certainties.

"*The Stranger* is the illustration of a book, without my real participation"[10]

Visconti called *The Stranger* "a child born with limitations." He agreed to bring the film to light because of the contract that he had already signed with Dino De Laurentiis, who wanted this film at any cost. But this time, the disagreement was not with the producer but with Camus's widow, Francine.

Whenever Visconti decided to bring to the screen a literary work, he remained only partially faithful to it, always exercising his freedom to change according to the difference of the medium and his own wish to manipulate the material. After the death of Camus in 1960 in a tragic automobile accident, Visconti decided to bring to the screen *L'étranger*. This was not an easy task, since this classic of existentialist literature combines with a simple form a cryptic content, mostly made mysterious by the personality of a man whose elusiveness has preoccupied the minds of readers and critics alike.

How did Visconti plan to bring to the screen the gripping feeling of "clear absurdity" that permeates *L'étranger*? First of all, he wanted to transpose it to modern times (*L'étranger* was published in 1938) and to place it against a background of the French-Algerian war.[11] With this intention he prepared a script with the cooperation of Georges Conchon. To his great disappointment, he found out that Francine Camus, the writer's widow, forbade any deviation from the original text. In light of this insistence, we can understand Visconti's lack of enthusiasm when he talks about the film, completed mainly to fulfill a contract.

Since the script prepared by Conchon and Visconti has not been published, it is impossible to say whether the free interpretation that the director wanted for *The Stranger* would have been more effective than the literal transposition of sentences taken from the novel and brought to the screen with a scruple that can hardly mask Visconti's resentment for not having been allowed to interpret. Since Visconti's intention was to enlarge the role of the Arab-French conflict that flickers throughout the novel and to have it burst into a war by transposing it forward twenty years, most probably the Arab rebellion, constantly but marginally present in *L'étranger,* would have played in Visconti's interpretation a much heavier role. Actually, the view of the Arabs in *The Stranger,* however limited by the script, is the most personal part of the film, especially in the brief but intense moments in which we are allowed to see the lively scintillating of dark eyes, the distant chants, and lamenting voices that convey the impression of a repressed group whose emotions are boiling in a tightly sealed pot. The violence at the beach would have had a political resonance, and its absurdity would have been related to the more universal absurdity of war.

However, Visconti found himself strictly tied to a great novel, a difficult novel, the simple form of which does not facilitate understanding. He was immediately confronted with the task of finding a face for Meursault, the protagonist, the stranger who is never called by his first name. To represent *L'étranger,* Visconti chose the familiar face of Marcello Mastroianni. This choice was definitely the first mistake in the reduction of the novel to the film. Mastroianni is excellent in his acting, especially in the second part of the film, when this actor, always associated with the melancholy playboy of *La dolce vita* (1960), projects surprising dramatic intensity. Paradoxically, this "good" acting does not help the film because the well-known and pleasant face of Marcello Mastroianni cannot generate in the audience the "absurd" mediocrity of the anonymous Meursault.

This absurd character, defined in so many different ways by so many critics, remains basically unexplained, unexplained according to the logical framework of the mind, always desiring to unify the fragments of reality. As Sartre said, "*The Stranger* is not an explanatory book. The absurd man does not explain; he describes. Nor is it a book which proves anything."[12] Meursault, the absurd man, escapes us in fact. His apparent indifference to his mother's death, his lack of commitment to Marie, the "help" that he gives to Raymond, a shady character with vengeful intentions against his own girl friend, create around Meursault a foggy curtain that breaks at times, leaving space that reveals a flickering of tender interest in life, but nothing more than this transpires in the first part of the book. In the second part instead, this man who had started reminiscing with the words, "Mother died today. Or maybe yesterday; I can't be sure," blossoms into a poet.[13] Faced with death he sings for the life that he barely skimmed.

Meursault definitely is absurd, but Mastroianni is not. As Lino Miccichè rightly says, "The absurd man Meursault . . . is transformed by Visconti into a too transparent good boy. . . . One ends up by empathizing with him, by being moved by human pity in front of his tears of fear . . . by understanding the mechanics of his crime."[14]

Mastroianni is clear. He is clearly tired and hot and in need of a cigarette in the mortuary. When the keeper offers to unscrew the lid of the coffin so that Meursault can see his mother for a last time, the expression with which he tells the keeper not to bother is also clear: it shows pain for the loss, even though mother and son did not have anything to say to each other for a long time. With Meursault, this is not clear: "While he was going up to the coffin I told him not to trouble. 'Eh? What's that?' he exclaimed. 'You don't want me to?' 'No,' I said"[6]. Short, telegraphic sentences complicate meanings, particularly with regard to Meursault's feelings. Who is Meursault? He never answers this question with insights into his feelings. He barely says that at that point he felt "rather embarrassed." We do not know whether he did not want to see his mother because he was moved (it does not seem to be so) or simply because he did not want to get up.

Mastroianni also provides an unexpected insight in an episode which in the book is as cryptic as everything else. When the employer calls Meursault and offers him a job in Paris, the response of the absurd man is as vague as ever:

I told him I was quite prepared to go; but really I didn't care much one way or the other. . . . As a student I'd plenty of ambition of the kind he meant. But, when I had to drop my studies, I very soon realized all that was pretty futile (52).

Camus does not tell us anything more about the episode, leaving us in the dark about the causes of the sense of futility that permeates Meursault's life. Is he bitter, sad, or light-hearted about it? Just as we cannot comprehend the reason why he did not want to take a final look at his mother, we cannot understand the reason for his feeling of futility.

In the film the printed words lose their ambiguity. Here, in fact, we see for the first time a light of great intensity on the face of Mastroianni. He says that everything is futile with a passion that leaves no doubt that the stranger is just a man who has been disappointed by life and is reacting with anger by trying not to get too involved with it. In Mastroianni's intense reaction of anger and sorrow, we can also see the pain caused by the loss of his mother and again the reason why he did not want the keeper to unscrew the lid of the casket.

In the visitors' room at the prison Meursault's attention is captured by the sight of an old woman and a very young man whose eyes "were fixed on the little old woman opposite him, and she returned his gaze with a sort of hungry passion." Meursault's attention returns to the couple several times during the visiting session. He notices that in the din an "oasis of silence was made by the young fellow and the old woman gazing into each other's eyes." He also catches the farewell between the two: "He called, 'Au revoir, Mother,' and, slipping her hand between the bars, she gave him a small, slow wave with it" (94). Nothing in the novel suggests that Meursault takes more than a passing interest in the scene. He simply appears to be intrigued by the silence of the two, and he examines them with the same detached interest with which he observed a meticulous woman at a restaurant. Meursault is so fascinated by this "little robot," who paid the bill in advance and ticked off items in a magazine throughout the meal, that he follows her in the street for a short distance, "having nothing better to do."

In the film, the prison scene is transformed by Mastroianni's eyes, which show more longing than those of the young man. Mastroianni's Meursault is not the stranger; he is a man who has lost his mother and, through a series of very unfortunate circumstances, finds himself in prison, separated from his girlfriend. Mastroianni's expression shows sadness and tenderness for the barrier between mother and son and for the one between himself and Marie.

Several times Mastroianni "explains" Meursault or, better, changes him into another man; paradoxically, with a strong dramatic interpretation he misses the point. And so when the absurd man is missing, *The Stranger* is also missing, and the literal transposition of the novel to the screen is only apparently Camus. Forced not to change anything, Visconti changed everything. As Lino Miccichè observes, "Visconti stepped aside, but Camus did not come in."[15]

There are other elements in the film that deserve to be considered. For example, there is the social background that Visconti wanted to modernize and transpose to the French-Algerian war. The main character is French, as are his friends, and the institutions, but surrounding the French social structure there is a simmering Arab presence. The chants, the language resounding in the streets, the glances, sometimes defiant, sometimes loving, the dark mysterious life lurking in the background—all these are links of a chain that surround the doomed colonial administration. The same feeling of the uneasy isolation of the European in another country is present in Antonioni's *The Passenger* (1975), especially in the opening scene where Locke (Jack Nicholson), stranded in the desert, finds nothing but empty stares and silence from the suddenly appearing and suddenly disappearing North Africans. The passenger is also a stranger, a stranger who exchanges the futility of his life for the futility of another life in a Pirandellian twist of identity. Like Meursault, he will be executed erroneously. There are interesting similarities between *The Passenger* and *The Stranger*, such as the feeling of not belonging and the ambivalence of the European in a world which does not belong to him.

It is unfortunate that Visconti was not allowed to expand this theme which in 1967, the year in which the film was made, could have had a great relevance to the international situation. The ambivalence of two worlds coexisting in love and hatred that is evident in the novel is also clearly seen in the film. When Meursault enters a cell full of Arabs, he is asked about his crime. "I told them I'd killed an Arab, and they kept mum for a while. But presently night began to fall, and one of them explained to me how to lay out my sleeping mat" (89). He has killed "one of them," and yet he himself is one of them. Camus was very well aware of the conflict of being a "pied noir," which he expresses here in the unfriendly silence of the Arabs and in the following friendly gesture of one of them. Visconti develops the scene through one of the few deviations from the novel in the film. The Arabs fall silent and stand away from Mastroianni, but subsequently a young man offers him a cigarette while another plays a little reed flute just like the Arab at the beach. This personal touch given by Visconti does not amount to much, but it is an indication of the road that the director would have taken if he had been allowed to interpret freely. The secondary characters surrounding Mastroianni are truer to the novel than the protagonist. The violent Raymond, old Salamano, Marie, and the old people at the house are all well represented, in part because their personalities are transparent in relation to Meursault's. Keeping pace with the novel, Visconti quickly introduces them with a disturbing realism, especially evident at the wake, where friends of the deceased come in and sit silently in front of the casket. The blinding light painfully underlines the wrinkles, the tears, the lifeless eyes, and the sadness of being close to the end: never have ghosts been seen so clearly. The wagging of their heads seems to suggest a reproach. "For a moment I had an absurd impression that they had come to sit in judgement on me." This silent trial is a preview of the noisy and chaotic one that, with its tautness and dramatic tempo, is the highlight of the film.

In the courtroom scene, an anxious and unruly public underlines with murmurs and titters the answers given by Mastroianni. The beads of perspiration on the foreheads of the actors, the frantic motion of the fans, and the shouts of the lawyers contribute to a feeling of confusion that makes the courtroom seem more like a Roman arena. The dramatic tempo is maintained through color as well as sound. The shirts of the crowd, the togas of the lawyers, and Marie's dress create a kaleidoscopic sequence of blinding white, black, and scarlet that provides the transition between the bright colors of the Algerian countryside and seashore and the somber shady world of the cell.

In the last part of the film, the world around Mastroianni closes in on him with the darkness and the constriction of prison. His face shows the strain by appearing older and unshaven in the greenish light. *The Stranger*, which started with a superabundance of bright colors, finishes in almost total darkness, with the exception of the fading rays of sunlight on the dark stones of the cell.

Contrasting with the final somber tone is the lightness of the Algerian life portrayed at the beginning. Here Visconti's attention to Camus's text is only apparent. While it is possible to perceive the heat of the sun and the vivid colors, the obsessiveness of the light extracting from the objects an independent existence is not there. Just as the absurd man Meursault has been transformed into the familiar Mastroianni, the "inhuman, discouraging" landscape has become the background for a normal human funeral inconvenienced by too much heat. In Visconti's version we see green fields, blue mountains, reddish earth, all enveloped by the dazzling rays of the sun and trembling waves of heat surrounding the pathetic silouette of Perez. These elements, technically well composed, fail nevertheless to convey the sensation of violence and hostility conjured up by Camus. In the novel, the death of the mother is more than a sad affair conducted under the oppression of the North African heat; it is an assault on life by a cruelly indifferent nature.

Similarly, the influence of the sun at the time of the murder is more than the extrinsically faithful transcription given by Visconti. The director shows the obsessiveness of the sun and Mastroianni's distress through a repetition of glaring images, but the sequence does not convey the powerful hostility suggested in the novel by the "sunlight splintering into flakes of fire" (70), by the thudding of the light in Meursault's head and by the "hot blast" (73) striking his forehead. The sun is attacking Meursault: "Whenever a blade of vivid light shot upward from a bit of shell or broken glass lying in the sand, my jaws set hard. I wasn't going to be beaten" (73). Visconti understates the violence of the landscape but maintains the dramatic tempo of the scene through his emphasis on the water and its sounds. The sound of the waves, which in Camus's words, was "even lazier, feebler than at noon" (74), is in Visconti's film a clamor similar to the reaction of the spectators at the trial, a pounding, rhythmical background to the sharper noise of the blows during the fist fight between Meursault's friends and the Arabs. Again, at the time of the murder, a small stream barely tinkling in the novel, provides a distinct and forceful noise of rushing water. Why did Visconti choose to give to the sound of the water an importance greater than the one given to it by Camus? Because of the director's reluctance in talking about *The Stranger* we do not have any specific information; we can only speculate on the reasons for the change. One possibility could be that Visconti, aware of the lack of pathos in the images, intended to fill the void with the cooperation of the significantly dramatic sound of water. Another reason, more remote but not too farfetched, could be a reminiscence of *The Leopard* (1963), or more accurately, a reference to a part of Lampedusa's novel that Visconti intentionally did not put in the film version. By stopping it at the ball, as we have seen, Visconti eliminated two chapters, one of them concerning the death of the Prince. In this chapter Lampedusa describes the dying of Fabrizio Salina, seen from the inside as the experience of the person who is dying and not, as more often happens in literature, from the observation of the spectators. The slow loss of vitality that Prince Salina has felt during all of his adult life intensifies: what was like a mild buzzing or the ticking of a clock in moments of silence is now like the dropping of a waterfall changing into the rushing of a river and finally turning into the clamor of the sea before the final great silence. Death, which had been compared by Fabrizio so many times before to light and scorching sun, is now water, whose symbolic meaning, absent from Visconti's version of *The Leopard,* seems to timidly appear in *The Stranger.*

Unfortunately this personal stroke, along with a few others, weighs very lightly on the total canvas. We can imagine the frustration of the director, whose good technical direction, especially visible in the trial and in the wake, could not compensate for that lack of freedom which was intended to keep him faithful to Camus, but which backfired, leaving very little of Visconti and very little of Camus. Presented without success at the Mostra of Venice, this frustrated film has not disappeared from circulation. It is often presented in film series related to contemporary French novels, and succeeds in gripping audiences with the tension Visconti has been able to bring to the screen, even though Mastroianni is not Meursault and the hostile cosmic irrationality presented in the novel becomes a commonplace series of senseless misfortunes. Criticized by almost every critic and, indirectly, by the silence of its director (usually very intense in the defense of his products), *The Stranger* seems to have had, nevertheless, some success "per absurdum."

8

The German Trilogy Launched: *The Damned*

AFTER *The Stranger,* Visconti begins his most "decadent" period of artistic expression. Giovanni Grazzini, in an intelligent article entitled "Visconti, the Career of an Artisan," perceives the direction which the director's work will take, analyzing the discrepancies between Visconti's political proclivities and his family heritage.[1] According to Grazzini, Visconti is faithful to the "red food" of his youth, but wants to incorporate it with the "ancient juices of his blue race." The result is, Grazzini continues, "a purple mixture," which is "the disquieting background of a sumptuous but ambiguous liturgy." The observation is indeed expressive and acute. From this point on, Visconti will be almost totally preoccupied with themes of death, solitude, and perversion, all presented with luxury and pomp. The social and political concerns, the emotional complexity of *Rocco,* the indignation expressed in *La terra trema*—the youthful passions— give way to a solitary, resigned passion.

In his article Grazzini perceives also a certain tiredness in Visconti and a disquieting feeling seething through the apparent luxurious perfection of the director's life. Having admired the elegance of Visconti's apartment, decorated with splendid works of art, Grazzini observes the director opening a box of marrons glacés: "There is a box of marrons glacés on the big sofa. Visconti opens it to offer them. But a lewd long line of ants nesting in the luxury comes out. They run on the carpets and they lightly touch his [Visconti's] hands."

However, the faltering inspiration sensed by Grazzini did not mean inactivity for Visconti, who, after the production of Verdi's *La Traviata* and the direction of another play by Giovanni Testori, *La monaca di Monza,* returns to the cinema to begin his German trilogy with the impressive *The Damned.*

127

The Damned, *before and after: the SA's gay party on the "Night of the Long Knives." (Credit: Movie Star News)*

The Damned (1967): The Plot

The rising power of Nazism in Germany during the early thirties spreads its influence on the Von Essembecks, a wealthy and noble family who owns a very productive steel mill. Aschenbach, a cousin of the Essembecks who is an SS member, helps Friederich Bruckmann, Sophie Essembeck's lover, to gain control of the steel mill. Joachim von Essembeck, the old patriarch of the family, is found mysteriously murdered, and Herbert, the only member of the family who vehemently accuses the Nazi party of violence and inhumanity, is falsely accused of the murder and narrowly avoids arrest by escaping through a window. One more obstacle stands in the way of the power-hungry lovers: Constantine von Essembeck, a coarse and beefy character who cannot understand his son Günther's love of music and who also has strong political support since he belongs to the SA. But the SS, led by Aschenbach, murders Constantine along with fellow SA members in a massacre obviously inspired by the real killing, which occurred during "the night of the long knives."

In the meantime, Friederich's nerves are unable to take the stress, the violence (he was present at the massacre), the constant struggle, the fear; thus another member of the family, helped by Aschenbach, is grabbing for the von Essembecks' power. The new man is Martin, a sexual deviant who seduces children, and who, up to this point, has been totally manipulated by his mother, Sophie. Martin hates his mother, who used him to convey all the power to her lover, Friederich, and decides to destroy her by raping her and subsequently keeping her under constant sedation till the day of her wedding with Friederich. The ceremony, orchestrated by Martin in an SS uniform, is indeed a funeral, since the son's wedding presents for his mother and new stepfather are two capsules of cyanide poison. After the instant death of the two, the film closes, with the fire of the steel mill in the background, as Martin gives the Nazi salute.

"I could not open any gleam of hope in that family of monsters. . ."[2]

Visconti did not introduce any positive elements in this film in which a family reflects the surge to power of Nazism. After viewing *The Damned,* one is left with the feeling of having watched a pit of vipers, reflecting through its personal battles the Nazi struggle for power on the outside.

As in *La terra trema* (1948), *Rocco and His Brothers* (1960), *The Leopard* (1963), and *Conversation Piece*(1974), the action revolves around a family, politically very powerful this time, to the point of being needed by the Nazis. While the other families, even the noble Salina group, are politically too insignificant to create a social impact, the Essembecks, with their steel mills and wealth, are shown to be a major factor in the life of Germany. Visconti observed, "I want to ask this picture where lay the responsibility for the Nazi in Germany. The most grave responsibility was with the bourgeoisie and the industrialists, because if Hitler had not had their help he would never have arrived to real power. Books say that the Krupps paid Hitler, so I don't invent."[3] And so he chose the very wealthy Essembecks and, as he very often does in his films, introduced them all together by showing them at dinner. "The dining-room as a place of reunion of the family, encounter and collision of the participant to this ritual, is in almost all of my films. It is like a beehive: every one works in his little cell, then they all congregate in a central place with the queen bee."[4] Visconti could not have described the situation better, especially in the case of the Essembecks, who, with their perpetual plotting, call to mind the industrious work of malevolent bees whose honey will be far from sweet.

The opening of *The Damned* is rather peaceful. We see the family members getting ready for the sumptuous dinner by donning elegant clothing, while blonde children wish happy birthday to their grandfather, Joachim von Essembeck. Visconti says that for this opening scene he was inspired by the dinner in Thomas Mann's *Buddenbrooks*, even if the stories are different.[5] And indeed they are, but at the beginning of the film there are also similarities. One is, of course, the fact that the story is about a wealthy Germany family (even if the Buddenbrooks are not as powerful as the Essembecks). Another concerns the heavy imagery and the slow and orderly pace of the beginning of the dinner, which, at this point, echoes Thomas Mann's words in *Buddenbrooks*: "They all sat on heavy, high-backed chairs, consuming good heavy food from good heavy silver plate."[6] But the Buddenbrooks are a "good" family, a family that loses its power because of the lack of strength in its members and because of unfortunate circumstances; the Essembecks are a bad family who gain power through unbridled and unscrupulous greed. At this point in the film we see the only gentle moments of the family gathering when the children recite a poem and when Günther plays the cello. Like Hanno Buddenbrooks his love of music is greater than his interest in the family wealth, and, like Hanno, who is swept away by typhoid fever, Günther will be swept away by another disease called hatred, which kills morally if not physically.

Constantine, who does not hide his sympathies for the Nazi, interrupts Martin's exhibition to announce that the Reichstag is burning. The young man who appears on an improvised stage, dressed as Marlene Dietrich's blue angel is indeed a disquieting apparition, which obviously shocks the solid bourgeois virtues of the old baron. In this disguise, Martin shows an arrogance that he will soon lose, when he falls again under his own mother's power. He regains his sense of superiority toward the end of the film, when he wears the Nazi uniform. The woman's disguise is just the beginning of Martin's mis-deeds, because during the same night he rapes his little cousin with whom he enjoyed playing games under the piano. Martin's pedophilic tendencies do not stop here; in fact, later on in an episode added by Visconti at a moment in which the film seemed to have reached a dead end, the young Essembeck seduces a little Jewish girl who, in shock, hangs herself.

Visconti describes this episode as a possibility of stepping out of the family environment and, at the same time, of explaining Martin's nature.[7] Although the sequence showing Martin and the girl is effective in presenting the squalor of the situation, emphasized by the starkness of the room, the wooden horse brought by Martin as a present (a veritable horse of Troy hiding danger and death inside its peaceful appearance), and the radio broadcasting an angry Nazi speech, alternated with waves of icy silence, the fragmentary episode turns out to be a slow and unnecessary interpolation. Martin's nature does not need more explanation: his disguise, the scream of his little cousin in the night and, later on, the rape of his own mother, would have been more than enough to convince the audience of his perversity.

From the very beginning also, the only possible positive character, Herbert, the one who could have had a good influence on Günther by saving him from falling in the pit of the communal hatred, is ostracized and forced to resign from the direction of the steel mill because of his fierce opposition to the Nazi regime. From this point on, the power struggle among the members of the family assumes gigantic proportions and everything is engulfed in a whirlpool of conspiracy.

Visconti's queen bee is Sophie Essembeck (Ingrid Thulin), the conniving woman who uses her sexuality to satisfy her thirst for power. This is Sophie's real passion, to which even love-making is subordinated, as is apparent when she takes possession of Friedrich, surrounding him with her strong arms and hands covered with jewels, while her mind is always involved in machinations. Angular features, feline eyes, blood-colored nails are details that, emphasized by heavy makeup, suggest the rapacious nature of this modern Lady Macbeth, who seems invulnerable at the beginning of the film, but who will collapse at the end like a queen bee who has flown too high in the atmosphere.

The internal battles of the Essembecks are developed in parallel with the political battles of the Nazis; however, this parallelism is often less than evident, especially to spectators not too familiar with the history of Germany during that period. Watching *The Damned* can be compared, at times, with entering a room covered with deforming mirrors, one reflecting the monstrosity of the other in a disconcerting entanglement of images presenting greed for power, violence, and sexual perversion. In an attempt to emphasize the parallelism, Visconti introduces the character of Aschenbach the Nazi, always present at the Essembecks' reunions, always blowing on the fire. From the opening scenes, in which he does not hide his satisfaction at the burning of the Reichstag, to the very end of the film, where he is Martin's mentor, the cruel and handsome Aschenbach is the deus ex machina of every situation, the original author of every stratagem, the bringer of evil into a family replete with it. Exuding a magnetic power, Aschenbach is the Nazi answer to the Macbethian witches, with whom he could chant, "Fair is foul, and foul is fair. Hover through the fog and filthy air."

However, the presence of Aschenbach is not enough to make *The Damned* an historical film on the rise of Nazism or on the responsibility of the industrialist class for those dramatic years in European history. The political events, with the exception of "the night of the long knives," are fleeting moments that can easily escape the attention of the spectator. The episode of the death of old Baron Joachim, for example, is not as politically clear as Visconti wanted it to be. "Joachim's death is a political fact," says the director, "it is the elimination of the free men in Germany. About this there is a remark made by Aschenbach." Before the flames of the Reichstag can be extinguished, the men of old Germany will be reduced to dust "that is all the liberals, all those who had open ideas, who were still tied to the Weimar Republic, and who were not Nazi."[8] But in the film, the relation between the state of the German nation and the state of the

Essembecks family is far from clear in Aschenbach's remark, and the old Baron's appearance is too brief to allow the spectator to identify him as a liberal still faithful to the Weimar Republic.

Most of all, Joachim's words at the dinner table do not come across as the expression of a man who is firmly anti-Nazi in his convictions, but rather as the compromise of an old man who will bend as much as possible to the will of people whose ideas he does not share, just to protect the prosperity of the mill. Certainly he does not appear to pose a threat to the Nazis, especially since, in order to keep in contact with the new political power, he asks Herbert to resign in favor of Constantine, who is a member of the SA. The banning and subsequent burning of books by the Nazis pass by too briefly to acquire political relevance on the screen, and the only link at this point between the murder at the Essembecks' house and the surge of the Nazi power is the flames at the mill combined with the somber gray of the sky and the black of the mourners at Joachim's funeral, which provide the same color spectrum of that ominous night during which, in smoking and flaming bonfires, so much of the culture of Germany was being burned.

The presence of Aschenbach is not enough to bridge the outside events with the inside ones, and the passions of the members of the family have a separate existence from the political shaping of the country: those bees would have stung one another even without the presence of the Nazi. As Lino Miccichè observes, "*The Damned* is not a film on Nazism, it is not a film on the great capital, but it is—and maybe this time more than ever—a great melodrama."[9] A melodrama indeed, but with no happiness, no sentiment, no hope.

Dantean Parallels

In *The Damned*, people move in an oppressive, closed-in atmosphere emphasized by camera shots from the top. The pit of vipers also recalls Dante's hell, a ravine in the shape of a cone inserted in the earth with its vertex at the center. There are, in *The Damned*, as many references to Dante's *Inferno* as there are references to *Macbeth* and *Buddenbrooks*. As a matter of fact, the Dantean similarities are the most strikingly visual features of the film. Gray, livid, leaden, black, red, and orange—the colors of Dante's *Inferno*—are, in *The Damned*, the tones setting the moods and conveying the vibration of inescapable evil. This reference to the *Divine Comedy*, which

Visconti, being Italian, could not avoid in a film called *The Damned*, also provides another insight into the original title: *La caduta degli dei* [The fall of the gods]. In Dante's "geography," hell is in fact formed by the fall from heaven of Lucifer, the most beautiful of the angels, who rebels against God. In *The Damned*, the evil settles around Martin, the strikingly handsome young man who, like Lucifer in the *Inferno*, rules the Essembecks at the end after his supreme rebellion against his own mother.

The Damned opens and closes with visions of fire in violent red flashes that appear rhythmically throughout the film in the Nazi armbands and banners, in the bonfires, and especially in the flames at the steel factory. The progression of evil follows the hierarchy of sins chosen by Dante: it starts with incontinence in the multifaceted passions of Friedrich, Sophie, and Martin; it continues with violence, and it ends with fraud, represented by the treason and deceit perpetrated by Martin under the orchestration of Aschenbach.

Hellish visions also compose the long and bloody episode representing the "night of the long knives." The SA meeting takes place in a Bavarian hotel, where we see members frenetically occupied with orgiastic actions and sad patriotic songs. An oppressive synthesis of color and sound provides the background against which half-naked reddish bodies move in a whirl of entangled limbs, glassy eyes, drunken laughter, waitresses thrown in the air, and handsome SA members wearing women's garters, while the Fuhrer's photograph watches from the wall. The homosexual overtones clearly refer to Rhom, the leader of the SA, and some of his early comrades, but the sadistic entertainment enjoyed by some of the participants could have been inspired by *Kaput*, a book written by Curzio Malaparte, a very well known Italian writer certainly familiar to Visconti. In *Kaput*, which is about the destruction of Europe during World War II, an episode describes Himmler and his SS in the vapor of a Swedish sauna, whipping one another while the swirling towels give a feminine look to their bodies, so defenseless now without uniforms. In *The Damned*, the SA members are indeed defenseless when, naked, exhausted, and drunk, they are confronted by the SS suddenly appearing from the fog of the lake.

Visconti, who was in Germany at the time of the real massacre, and who retained a vivid memory of the atmosphere of the time, presents this shocking episode, a veritable bloodbath, with a style in which it is possible to discern a certain self-indulgence in portraying violence

The beginning of the horrors in The Damned: *The SS troopers arrive to eliminate the rival SA after the party on "The Night of Long Knives." (Credit: Movie Star News)*

aesthetically. The naked bodies of the SA are carefully grouped in entanglements that could have been conceived by a Renaissance painter, and they are systematically slaughtered in what is a disquieting combination of horror and artistic expression. It is almost as if the SS men had burst in with their machine guns in Michelangelo's *Last Judgment,* anticipating God's wrath. Because of this studied presentation, violence here does not have a sudden breathtaking impact, but in its systematic horror it conjures up the programmed elimination of human beings which was later devised by the Nazis.

In the group of the murderous SS we see the ambitious Friedrich and the ever-present Aschenbach, who leads the massacre in which Constantine dies. The elimination of the hard-drinking and loud-talking Constantine will not only leave the field open for Friedrich, who will subsequently capitulate to Martin, but will make a Nazi of his own son, the gentle Günther, whose hatred for his father's murderer will be "industrialized," in Visconti's words, by Aschenbach and directed to the construction of that gospel of hate through which the Nazis are founding their religion. "The Nazi party," Visconti says, "which first chooses as its pawn the violent, noisy, brutal, but after all quite naive Constantine, later uses Friedrich as a technician . . . and at the end prefers as its last solution Martin, a boy without a conscience, a degenerate." Visconti explains in the same interview that "Martin and Günther are the people who brought Nazism to its complete development, to the war, to the destruction of the world, to the final solution of the Jewish problem."[10] The sequence of the characters, Constantine, Friedrich, Martin, and Gunther, is psychologically well chosen by the director to express the consolidation of power that originated with brutal but relatively naive people, developed in the hands of more astute politicians, and ended in monstrous inhumanity. However, this succession fails to provide as strong a political emphasis on the rise of Nazi power as the director intended. Politics remain in the background of the shocking internal struggle among the Essembecks. The Nazi takeover has little to do with the impact of the scene in which Martin rapes his own mother. We see in Martin not the perfect Nazi but a young man whose mixture of love and hatred for his mother, combined with his sexual perversity, brings him to this outrage.

Martin and Sophie, the degenerate son and the powerful mother, now face each other in an unavoidable showdown. For Martin, the time has come to avenge himself for all the humiliation that, he says, he has suffered at the hands of his mother, who does in fact exploit the excessive attachment of her son by keeping him under her complete control in order to gain more power for Friedrich. In the original plan for the film, the character called Sophie was Friedrich's wife, an ambitious woman not related to Martin, whose mother was a melancholy widow named Amalia. In the final version Sophie Essembeck, combining the roles of mother and lover, becomes much more powerful ruling the Essembecks.

The scene in which we see Sophie's strong will and astuteness at their best is the conversation she has with Aschenbach when the two meet in the Nazi archives. Here, surrounded by dossiers containing information on so many lives, Sophie and the Nazi elegantly trade mundanely sophisticated words that cannot hide their arid souls, so hungry for power and so unscrupulous are they. The two are like parts of the same machine, perfectly synchronized in their phrases, gestures, and appearance. Both of them are impeccably elegant, Aschenbach in a black Nazi uniform that makes his lean body leaner and his blonde hair blonder, and Sophie in her black and pearl gray dress, so charming and so cruel. The woman is so sure of herself that nothing seems to be able to nick her steely will power in the course of the foreseeable events. But Sophie does not realize that a killing blow would come to her from her own son, from Martin, who so often, even in his adult life, ran to her shakingly and like a baby held on to her for reassurance.

In the incest scene the once–powerful woman becomes a shaking figure in the penumbra of the room. She acquires the appearance of a frail blue flower, a scared blue angel as Visconti's camera lingers on the forbidden union, presenting it as a desired sickness, a mixture of pleasure and pain, exaltation and disgust.

The censors did not remain indifferent to the daring scene. They wanted it cut, to the great distress of Visconti, whose defense was that even between Hamlet and his mother "there are many things," and that the scene in *The Damned* is "very eliptic."[11] Eventually they were satisfied, and Visconti had to endure only a "little cut." Although Visconti was plagued by censorship throughout his career, contemporary standards bear out the director's assertion that "History demonstrates that the censors are always wrong."[12]

After the incest, Sophie, kept in a state of sedation, becomes a shadow of the strong woman she once was and lives in her pathetic memories of her son's childhood: carillon music, Martin's blonde locks and early drawings. Sophie, Visconti says, "returns as a mother to her baby after having been possessed by him. This is an absolute Freudian return."[13] Visconti adds that in order to establish Martin's deviant personality, he included among Sophie's keepsakes Martin's drawing of a child killing his mother. A little girl was given the assignment by Visconti to draw a picture of a boy killing a woman, but the girl, after having drawn the two figures, refused to put the knife in the boy's hand. "I had to draw the knife," confesses Visconti. "This is quite funny. Then under the drawing I wrote what the child would have written: 'Martin todd Mutter,' [Martin kills Mother] and then under that, 'Mutter und Martin,' [mother and Martin]."[14]

Martin kills his mother at the wedding of Sophie and Friedrich. An already ethereal figure, the woman is, at her wedding, the image of death: her face is chalky white, her expressionless eyes gaze into nothingness, her mouth is as red as a wound, while Friedrich, now that he has lost Sophie's help and support, is only a shadow of the ambitious technician who did not stop at murder to achieve his goal. Equivocal guests abandoning themselves to lascivious dances, the darkness of the hall, and the red Nazi banners hanging from the walls provide the wedding with the atmosphere of a somber orgy; the proud and aristocratic Sophie Essembeck is receiving congratulations from shadowy characters invited by Martin. In representing the death of the newlyweds Visconti was inspired by the suicide of Hitler and Eva Braun in the bunker right after their wedding, and indeed the way in which the two bodies are found by Martin—Friedrich's lifeless on the couch, Sophie's sitting and staring ahead—fits the descriptions in several accounts of the last hours of Hitler and Eva.

The wedding in *The Damned* is a veritable funeral, the second one in the film. The first funeral, the one for old Baron Joachim, also murdered, does not have the psychological sadism of the second, but it shares the somber tone, heavy with conspiracy. The baron's burial is the first outside scene in *The Damned*, but the open space is hardly a liberation from the dark decor and shadows of the Essembecks' house, which seems turned inside out to provide a leaden low sky and the iron background of the factory against which the Essembecks march in their black attire.

Visconti has not left any hope for "that family of monsters," who eliminate each other one by one, weaving their murderous webs in which, at times, they entangle themselves. "They all had to be asphyxiated, closed in a gas chamber without leaving any air-hole,"[15] remarked the director. *The Damned* is indeed a shocking film that cannot be seen as simply entertainment. Its scenes linger on in one's mind; the spectator is caught in the webs spun by the Essembecks and Aschenbach, since the evil, so tautly represented without even a glimmer of hope, has a choking and oppressive effect on the audience.

Reception of *The Damned*

As Visconti probably expected, *The Damned* provoked at its appearance distinctively different opinions among critics and public. Among favorable responses are those of Peter Cowie, who sees *The Damned* as being "much underrated" and "close to being Visconti's masterpiece,"[16] and Brad Darrach, who finds the script "a lesson in dramatic structure."[17] On the negative side, *The Damned* is viewed by Robert Hatch as a "family chronicle, but at the hack level— crushed by a monotony of facts that do not inform, sodden with greed, perversion, hatred and treachery,"[18] and by Richard Schickel, who reacts to Visconti's historical perspective writing that "To imply a cause-effect relationship between sexual perversion and political perversion is historically inaccurate and socially irresponsible."[19] These are just a few of many examples of the extreme reactions provoked by *The Damned* among critics and public alike.

The differences in reactions and in interpretations stem, in my opinion, from Visconti's intensity and from the complexity of his films, so rich in their substance as to create, at times, what I call a positive ambiguity, a possibility, that is, of various interpretations of the director's rich imagery based on a fermenting substratum. Visconti in fact made day-by-day changes that resulted in a film partially different from the one intended at the beginning of the shooting. This is the reason why it is at times quite baffling to read in an interview given by the director an interpretation that appears to have nothing to do with the film itself. In the case of *The Damned*, the film was supposed to have many more connections with the rise to power of the Nazis than are evident; but its political content is elusive compared to the real substance of the film, which is undoubtedly the tragedy of the Essembecks. Their sexual perversions were meant to have a more evident relation to the Nazi's crimes as a metaphor for "a scandalous underlining . . . to the establishment of Nazism."[20]

By comparing the summary of the original script published by Cappelli to the final product, it appears obvious that, more than other films, *The Damned* was subjected to changes and revisions that resulted in contradictions between the intention and the result. Visconti once told Stefano Roncoroni that "Marx here is not interpreted and understood superficially, but he is interpreted and understood profoundly; the situation of the family is seen with a Marxist eye because there is no way out in such a family. The film is more Marxist than ever because Marxism here is assimilated, understood, and remembered with a detached eye."[21] *The Damned*, a Marxist film? Again, Visconti may have had an intention that he did not realize.

With *The Damned* Visconti succeeded in showing the struggle within a big and powerful family at a time of political turmoil, but the parallel between the "beehives," the Essembecks and the Nazis, is not well established. *The Damned* is a powerful film tarnished by fragmentation. Like a mosaic with vivid and valuable tiles that have not been put together properly, it offers the spectator intense images that do not always cohere as a whole.

9

Death in Venice:
Rational Man Among the "Devils"

FOR A LONG TIME, Visconti intended to make a film about Milan, specifically on the Milanese bourgeoisie, whom he knew so well, since he had been born and raised in the northern Italian metropolis, where his mother belonged to one of the best known industrialist families. "I always dreamed," he said to Guido Aristarco, "of doing the story of the Milanese bourgeoisie, taking my family as a cue, my mother's family. I would like to film the development of that bourgeoisie, which later became the rich bourgeoisie. That atmosphere I remember very well. I lived in it as a child. I can smell it."[1]

But what could have been a cycle on the life of Milan never came to the screen because, after *The Damned,* Visconti abandoned the idea and decided to continue his cultural and artistic affair with German history and literature. In the second film of what will be his German trilogy he decides to represent one of the better–known works of a writer whom he had always loved, Thomas Mann's *Death in Venice.*

Already in 1956, Visconti had presented a ballet inspired by Mann's short story *Mario and the Magician,* and now, fifteen years later, he finally felt mature enough to tackle the very complex *Death in Venice.* "I always waited to have enough maturity and experience to face the rendering of accounts which is in Mann's novella. The right moment is now, after *The Damned.*"[2] But in Italy Visconti could not find a producer willing to take a chance on financing the film.

Mario Gallo, the coproducer who helped Visconti in this predicament, summed up the situation: "Some people took the proposal under consideration (the title made them think of a thriller or of a story about violence), but as soon as they read the short story, they drew back. Someone even suggested the substitution of a beautiful girl for Tadzio. In this situation I accepted with enthusiasm the offer of organizing this film, that is, to make it financially possible."

141

The film was, in fact, made possible by Warner Brothers. "The president of Warner took our project into consideration," continued Gallo, "we had to overcome many obstacles . . . but Visconti was able to realize his work in total freedom."[3] Grateful to Gallo for his help and to Warner Brothers ("The Americans did not even want to read the script, and they gave their approval on the basis of Mann's novella and of the guarantee which we offered."[4]), Visconti started work on *Death in Venice.*

Death in Venice (1971): The Plot

Gustav Aschenbach, a musician at a difficult moment in his career, arrives in Venice for a vacation during which he seeks to find answers for all the doubts obsessing his mind in order to obtain solace and peace. At the Hotel des Baines, frequented by European high society, his attention is riveted by the stunning beauty of Tadzio, a Polish boy who, with his family, is also a guest at the hotel. Aschenbach, a man who in conversations with his friend Alfried has always defended purity and rationality in artistic creation, is disturbed by his feelings toward the boy.

Overcome by a strange feeling of uneasiness, Aschenbach decides to leave Venice, but a mistake in the shipment of his trunk, which was sent to Como, provides him with the excuse to come back to the city. He will not leave unless he can leave with his trunk.

While Aschenbach's feelings for Tadzio grow to the point of becoming infatuation and even love, a few cases of cholera appear in Venice but are kept secret by the authorities because of the need not to frighten away the tourists. Aschenbach is informed of the presence of the epidemic by an English clerk at a travel agency but decides to stay and not to reveal his discovery to anyone. In love with Tadzio's beauty and increasingly concerned with his own appearance, Gustav Aschenbach tries to rejuvenate himself with the help of hair dye and makeup.

But the sickness reaches the musician, who, having followed Tadzio through the streets of Venice, collapses on his lounge chair on the beach with the vision of the beautiful boy pointing to a far-away place on the horizon.

"Certain goals are reachable only through Eros."[5]

With these words Visconti sums up the intent of his cinematic rendition of *Death in Venice,* the celebrated novella written in 1911 by

Thomas Mann, a writer whom Visconti admired to the point of wanting to conclude his directorial career with the filming of *The Magic Mountain.* "There are things which I have been carrying with me for a long time," says Visconti, "and I need to free myself: then I can kick the bucket."[6] He did not elaborate, but he may well have been referring to his preoccupation with decadence and ambiguity, which, discreetly present already in his early works, became more and more pressing and pervasive in his later films. The social engagement of early works like *La terra trema* (1948) and *Rocco and His Brothers* (1960) now makes room for the individual dimensions of the struggle within the soul of an artist. Through Mann, Visconti wants to free himself, only a few years before his death, repeating in a chronologically longer struggle Aschenbach's search for beauty through the deadly streets of Venice. The director's desire to find artistic freedom with the help of Mann's Aschenbach explains Visconti's paradoxical assertion that "My film describes an intellectual adventure balancing between truth and imagination in a key totally realistic and completely fantastic."[7]

As usual, when a literary work is brought to the screen, changes are made because of the director's interpretation and because of the differences in the medium, which is more dramatic and immediate. Because of time limitations, a director must eliminate or condense several parts of the literary work to fit the two-hour span of a film. The time factor, however, is not very relevant in *Death in Venice* since the novella is also short and consists of a description of mainly psychological states rather than a dramatic portrayal of actions.

Visconti makes two major changes: Aschenbach's profession is altered and flashbacks are used. In Mann's novella the protagonist is a writer, but in the film he is a composer. In an interview with Lino Miccichè, Visconti explained the reasons for the change: a musician is first of all more "representable" in a film because it is possible to have his music as a background. Off-camera readings of literary works are not as expressive and are often tedious. Another reason is that Mann himself was influenced by Gustav Mahler, the musician who died while Mann was in the process of writing the novella and whose death profoundly shocked the writer. Visconti wanted to use Mahler's music for *The Damned* (1967) but was at the time dissuaded. *Death in Venice* provided the opportunity which the director reluctantly abandoned four years earlier.[8]

The flashbacks Visconti introduces also depart from the original. They present a young prostitute and painful arguments with Alfried, a "friend," on the nature of art. Quick and very vivid, the flasbacks, with the exception of the ones concerning Alfried, provide only fragments of memories in which love, serenity, grief, and shame appear unexplained and inconsistent. The family scenes in which we see a happy young Aschenbach in the clear surroundings of the Tyrolean Alps and the shattering loss of his little girl are too fleeting and fragmentary to contribute to the understanding of Aschenbach's soul. The encounter with the young prostitute is downright confusing since it is impossible to discern whether Aschenbach's shame is due to a sexual failure or to a recognition of the weakness of his senses.

The flashbacks concerning Alfried, which Visconti characterizes as "ideological," provide the metaphorical dimension of the passionate involvement of Aschenbach. Alfried, who in Visconti's words is Aschenbach's "alter ego, his good or bad conscience,"[9] is trying to destroy Aschenbach's rigorous artistic ideology, which refuses to see irrationality in the artistic creation. In Mann's words, Aschenbach, the man of letters, "had done homage to intellect . . . had turned his back on the 'mysteries,' called genius itself in question."[10] In Visconti's film, during a heated discussion, with the relentless Alfried, Aschenbach contends that "the creative act is a spiritual act." "Beauty belongs only to the senses," insists Alfried. "Evil is a necessity. Art is ambiguity, always. And music is the most ambiguous of all arts. It is ambiguity made into a system." The ambiguity of the artistic creation which Aschenbach refuses to acknowledge resides in Eros and is antithetical to Logos, the power of reason.

All his life Aschenbach has kept his rigid views as a defensive barrier around himself, a bulwark of dubious strength that will collapse in a city built on water. The vulnerability of Aschenbach is evident from the first pages of the novella, specifically when the reader is informed that the protagonist's hero is Sebastian, who reflects a "conception of an intellectual and virginal manliness" standing "in modest defiance of the swords and spears that pierce its side."[11] In this symbol, favored by Aschenbach, the modesty and the virginity disguise the erotic significance illuminated by more than one Italian painting of the Renaissance. In Visconti's film, Aschenbach's vulnerability appears in his fastidiousness, in his methodical gestures, and in his irritability at the inconvenience of the trip. For the dignified Aschenbach, for whom love no longer seems to exist, the metaphorical voyage into the recognition of the irrational elements acting on the artistic creation of beauty has the effect of making him fall in love with the beautiful Tadzio.

Several critics have harshly criticized Visconti's treatment of the involvement between Aschenbach and Tadzio, complaining that the homosexual theme is too overt, especially on the boy's side. The encounter with the prostitute, coming to Aschenbach's mind when he hears "Für Elise" played by Tadzio at the piano in the hall of the hotel, is indeed cumbersome. Since the young woman in the brothel plays the same piece, and since her features are similar to Tadzio's, the implication is evident. To balance the sinfulness of this association, Visconti provides another flashback in which a paternal attraction on Aschenbach's side is suggested by the similarity between Tadzio and the musician's little daughter. Again, the flashbacks interpolated by the director prove to be totally unwarranted, adding ambiguity to a story that does not need more complications.

Flashbacks aside, the rapport between Aschenbach and Tadzio, if more "vivid" on the screen, is not as heavy handed as many critics claim. It is true that the glances of the boy can be interpreted as sexually significant and, because of the medium, are certainly more graphic than literary descriptions. As Lino Miccichè rightly says, "a literary glance is not a cinematographic glance;"[12] therefore Tadzio's incredible beauty, his presence, his long glances, his awareness of being followed through the sickly streets of Venice are much more sensual in the film than in the book.

But the novella itself is quite explicit about the involvement developing on both sides. Mann himself, talking about the genesis of *Death in Venice,* which should have told the story of Goethe's love for a very young girl he met at Marienbad, says that the real subject of the novella is passion as perturbation and degradation. A personal experience of a lyrical voyage made him decide to bring things to the extreme by introducing the theme of forbidden love.[13] But "the artist's dignity" and "the tragedy of supreme achievement,"[14] which are essential themes of *Death in Venice,* are strictly related to the fall of Aschenbach, which in all its implications and realistic aspects has been forcefully but not tastelessly presented by Visconti. If in the novella Tadzio's responses are less graphic, Aschenbach's involvement clearly develops from pure admiration of perfect beauty to a sensual appreciation: "How dare you smile like that! No one is allowed to smile like that," Aschenbach silently reproaches before

A moment that captures the essence of Death in Venice: *the fading Aschenbach (Dirk Bogarde) looks longingly at the youthful beauty of Tadzio (Björn Andresen). (Courtesy of Museum of Modern Art/Film Stills Archive)*

whispering, "I love you."[15] Defending the frequency of the glances and their greater intensity on the screen, Visconti rightly says that even in Mann the rapport between Tadzio and Aschenbach is ambiguous. Even though Aschenbach's adventure is "cerebral and intellectual," it contains "elements that move Aschenbach and break his equilibrium."[16]

Mainly because of the impossibility of introducing into the film Mann's philosophical insights, the lack of which creates a vacuum not filled by Mahler's music, the disturbing elements do outweigh the "intellectual and cerebral" adventure, which is represented only by the flashbacks of arguments with Alfried and by Aschenbach's dying words, the content of which is overwhelmed by the shocking vision of his demeaning death. Nevertheless, Visconti's screen rendition of Aschenbach's adventure is neither tasteless nor pedestrian. It would have been if the director had chosen to introduce in the film Aschenbach's nightmare, to which Mann dedicates two pages filled with visions of Dionysian rites, in which human beings and animals participate to the sound of primitive instruments throbbing in honor of a savage god. Visconti, who had actually filmed this episode in a

Monaco night club, decided not to include it in the film but to substitute instead a flashback concerning a musical fiasco that Aschenbach experienced, after which Alfried, the cruel alter-ego, poured salt in the wound by dismantling Aschenbach's rigorous and purist conception of art. "Pure beauty, absolute rigor . . . abstraction from senses. Nothing is left, nothing." Alfried has won. Aschenbach's resistance is gone, and at the end of his life he finally sees that his religious worshipping of purity and rationality was only self-deception. As Alfried has told him, "Beauty belongs only to the senses," and Eros is at the core of artistic creation, which is irrational in its real nature.

Aschenbach's impotence in the presence of ambiguity is clear in the episode at the barber shop, where a sly barber who seems to "know" has little trouble in convincing the dignified old gentleman to allow him to make him young again. In a shattering scene we see the real fall of Aschenbach, powerless and totally devoid of the hauteur that made him scorn with no touch of compassion the old-young man he meets on the boat at the beginning of the film. The grotesque appearance of the old man, who singles out the austere Aschenbach in the crowd of the passengers and mellifluously wishes him a very happy sojourn, tragically foreshadows Aschenbach's visit to the barber shop. The Mephistophelian barber dyes the musician's hair and moustache, covers his face with makeup, and puts rouge on his lips. As a final touch, he places a rose in Aschenbach's buttonhole, clearly dressing him for his own funeral while the soft background music and the whispering word create a funeral parlor atmosphere. Aschenbach becomes a marionette; his dignity and his meticulous attention to forms, which made him intolerant of any human weakness, give way to produce a frivolously dressed old man hysterically running through the bluish streets of Venice, trying to hold in his view the slim figure of a young boy. The chase ends on the now–deserted beach, where Aschenbach collapses on his lounge chair like a wireless marionette, the makeup and hair dye running down his face. He addresses Tadzio: "Morality of shape, fame, trust in other people, the pretense of educating—lies, Tadzio, only lies. The abyss is our goal." The puppeteer's wires holding Aschenbach's rigidly pure view of art have broken. Alfried, the prophet of irrationality, the disturbing alter-ego, has the last word.

"Certain goals are reachable only through Eros," says Visconti, but the hymn to Eros in *Death in Venice* is also a hymn to death, since it brings us, in Aschenbach's words, to the abyss. Beauty, Eros, and

Death are the three coalescing entities whose relation, consciously denied by Aschenbach during most of his life, unfolds in front of him on the deserted beach in his last vision of Tadzio turning his "head of Eros"[17] and pointing to a far-away goal on the horizon.

The Structure of Aschenbach's Journey

The moral, philosophical, and physical collapse of Aschenbach is narrated by Visconti through a series of tableaux, in which powerful imagery conveys an overwhelming feeling of death. From the beginning of the film the black smoke of the *vaporetto*, with its silent and dream-like motion, is a bad omen reinforced by the slow entrance into Venice. The traditional vision of golden palaces, blue sky, and polychromatic marbles is replaced by a view of a city buried in fog and humidity. In this swaying liquid world the gondolas, usually a romantic means of transportation, are funereal black silhouettes on the murky water of what Mann calls "the most improbable of cities." Its ambiguity encircles Aschenbach, who, from the very beginning, has lost control of his destiny, while the local characters, with their smirks and sly glances, seem to "know" already.

The Venetian journey is in fact a crossing into another world, where Aschenbach's intellectual categories are worthless and where an atmosphere of conspiracy entangles the musician. "In my opinion," Visconti says, "the old man of the boat, the gondolier, the hotel manager, all are little devils which are concurring in Aschenbach's destiny."[18] The local inhabitants, in fact, often appear grotesque and behave with sheepish politeness, sometimes with cruel jeers that deny the presence of the "sickness" and attribute the disinfection of Venice to simple precautionary measures. "It is the sirocco, sir. Disease? What disease? Is the sirocco a disease?" So says the head musician of the coarse little group serenading the guests at the Hotel des Baines. Gesticulating, exhibiting toothless smiles, playing with cruel cheerfulness, the group is a veritable representation of the devils who jeer at their impotent guests in the Malebolge ("evil pouches") section of Dante's *Inferno*. At times Aschenbach really seems to have fallen into this Malebolge, where, in the fifth pouch, grotesque devils with names such as Barbariccia ("Curly Beard"), Cagnazzo ("Bad Dog"), Malacoda ("Evil Tail") torment sinners whose punishment consists of being immersed in boiling pitch. Interestingly enough, when Dante describes the huge cauldron full of pitch, he compares it to a vision of the Arsenal in Venice, where pitch is used during the winter to repair the boats.

The performance of the four "musical devils" increases Aschenbach's uneasiness, already awakened at the beginning of the film by the mysterious gondolier muttering incomprehensible words to himself and totally oblivious to Aschenbach's protests: "I want to go to the wharf." "You are going to the Lido." Aschenbach is brought to the Lido, to the improbable world of swaying water, by Charon who disappears before getting paid. "He is the only gondolier without a license," an old sailor explains to Aschenbach. "You have travelled free of charge." Frowning, Aschenbach drops coins in the hats of people of undefined profession and reacts to the sheepish courtesy of the hotel workers with a curtness close to rudeness. But his apparent Nordic detachment is constantly assailed by the "devils" who, as the film progresses, take Aschenbach completely in their power, robbing him of his dignity and preparing him for his death in clown's makeup.

Especially in the scenes of Aschenbach's frantic pursuit of Tadzio, Venice has the aspect of a hellish city decaying from sickness, its crumbling walls splattered with disinfectant and plastered with ominous warning posters. Angry voices and glimpses of violence are heard and seen in the streets of a city whose splendor has now been swallowed up by a desolation presented in bluish hues reflecting the reddish tones of the bonfires burning the scattered garbage.

The flickering, disturbing world of the "devils," with their exaggerated gestures, accentuated features, and grotesque gait, is counterpoised by the elegant transience of the aristocratic group at the Hotel des Baines; in the improbable city we find not only Dante's Malebolge but also Virgil's Kingdom of Hades, inhabited by the shadow-like tourists. Amidst the elegant decor of the dining room of the hotel, the perfectly attired guests whisper to one another in a strange Esperanto composed of fragments of exotic languages and delicately manipulate the utensils with which they bring food to their mouths. Eating is a ritual of ethereal gestures and nothing more; the elegant shadows do not swallow the food. Yellow lamps, glass-stained windows, ivory–colored vases holding oleanders and hydrangeas, very delicate flowers in bluish and pink tones that quickly vanish after a glorious blooming constitute the frame for this brilliant fresco, painted by Visconti, in which we see the doomed European aristocracy surviving in a bubble that will soon break. It is impossible not to realize that only a few years later the First World War will drastically

"The elegant transcience of the aristocratic group at the Hotel Des Baignes": Tadzio's mother (Silvana Mangano) dines with her perfectly attired family. (Credit: Movie Star News)

end the "belle époque" and that during the same war, the Russian revolution will eliminate the nation's aristocratic class from its socety. The sad Slavic song sung at the end of the film on the deserted beach is poignant and pathetic, and the Venetian "sickness" is the bad omen announcing worse times. From the attention given to these details it is obvious that Visconti wanted not only to tell the story of Aschenbach, but also to portray an aristocratic society close to death, oblivious to the real world, and already shadowlike. "Vitaque cum gemitu fugit indignata sub umbras" ("And life, sobbing, fled indignant to the shadows"), says Virgil twice in the *Aeneid*, once for the death of the young woman warrior Camilla, again for the death of the hero Turnus. When we observe the beautiful children building sand castles on the beach, and we think of their dark future, it is Virgil who comes to our minds with his poignant verse expressing the bitterness of an early death.

The burden of the acting falls on Dirk Bogarde's shoulders, since Björn Andresen (as Tadzio) is never heard saying a word, and the secondary characters make very brief appearances. Romolo Valli, playing the director of the Hotel des Baines, is only a shadow of his excellent don Pirrone, the Jesuit father in *The Leopard* (1963), and Silvana Mangano makes a cameo appearance as Tadzio's mother.

Björn Andresen's physical features exactly fit Mann's description of Tadzio: an adolescent of stunning beauty, whose androgynous features betray tender frailty. "Imperfect" and "bluish" teeth are the only flaw which Mann attributes to Tadzio and which is faithfully reproduced on the screen, along with the youngster's stooping gait. The fight he loses at the end of the film when Jasciu, the robust older boy, almost suffocates him in the sand suggests that Eros and Beauty are frail and probably short-lived. Dirk Bogarde's performance is a tour de force. His Aschenbach is too jittery at the beginning of the film but gains consistency and achieves its greatest effectiveness in the scenes in which the dignity of the musician has collapsed behind the mask of a clown.

Visconti's direction is also a tour de force. There is no doubt that his love for Mann and the few years spent thinking and hoping to be able to bring *Death in Venice* to the screen contributed to the care and the attention he obviously devoted to the film, which was received, as usual, with mixed reactions. Many critics expressed dissatisfaction with the interpretation of the relation between Aschenbach and Tadzio but have admired the imagery. *Death in Venice* periodically appears at revival houses and always attracts good attendance and favorable comments. It is a powerful work that leaves one with the dramatic imagery of "improbable" Venice, where Malebolge and the Kingdom of Hades coexist side by side, while the irrational core of beauty and Eros and its relation to death are personified by the godlike young boy followed through the sickly streets of Venice by an older man frantically crisscrossing the two realms.

10

Ludwig: The Flight from Reality

IN 1971, RIGHT AFTER the completion of *Death in Venice*, Visconti was fascinated by the idea of filming Marcel Proust's *A la recherche du temps perdu*, an idea that has also attracted Joseph Losey. Just like Mann, Proust was a great love of the director, who started reading the French author at a very early age and kept rereading him for the rest of his life. During the filming of *Death in Venice*, Visconti was seriously thinking about Proust's masterpiece, which he planned to begin to film in Venice with "the Venetian sojourn of the author-protagonist Marcel and his mother after the death of the beloved Albertine. . . . I decided to leave aside the theme of childhood and the mundane one in order to follow one of the fundamental feelings in the work: love, jealousy." Visconti already had the precise cast in his mind. Alain Delon would be Marcel ("In his beauty there is something mean and furtive. I will give him a beard and make his eyes dark with contact lenses"), Laurence Olivier would interpret Baron Charlus, and Helmut Berger would play Morel.[1]

During the spring of 1971 Visconti spent about a month in Normandy researching *A la recherche* and preparing a script with the cooperation of Suso Cecchi D'Amico. But financial problems and copyright difficulties (which, even later on, were never resolved) forced him to abandon the project and to focus his energies on another film he had in mind. This too proved difficult to complete for financial but especially for health reasons. In fact, *Ludwig*, the third part of the German trilogy, was unfortunately complicated even more by Visconti's severe illness.

Ludwig (1973): The Plot

With *Ludwig* Visconti brings to the screen the sad story of the mad king of Bavaria who lived between 1845 and 1886. Succeeding his

Helmut Berger as the alienated King Ludwig II of Bavaria driven at last to madness in Ludwig. *(Credit: Movie Star News)*

father, Maximilian II, Ludwig became king in 1864 at the very early age of 19. The opening o the film shows him at confession, during which he confides to Father Hoffman his anxious idealism. This is followed by the coronation of the strikingly handsome young monarch. At this time there are two great loves in Ludwig's life: his cousin, Elizabeth of Austria, Emperor Franz Joseph's wife, with whom he shares his romantic dreams, and Richard Wagner, who, with his music, soon becomes an obsession for the young king. Ludwig does not hesitate to bleed the Bavarian state treasury to finance the greedy genius who, naturally, does not enjoy great popularity with the populace. Wagner's scandalous personal life and "his cost" provoke strong popular opposition, and the composer is reluctantly ordered by Ludwig to leave Munich but also assured of continuing devotion and friendship on the part of the king.

Another crisis appears in Ludwig's life when he finds himself involved in the Austro-Prussian war on the Austrian side. After this brief war (called the Seven Weeks' War) in which the small Bavarian army is defeated, Otto, Ludwig's younger brother, who had led the troops in the king's place, develops a mental disease. At the same time Ludwig discovers in himself homosexual tendencies, and, feeling terribly guilty, he decides to defeat them by getting married. He suddenly announces his decision to his mother and chooses as his future wife his cousin Sophie, Elizabeth's sister. During this period Ludwig develops his passion for building, which will lead him to squander the Bavarian treasury on the construction of the castles of Linderhof, Herrenchiemsee, and Neuschwanstein. Ludwig retires in seclusion to these extravagant castles after breaking his engagement to Sophie, who painfully realizes that the only woman who is able to stir loving feelings in Ludwig is her sister Elizabeth. During the Franco-Prussian War of 1870–71, Ludwig is on the victorious Prussian side, and in 1871, reluctantly but politically not unwisely, he submits to Prussian Prime Minister Bismarck's concept of a unified empire and allows the inclusion of Bavaria in the German Confederation.

Constantly more isolated in his castles, Ludwig refuses any human contact (he does not even want to receive Elizabeth) with the exception of special guests, such as the actor Kainz, and contracts more and more debts because of his insatiable thirst to build monuments. This tendency and the news of the king's participation in orgies with his servants convinces a commission led by Count von Holstein to declare him insane and to keep him under surveillance at the castle of

Berg while his uncle, Prince Luitpold, takes the regency of Bavaria. During a walk in the castle's park, Ludwig and his psychiatrist, Professor Gudden, disappear. After a frantic search their bodies are found in the lake, giving origin to different theories on the circumstances of their deaths (which still have not been clearly explained).

"I prefer to tell about defeats, to describe solitary souls and fates crushed by reality."[2]

Among the solitary souls presented by the director, Ludwig is the most solitary and the most clearly destined to be crushed by reality. The film follows Ludwig from the time of his coronation to the time of his death, and the unhappy figure of the young monarch is the undisputed protagonist in a work in which Visconti put a tremendous amount of energy.

"For me *Ludwig* has been particularly wearisome, in preparation and in realization, because of other people's uncertainties," Visconti once remarked.[3] The director revealed that the constant doubts "broke his nerves" in a fight that lasted six months, mainly because of the producer's objection to the cost. Finally people willing to invest were found, and *Ludwig* began as an Italian-German coproduction in which an Italian, a French, and two German companies shared the financing. "Then we started looking for the places," Visconti continues in the same interview, "and we started filming, always at night and in terribly cold weather. . . . I really cared about this film for several reasons. Because with *The Damned* and *Death in Venice* it would have represented my kind of trilogy on modern Germany: the radical transformation of a society which succumbs to leave its place to a new society, the disintegration of a powerful family, the psychological evolution of a character."[4] The sympathy that Visconti felt for Ludwig ("because he is defeated, a victim of reality. . . . In Bavaria there are young people's clubs dedicated to the cult of this monarch")[5] and the fact that at this time in his life the director was dedicated to the career of Helmut Berger, who had already interpreted Martin in *The Damned*, were also strong reasons for the determination displayed by Visconti to have Berger play Ludwig. The relationship between Visconti and the actor was so strong that, exactly one year after the death of the director, Helmut Berger tried to commit suicide in Rome.

The harshness of the Bavarian winter and the tension before the beginning of the film took a heavy toll on the director's health.

Already under a doctor's care because of a very mild stroke suffered a year before and rebellious as usual, Visconti not only worked with the energy of a much younger man, but also discarded the medicine that had been prescribed to him because carrying it annoyed him. "It was always spilling in my pocket. One day I was so upset that I threw it away, saying, 'It is not possible to always have wet pockets because of this damned medicine.' See how stupid I was? I paid for it dearly"[6] On July 27, after the completion of the shooting of *Ludwig* but before the editing, a very serious second stroke hit the director in a restaurant in Rome. He immediately realized its gravity: "I remember everything exactly. I never had a moment that was not clear. Everything was very clear for me," he told Costanzo Costantini. "I remember that Enrico Medioli took off my shoes while I was on the bed. I was wearing socks of a brilliant blue. "How could I have made such a mistake?' I asked myself."[7] Of course the elegant and sophisticated director is not thinking here about the overworking and the discarding of the medicine, but rather, he is questioning his own taste in choosing socks. In a Zurich clinic, where he was taken from Rome, Visconti worried about something much more important than his clothes. "The film, the film, the film. The fear of not being able to finish *Ludwig*, the fear of not seeing it come out. The thought of *Ludwig* did not leave me for a minute. Actually, I have to say that this thought gave me strength to react to my infirmity. For this, *Ludwig*, is the film that I love the most."[8] And so, sustained by a heroic willpower, the undefeated Visconti came back to his film to complete the story of the defeated king.

From the very beginning, we see Ludwig doomed. The film starts by showing us the very young and beautiful king, then switches intermittently to the very gloomy future of the monarch, until the two lines of narration coincide in the park of the castle of Berg. "I will be able to call the real wise men, the great men of genius, the great artists. This is what the great monarchs of antiquity did. I will become better," says Ludwig to the father confessor. The beauty of these ideas is followed by the episode of the coronation, where Ludwig appears as the perfect king: young, handsome, and incredibly elegant in his white buckskin pants, blue jacket, long black boots, and ermine cloak. He confidently moves toward his new subjects to deliver his first speech as king. His clear and solemn words echo throughout the following scene in which a much older Ludwig, showing on his face the deep marks of dissipation, is told that he is

The "Visconti Touch" at its most sumptuous: The old queen of Bavaria, Ludwig's mother (Isabella Telezynska) receives a richly dressed company at a royal levée in Ludwig. (Credit: Movie Star News)

about to be arrested. Visconti fuses the beginning and the end, the glory and the humiliation, the idealism and the folly.

The action unfolds at a slow pace, interrupted by sudden changes of time and place that do not facilitate understanding, as the film tries to follow the disintegration of Ludwig's soul. Particularly vulnerable to disappointments because of his great expectations, his acute sensitivity, and a hereditary mental weakness—his grandfather, Ludwig I, was said to be peculiar, and his brother Otto died insane—Ludwig is crushed by crises that could have been overcome by less "artistic" but more stable people. While the film stresses the painful events as the cause of Ludwig's unbalanced behavior, in Ludwig's real life those crises simply exacerbated a condition already present in the young monarch. They were pain added to pain, sorrow added to sorrow.

Ludwig's first crisis in the film is his relationship with Richard Wagner. Interpreted by Trevor Howard, whose features are very similar to those in the musician's portraits, Wagner's personality on the screen reflects what has been said about him: he is a genius, but also a sensualist. The sanguine Wagner who plays on the floor with a beautiful shaggy dog is as much interested in sensual comfort as he is in musical creations, if not even more so. He is an egotist who assumes that his greatness elevates him above other mortals. In the first scene we see him already benefitted by Ludwig's generosity, sitting in an expensively decorated room and wearing a silk jacket, which he obviously enjoys caressing while talking to Von Bülow, his orchestra director, and Von Bülow's wife Cosima, Liszt's daughter. The scene delineates a ménage à trois, in which conniving is the name of the game. Very significant glances occur between Wagner and Cosima (who was twenty-four years younger than he), while Von Bülow pretends not to see because his wife's unfaithfulness means a successful career for him. Very indicative of the tense situation in this respect is the moment at which Cosima, with particular intensity, tells Wagner of expecting another child, and Von Bülow, standing up in front of the piano, controls himself by playing a few chords. Cosima, while married to Von Bülow, had four children by Wagner; the last one, a daughter named Isolde, had the musician as her godfather.

Wagner's greed ("Nothing is too beautiful for me. . . . I cannot be satisfied with a mediocre life. I need all this to work. As a matter of fact, I need much more. I need security") is presented by Visconti in absolute contrast to Ludwig's idealism. The king adores the musician, whose music he considers one of the greatest achievements of mankind. No price is too high for Ludwig; his idol must create under the best possible conditions. Even though Wagner seems to nourish a genuine feeling of admiration and affection for the young monarch ("He moved me. He is an extraordinary boy, adorable. An angel descended from the sky."), he also takes advantage of the angel's generosity. This is obvious in a subsequent scene, where the musician and Cosima, with transparent opportunism that Ludwig does not appear to notice, ask for the huge sum of two hundred thousand gulden. The woman tells Ludwig that Wagner's health is affected by financial worries, while the musician pretends not to want to disclose his problems, but it is clear that his reluctance is just part of the act. After Ludwig leaves he says, "They promise everything, they profess friendship and love, but who are these Maecenas? This is a brainless little boy. The last madman of a family of madmen." For the "brainless little boy," friendship and love are supreme virtues, and Wagner and his lover obtain what they want.

In the next scene, cut by Visconti but retained in the script, Cosima supervises the clerks of the National Bavarian Bank who carry sacks full of money into two waiting coaches while a little crowd observes the operation and makes sarcastic comments. When the ménage à trois is made public by a newspaper and the three persons involved ask Ludwig for a letter of support, the king's bitterness and disappointment are evident, and the shadow of sadness that appears for the first time in the film on Ludwig's face, will not leave him from this time on. "Wagner knows how much I appreciate real friendship," he says with a tired sarcasm.

Visconti makes a point of contrasting Wagner's egotism with Ludwig's delusions about human nature in a sequence of scenes covering several years. The sequence is too long because of cumbersome dialogue and too short to clarify for the uninformed viewer the complex nature of that friendship. The film by itself is not adequate to explain the situation, and it shows once more the progressive detachment of Visconti from the general public, which generally speaking, would not be well-informed about the intricate relations between Wagner and Ludwig. It is true that several times before Visconti used unfamiliar historical events in his films. *The Leopard*, for example, presents a story with a background very well known in Italy but almost unknown in the United States. However, *The Leopard* is marked by emotional intensity while *Ludwig*—and this is the real flaw of the whole film—is pervaded by coldness and detachment. The relationship between Wagner and Ludwig leaves us cold because its nature is not clarified enough intellectually and, especially, because it does not have the emotional impact that would compensate with imagery for the lack of historical explanations.

Another important person in Ludwig's life is his cousin Elizabeth, Empress of Austria. Elizabeth's life was marked by tragedy: her sister Sophie, Ludwig's fiancée, died in the fire of Bazar de la Charité in Paris, and her son Rudolf, the heir to the throne, committed suicide with his lover Maria Vetzera (an affair treated in two films entitled *Mayerling*). Elizabeth herself was murdered by an anarchist in Switzerland. In the film we do not see any of these tragedies, with the exception of a glimpse of the dead body of the empress, right after she has pronounced some words which sound like a gloomy prophecy: "Monarchs like us," she says to Ludwig, "do not have a history. They are good for parades. Posterity will remember us only if someone, giving us a credit which we do not deserve, will take the trouble to kill us." The outspoken, lively, and extravagant Elizabeth is interpreted by Romy Schneider, whom we see for the first time riding a horse in a circus. Elizabeth was also a sportswoman who loved physical exercise and horses. This scene, in which we admire the elegance of Elizabeth, dressed in black on a beautiful white horse against the warm reddish background of the small circus, was the first episode filmed by Visconti in Bad-Ischl, Austria. Giorgio Ferrara, who kept the journal of the filming, describes Visconti's technical attentions to all the details and his mathematical precision in their coordination.

Many were the difficulties encountered in the filming of this scene. First of all, the very cold weather had frozen the surface of the performing area, which had to be defrosted by the installation of about thirty gas stoves. But the greatest difficulty was the synchronization of the dialogue and the actions of the actors with the evolutions of the horse, Lola, which became more and more nervous with the passing of time. Finally the scene was completed to the satisfaction of Visconti, whose perfectionism also required fresh (not plastic) little bouquets of violets on the temples of the horses; Romy Schneider, however, needed two days to recuperate.[9]

The feelings between the cousins appear very strong in this scene. The king is timid and tentative as a teenager on his first date; the empress, apparently sure of herself, hides under a jocular sarcasm tender feelings for Ludwig and bitterness about her own life. Elizabeth apologizes for not having been present at Ludwig's coronation: "I was about to come," she says, "but then the idea of all those relatives." Later on, outside, in the clear stillness of the cold night, the empress confides her bitterness. "I defend myself by escaping. They say I am extravagant. I am criticized for anything I do or say." At this point it appears that Ludwig is in love with his cousin: "I believe that all men fall in love with you," he says to her without taking his eyes from hers. "Is it true," she asks rather tactlessly, "that you never had a woman? They say that you love to be alone. That you despise all the people surrounding you. That you go horseback riding in the night, and for this they call you the lover of the moonlight. But I also do all these things." Even though Elizabeth shares with Ludwig the pleasure of nightly equestrian excursions, her reality is never so entangled in a dream. She shows skepticism toward Ludwig's enthusiasm for Wagner: "What do you want to create? A people of musicians? You are a boy, Ludwig. And a little bit crazy. We are all a little crazy in the family."

Because of her opposition to Ludwig's patronage, Elizabeth does not attend the presentation of Wagner's *Tristan*. "How much did it cost?" she inquires. "This spectacle, Wagner, his orchestra director, the family of the orchestra director—what kind of aspirations do you have? To be remembered in history because of Richard Wagner? You must have the courage to build your own reality. You cannot be alone and I cannot be anything for you. Get married. Marry Sophie." Elizabeth understands Ludwig, and she tries, unsuccessfully, to help him deal with that reality from which the king is becoming more and more alienated. A very powerful scene that reveals through its imagery Elizabeth's inability to help her cousin and his alienation is the visit that the empress tries to pay to the secluded king several years later. She walks through the cold magnificence of the gallery of the mirrors in the Herremchiemse castle. Sixty-five mirrors and one thousand candles reflecting and illuminating the emptiness, a huge bronze peacock with green and blue eyes, a piano covered with black velvet and silence. Silence is here and in the castle of Neuschwanstein, the fortress in the clouds where Ludwig hides away from the cousin whom he loved.

Ludwig's escape to a world of clouds and dreams starts manifesting itself after the conference with Elizabeth, when, having agreed to participate in the Austro-Prussian war, the Bavarian king refuses to acknowledge its existence by not receiving his generals and by letting his very young brother take his place on the battlefield. When Otto, the starry-eyed adolescent brother, comes to Ludwig in his military uniform, the king is listening to a carillon playing the prelude of the *Lohengrin* in a bluish room receiving its light from an artificial moon suspended on the ceiling, across which clouds are slowly passing. Ludwig's interest is totally concentrated on the music of his idol and on the architectural gimmick, a very modest preview of what will happen in his future constructions. "For me the war does not exist," he says to Otto. "Go back to the front. And if the general asks you about this you must answer: the King does not know that there is a war." Later on Durkeim, a man who will be faithful to Ludwig till the end, brings the news of the defeat and of Otto's incipient mental disease. "He lives in anguishing solitude," Durkeim says referring to Ludwig's young brother. "He looked for happiness in the impossible, for security in the exception." "Why should he not have done it?" replys Ludwig. "The world around us is incredibly base. I want to be free. Free to look for happiness in the impossible." Apologizing for his frankness, Durkeim warns the king about that dangerous freedom which could bring him to a point of no return and tells him that it takes courage to accept mediocrity: "It is the only hope for saving oneself from an impure solitude."

But a dismal isolation starts to envelop Ludwig, who at this point makes an attempt to normalize his life by becoming engaged to Sophie, Elizabeth's sister. However, this misguided endeavor brings the king to another crisis, which will alienate him even more from reality. Ludwig's decision to take Sophie as his wife is based on the advice of Elizabeth and Durkeim, both of whom stress the necessity of finding the courage to deal with life, and on his own attempt to suppress his homosexual feelings.

We understand from the king's conversation with the Jesuit Father Hoffman that Ludwig had such feelings earlier, but their manifestation appears in the film in a pictorially expressive scene. Walking in the moonlight toward the lake in the park of the castle of Berg, Ludwig sees someone swimming naked in the lake. The moonlight swimmer, who at the king's call emerges from the water like an aquatic creature, is a young valet, Volk, whose naked silhouette, illuminated by the clearness of the night, stands out against a heavy and thick vegetation, giving to the whole scene the intriguing effect of a mysterious forest painted by Henri Rousseau. The king stares at the young man reproachingly and leaves in anger. The original scene, cut by Visconti but described in the script, explains more about the reasons for Ludwig's hostility. During a swim that the king, also naked, takes with the valet, the latter, an unexperienced swimmer, holds onto Ludwig's body. During the playful embrace the hilarity of the king soon changes into a sudden stare of hatred, and Volk is suddenly abandoned in high water where he almost drowns, while Ludwig leaves the scene without paying any attention to the struggling of the young man. Obviously the emotions provoked in him by the valet are very disturbing to Ludwig, who, in a subsequent scene, tearfully asks for help in front of the crucifix.

To counteract these unwanted feelings the king suddenly decides to marry Sophie, and at dawn, while his mother (whom he always despised) is still in bed, announces his choice to her. The queen is overwhelmed with joy, but her enthusiasm is not shared by Father Hoffman, Ludwig's confessor. The young monarch himself shows only preoccupation and unhappiness during the engagement. "Our engagement is more tiring than a military campaign," he says to Wagner in Sophie's presence. "A martyrdom. A real martyrdom which Sophie endures without a lament. She is a perfect fiancée." Sophie's endurance is not tested by the social duties of showing up at balls, family reunions, and ceremonies, but by Ludwig's cold, strange behavior. "Often he comes during the night," Sophie says to Elizabeth. "Mother asked him to change the time of his visits. For him it was an excuse to diminish them. Sometimes he comes by at night and he leaves a bouquet of flowers for me. Without a note." Elizabeth encourages her sister to help Ludwig. "He has many faults and many virtues. He is vulnerable. You can save him. You must. But you must be strong. Don't accept any delay to the wedding."

But Ludwig has already made his decision, which he communicates to Father Hoffman. The latter tries to convince the king that it is his royal duty to get married and to have children and encourages him by expressing a certainly compromising view on sexual preference: "You must use the temptations of the devil against him. You must use them for the honor of God. In the darkness of a room, helped by the imagination of sin, you will realize that the warmth of one body is just like the warmth of another." "You are teaching me something new, Father," replys Ludwig, unconvinced. Father Hoffman continues, saying that Ludwig must be an example for his people. "If you are different, they will never forgive you. I know that so far you have had the strength to reject the temptation of sin. I want to know if it is still true." "Yes," answers Ludwig, while we see images of his "fall" with Hornig, one of his grooms.

After this crisis Ludwig retreats forever and completely into his world made of frozen dreams. He refuses to live in Munich, the capital, and spends his life in the darkness of the extravagant castles he builds by squandering the Bavarian treasury on spectacular displays of frozen magnificence. Guy de Pourtales describes Ludwig's love for porcelains that did not represent anything, for bed covers so embroidered with gold that he could not rest on them, and for pen holders so ornate and complicated that he could not use them for their purpose.[10]

The extravagance of this very lonely man, surrounded by a court of lackeys and grooms who receive, according to his mood, generous gifts or whippings, is presented by Visconti with images that, compared to Ludwig's excesses, show a degree of restraint. The king carries his obsession through his luxurious and useless living quarters: the largeness of the rooms that Ludwig fills with a surplus of mirrors, useless ivory, and gilded objects emphasizes the emptiness of his soul.

The second part of the film portrays the progressive emptiness of Ludwig's life as he decays as a person while as a king he tries to fill the void with the coldness of precious objects, gimmicks, and imitations. The luxury of the castles is nothing but a protective shell for this man whose appearance is also a mark of his deterioration. The handsome Ludwig who royally marched toward his subjects the day of his coronation is now an overweight, middle-aged man (in real life Ludwig had ballooned to huge proportions) with swollen red eyes and rotten teeth. He drinks heavily and lives in the darkness of the night. The lover of the moonlight has lost every romantic appeal and hides shamefully in his kingdom of snow. He has become a nocturnal creature, filling his lonely nights with debauchery, as we see in the scene at the hunting lodge, where a drunken Ludwig, showing in his laughter his decayed teeth, tries to recognize by the touch the identity of the half-naked valets and lackeys with a blindfold over his eyes.

Sometimes his old passion for the arts returns, but in a way in which it is possible to discern the king's complete estrangement from reality. The king's delusions are evident in the episode concerning Joseph Kainz, the actor who arrives at the castle of Linderhof after receiving an invitation from Ludwig. The latter receives Kainz with a coldness which surprises the actor until the explanation is given to him by a servant. "The king wanted to meet Romeo, not Mr. Kainz. He has invited Romeo to Linderhof. If you will be able to be Romeo or Didier, one of his heroes, it will be a sure victory." The actor does his best to humor the king's delusions, but the effort proves to be too much for a mere mortal. The actor is asked to recite without interruption from Schiller and from Hugo, while in the king's mind the characters become real, arousing even more his state of excitement. When Kainz, exhausted, asks for permission to get some sleep, the king takes him to see his kingdom. On the sled dragged by four gray horses the actor can still master enough strength to recite verses that appropriately speak of glaciers in a land where Spring will never arrive, but on the Tristan, Ludwig's boat, he collapses. "You snored," says Ludwig, hurt. "This is not the poem which I wanted to hear from you." When the actor, exhausted, refuses to go on with the recitation, Ludwig takes it as another betrayal. His face acquires an expression of deep sorrow while he says to the actor, addressing him formally, "Then if you are tired get some rest."

Ludwig's mind is now so vulnerable that even a very legitimate excuse is taken as terrible disappointment and treason. Only his precious ornaments and his mountain kingdom, where Spring will never melt the snows, do not hurt Ludwig. His sled, dragged by beautiful horses lifting clouds of powdered snow with their hooves, takes the sorrowful king across his white and cold land of which Visconti gives us the dreamy mood with soft nocturnal images. But Ludwig's behavior is worrying the members of his government, and with reason. In real life, Guy de Pourtalès tells us, this king who at night dressed up like Louis XIV, thought of founding a far-away new kingdom of luxury and voluptuousness with himself as absolute monarch and of paying for it by "selling Bavaria."

Problems of Interpretation

Visconti does not present in his film Ludwig's most striking oddities, preferring to emphasize the king's sadness and alienation rather than his insanity. This presentation of the king results in some peculiar interpretations of the film. For example, Pietro Bianchi, in his introduction to the script, says that "Ludwig is relevant, and Visconti has understood this perfectly, because he represents all that Nazism is not. He favored dream, generosity, particularism, solitude from the nationalists who are drunk from beer and slogans. He even lost a war."[11] First, to talk about Nazism in reference to Ludwig (1845–1886) seems to me anachronistic. Second, since when is it meritorious to lose a war? Merit would have been finding a way of staying out.

Ludwig favored the dream, because he could not deal with reality. As his friend Durkeim warned him, dreams left him isolated. He was generous, but with the money of his subjects. Wagner's expenses were paid not by Ludwig but by the Bavarian people, and the king's solitude was one of unconcerned noninvolvement, as is evident when he lets his adolescent brother lead his soldiers to die while he looks at the clouds of his dream room. Finally, in presenting the nationalists drunk on slogans and beer as the evil opposing Ludwig's good, Bianchi unintentionally critizes Ludwig. Ludwig was not a nationalist, but he was drunk in more than a metaphorical way: he was drunk with his own slogans (the dream, Wagner, his pure kingdom), and he was often drunk on champagne. He left impressive castles to posterity, and yet, without his questionable taste and his mania for imitation, he could have left better artistic products.

"I am an enigma," says Ludwig. "I want to remain an enigma. Not only for other people, but also for myself." Ludwig's personality is less than an enigma: his loss of touch with reality, his delusions, his megalomania are quite consistent in his behavior. An enigma, however, his death remains. It is presented in the last scene, filmed almost in total darkness as torches struggle against the wind and the rain. Visconti directed this episode masterfully, creating a dramatic tableau with the drumming of the rain on the swamp, the flickering of the flames, and the frantic search contributing to the gloom in which the twilight of the king's existence has finally turned into an unredeemable night. The search is led by Count Holstein, who finds Ludwig's and Dr. Gudden's bodies and announces the macabre discovery with two gunshots. The floating corpses are hoisted on the boat and subsequently laid on the shore. Their ashen faces are illuminated by the reddish light of the torches and beaten by the incessant rain while Holstein announces the official version of the two deaths: "The king committed suicide, and in order to do it he had to kill Dr. Gudden."

Since nobody was present, the end of Ludwig's life has remained a mystery which Visconti encourages by having Holstein behave in a suspicious way. The count is presented as a man who not only has no pity, but who seems to nourish a personal animosity for Ludwig, probably because of what occurred in a scene cut from the film. In the deleted episode, an outraged Ludwig literally kicks the drunken Holstein out of his room for having congratulated the king on his victory over his enemies, his mother ("You hate her with all your strength") and his brother, now in a mental institution ("They were all ready to tie the little brother to the throne")[12]. Ludwig interrupts Holstein, hitting him with fury and ordering Volk to spit at the count's face. Because Holstein is alone when he discovers the bodies and shoots twice, the two shots may have been more than signals. The film ends with Holstein's official explanation, but Visconti had filmed two more scenes, both cut. In the first one Elizabeth receives the news of Ludwig's death and screams, "They killed him. Assassins! Assassins!"[13] In the second one, a servant holds Ludwig's coat and shows a hole made in it by a bullet.[14]

Several scenes retained in the script have been cut throughout this very long and complex film, which was received generally well in Italy, mainly because of Visconti's professional ability. Several critics commented negatively on the director's increasing attention to themes of alienation and destruction. The success of *Ludwig* in the United States was minimal. While *Death in Venice* and *The Damned* periodically resurface, *Ludwig* has disappeared from revival house screens and is not even shows in series dedicated to the director. Reviews have also been scattered and brief. One typical response, from an issue of *Films in Review*, admires the "opulence, exquisite sets, beautiful and interesting costumes" but finds the film "too long," Berger "pitiful," the English dialogue "laughable."[15]

Care, preparation, and professionalism of approach cannot be denied Visconti who, as we have seen, even gambled on his health to film *Ludwig* on his own terms and with his own painstaking direction of the actors, all of whom perform well, Helmut Berger included. But the film is emotionally cold. Its magnificence, just like that of Ludwig is an artifice which vainly struggles to fill the images with the sympathy for a lost soul that Visconti wanted to communicate to the audience. The undeniable beauty of some scenes (the encounter with Elizabeth in the circus, the gallop of the horses on the snowy ground, the mysterious atmosphere pervading the Bavarian mountains, and the dramatic search for the bodies) are not enough to redeem a film based on the remoteness of a king whose royal sorrow is too detached from reality to provoke in the viewer more than cold pity.

11

Conversation Piece:
A Film about Impossibility

VISCONTI'S STRUGGLE WITH ILLNESS was long and difficult, but the director fought gallantly with the help of his work, which kept his intellect alive and gave him the psychological strength to accept his physical limitation. "Only if I cling to the capacity of an intellect which, luckily, has not been hit, can I continue living," he said to Lina Coletti. "I was free before. I was abusing my body as if it were the most natural thing in the world. Then the slap. I hate my illness because it deprived me of my freedom, because it humiliated me and it keeps humiliating me."[1]

A man as active and independent as Visconti must have found it especially humiliating to have to learn how to walk again, how to move his hands, how to comb his hair. But his spirit proved indomitable. "I swear that neither old age nor illness have bent my desire to live and to work. I feel fresh for another ten films. Films, theater, musicals—I want to confront everything, everything. With passion. Because one must always burn with passion when one starts something. We are here for this: to burn until death, which is the last act of life, completes life's work transforming us into ashes."[2] Very passionate words indeed, coming from a man who is, as he defines himself, "old and sick." Visconti expressed himself in these terms right after the completion of *Conversation Piece* in November 1974. This, however, was not his first work after his illness, because in the spring of the same year, he had presented at the Teatro Argentina in Rome Harold Pinter's play *Old Times*. "It's a tragedy about the inability to communicate," he explains, "even though the characters continuously talk. . . . I hope I have interpreted it correctly."[3] Unfortunately, Visconti's interpretation did not please the author.

The director had chosen to present an Italian version that was not approved by Pinter's agent in Italy and was forced, after the first two

The distraught "Professor" (Burt Lancaster) breaks down over the murdered body of young Konrad (Helmut Berger) in Conversation Piece. (Courtesy of Museum of Modern Art/Film Stills Archive)

shows, to stop the play. Harold Pinter, who arrived from London during the peak of the controversy, imposed modifications upon Visconti. (Pinter's indignation referred mostly to the sexual acts which Visconti had introduced.)

Although Visconti's return to the theater was not happy, the disappointment and the incomprehension were soon to be offset by the smoothness of the work in his next film and by the demonstration of solidarity and affection which he received from colleagues, friends, and the public, who all awaited the completion of his next film, *Conversation Piece*.

Conversation Piece (1974): The Plot

In an elegantly furnished apartment, situated in the center of Rome, a professor lives a solitary life surrounded by beautiful books and paintings. He is in the process of buying a new "conversation piece" from two antiquarians. He decides not to buy it, however, because the price is much too high. During the negotiations the professor hardly notices the presence of a beautiful and elegant lady whom he believes to be with the antiquarians; the woman instead came on her own with the intention of renting the attic from the professor. The latter is adamant in his refusal and is disconcerted by the rude insistence of the woman (Bianca Brumonti), who is soon joined by her daughter Lietta and her fiancé Stefano. A few moments later the invasion is completed by the appearance of Konrad, Bianca's young lover, who announces to the woman that the police are about to tow her car, which provokes the precipitous departure of the group. The professor returns to his favorite occupations of reading and contemplating works of art. Overtaken by the sudden desire to possess a painting shown before by the antiquarians, the professor decides to buy it, only to be disappointed by the discovery that the conversation piece has been sold. The following day Lietta and Stafano return with the painting (they were the buyers) and succeed in convincing the professor to take it as a payment on the rent of the attic.

One night, returning from a concert, the professor notices pieces of plaster and water in his own apartment, obviously the result of modifications made in the attic. Determined to find out what is going on, he decides to take a look and is shocked by what he sees: a demolished wall, piles of bricks and plaster—an enormous confusion, in the middle of which Konrad sleeps, enveloped by a sumptuous fur blanket. The intrusion wakes the young man, who is furious when he finds out that the apartment was not sold but merely rented and who, subsequently, in an agitated telephone call to Bianca, unpleasantly severs his relations with her.

A few days later, after several explanations, the situation is "normalized" again: the apartment is rented for a year and the group, Bianca and Konrad included, leave for Fiumicino for an extended yacht vacation. Slowly the professor becomes involved with this eccentric family. One night, hearing noises and moaning upstairs, he finds Konrad beaten and bloodied and keeps him in his own apartment for a few days. When the young man, on his way to Monaco, is stopped by the police at the border, the professor is called to confirm Konrad's alibi. From the police and from Bianca later on the professor finds out that Konrad is involved in several kinds of shady deals, and he reproaches Bianca for allowing her young daughter to associate with such a man.

The conflict which is slowly mounting explodes after a dinner that the professor offers to the group: Bianca announces matter-of-factly that her husband requires that she leave Konrad and that she is thinking of divorce. When Konrad, who is unusually tense, asks her to marry him she answers that he is not the type that a lady marries. This provokes rage in the young man, who accuses Bianca and the society in which she lives of being false and corrupt. He also accuses her husband, a well-known fascist, of having plotted and failed in a right-wing takeover. He, Konrad, is the one who warned the police of it. The following day, an explosion is heard by the professor, who runs upstairs and finds Konrad dead. In the final scene of the film we see the professor on his deathbed receiving the visits of Bianca and Lietta, who expresses her conviction that Konrad did not kill himself but was murdered and asks the professor to have some faith in the young man.

"It is the tragedy of solitude."[4]

In his next–to–last film, Visconti returns to the theme of loneliness, which he has already presented as a total separation from reality in *Ludwig*. The director switches from the snowy kingdom of Bavaria in the nineteenth century to an apartment in modern Rome, where, amidst elegant surroundings, he follows with the camera the clashing of two worlds and two different life-styles. *Conversation Piece* is vaguely inspired by *Conversation Pieces*, by Mario Praz, an Italian critic who is mostly known for a book of literary criticism translated in English as *The Romantic Agony*. A "conversation piece," as Praz explains, is a term "used in England for paintings, usually not of large dimensions, which represent two or more identifiable people in attitudes implying that they are conversing or communicating with each other informally, against a background reproduced in detail."[5]

Praz's book, a series of domestic scenes in which characters appear in groups playing music, sitting at the dinner table, reading books, gave Visconti an idea for the background against which his characters move and interact. The apartment of the professor (played by American actor Burt Lancaster, with whom Visconti had already worked in *The Leopard*) is nothing short of an elegant little museum where richly bound books, tasteful pieces of furniture, and bronzes mingle their sienna and ochre hues while hundreds of eyes look down from the conversation pieces covering the walls. A little army of painters, plasterers, sculptors, and specialized artisans worked at the creation of this museum, where a solitary man lives surrounded by painted family lives. We do not know his name, since his identity is expressed only by what he does: he is the professor who goes to concerts, listens to rare records, contemplates his paintings, and reads his books. His means allow him to lead a very comfortable life away from the crowd. "Living with men," he says, "one is forced to think about men rather than about their works, to suffer with men and to be preoccupied with them. . . . Someone wrote, 'Crows go in flocks! The eagle flies alone!'" And in his eagle's nest the professor lives in gilded solitude.

At the time when he was filming *Conversation Piece* Visconti was also thinking about Thomas Mann's *The Magic Mountain*, which he wanted to bring to the screen as the conclusion of his career. We can certainly see a parallel between Hans Castorp and the professor, both living in an isolated environment, both occupying their time with unnecessary but pleasant routine, both inhabitants of a somewhat magic world inhabited by unreal people—the other patients in Castorp's case, the families in the conversation pieces in the case of the professor. If the professor does not have Hans's moist spot on the lung, he certainly has his own kind of sickness which, just like the slight "tuberculosis pulmonum" keeps Mann's protagonist in the Grisons, keeps the professor in his museum apartment. The professor's disease is solitude bordering on misanthropy. "I did not want to let the apartment," he confides to Lietta, "because I am an old maniac, an eccentric who is disturbed when he hears noise, when he sees people at the front door, and when he has to maintain relations of convenience."

The luxury with which the professor surrounds himself, his cultural interests, and, naturally, his wanting to be alone have led many interviewers to draw a parallel between the professor and Visconti himself, which the director has always been quick to deny. "There is nothing autobiographical in the film. Maybe an identical substratum of sensitivity; I always avoided total solitude, and I look for the other kind, the one which you choose, selecting a few friends and giving preference to staying by yourself with your books and your music rather than among people who cannot give you anything and to whom you could not give anything."[6] In another interview Visconti calls the professor a "selfish man," a "maniac about things," a man "incapable of establishing relations with other people, and a man who abandons his family to isolate himself completely." But he admits that "the only autobiographical element is the solitude."[7]

The professor maintains a tranquil existence until his nest is jarred by a flock of crows. Bursting, uninvited, into the professor's apartment, (flying in, almost, since they just materialize out of nowhere) Bianca, Lietta, Stefano, and Konrad shatter the silence of the professor's life. He is mesmerized by the frivolous chatting and increasingly frustrated because his brief but firm denials on the availability of the attic do not seem to be heard by "the crows," probably deaf because of their own vocal fluttering. During the intrusion Bianca moves to the balcony, from where we see a spectacular (painted) view of Rome. The most striking details, however, are the statues decorating the balustrade: enormous double-faced busts which Visconti evidently chose not only for decoration but also as a symbol of the struggle that will occur between the two worlds. The two-faced head is an obvious representation of Janus, the Roman god whose temple was open during wartime and whose faces, looking in opposite directions, were one young and one old. The radical fracture between the young and the old which Visconti wanted to present in this film is paradoxically apparent in the impossible relation of two faces frozen in stone and unable to look at each other. They are united and divided at the same time.

Among the invaders Konrad is certainly the most complex person, and he does not really belong to Bianca's world. He is what is called in

Italian *un ragazzo di vita* ("a boy of life"), a usually very handsome and charming young man who uses his physical appeal to earn a living. His sexual exploits must be numerous, because Lietta and Stafano, joking with Konrad about the people who would miss him in case of his death, talk about a funeral participation of all "the prostitutes of Rome . . . loan sharks, drug addicts, and a gay delegation." (They do not add, but they should, "rich middle-aged women.")

There is something more to Konrad, however. During a telephone conversation with Bianca in the presence of the professor, he becomes angry with the woman because she has not bought the apartment for him. Konrad addresses her with a stream of vulgarities (and Bianca is more than happy to reciprocate), but as soon as the exchange has ended, his attention is suddenly attracted by a record ("I have a passion for Strauss") and by a painting which he identifies, showing a surprising knowledge to the professor. Later on he says that he was once an art student at the University of Berlin. "I was with the student movement. I had to run away, and I don't know how, but I landed on very different shores." The new shores are not only different but also dangerous, as we can see from the beating that the young man receives. This episode is a real turning point in the film, not because of Konrad's unfortunate experience, but because it represents a change in the feelings of the professor. Slowly, almost without realizing it, the old man is developing an interest in the "crows" who are so different from him, so vulgar and yet so alive. When they do not show up for a dinner to which he has invited them, the professor, obviously disappointed and angry, complains to Erminia, the housekeeper, that "They are not refined people. They are impolite, silly, and useless." But his return to noninvolvement is brief, and his eagle's nest is once again shaken by the jarring events of the outside world.

For the first time, while taking care of Konrad's bruises with cold compresses, the professor confides a detail of his past. "I was in war, and I have been afraid. My mother, who was Italian, was here during the war. My father and I were in America, and I came back to Europe only with the V Army." Referring to the secret room where Konrad now rests, which, during the war, was a hiding place for political refugees, the professor calls it "the fruit of fear." Actually, that room is not the only "fruit of fear." The whole apartment, because it protects its owner from the pain of emotions, gives him a feeling of warmth, enhanced by the many family portraits hanging from the walls.

Konrad's presence in his apartment brings back memories to the professor. In one flashback he remembers himself as an uncooperative child who does not want to say anything, despite his mother's insistence; in another he sees his wife crying and asking for his help. Affected by these memories, but not enough to change his attitude toward other people, the professor freezes at the first glimpse of closeness coming from Konrad: "Today I did not sleep all the time," says the young man. "I was imagining that I was telling you everything of myself and that I was asking you for advice." "I don't have any advice to give you. And besides, a man of your age and of your intelligence knows by himself what he has to do," the professor replies coldly. He knows better than to get involved with a complex young man who was once a brilliant art student involved in politics, who is now the "kept man" of a rich and spoiled older woman, and who is also suspected of participating in shady deals involving gambling and drugs.

"I have my preferences," says the professor, referring to his paintings. "I even have my infidelities. I had a long predilection for the Sitwell family. I even took it to my bedroom. But a deeper knowledge did not help our rapport. I started arguing with the older daughter." The professor continues to fantasize about the conversation pieces, the purified artistic expressions of privileged moments in a family's life.

The family that introduces itself into the professor's life, however, is not a model of morality and convention. Not only do Bianca and Konrad continue their relationship without any discretion, but Konrad, Stefano, and Lietta indulge in erotic games which they do not even try to hide when the professor, awakened by the music, finds them naked and smoking marijuana in his living room. Smiling, Lietta recites some lines by Auden: "When you see a fair form chase it / And if possible embrace it / Be it a girl or a boy. / Don't be bashful be brash, be fresh. / Life is short, so enjoy / Whatever contact your flesh / May at that moment crave / There is no sex-life in the grave."

A methodical intellectual like Aschenbach in *Death in Venice*, the professor believes that he has solved the problems of his life by excluding human involvement and filtering his emotions through the categories of his intellect. Just like Aschenbach, he is confronted here by the irrationality of Eros, which does not seem to be limited by the power of reason. Struggling to keep a balance between feelings and disciplined thoughts (it was not difficult when he conversed only with books and paintings), the professor is challenged by the life-style of people who have defied conventional morality. "There is nothing wrong," says Lietta. "How were you when you were young? Weren't you like us?" "No. Definitely not," answers the professor. He disapproves of their life but at the same time sees that his own, at the other extreme, is also deficient. "I have little time left," he says. "I would need a son already grown to be able to tell him all I know." Lightheartedly, Lietta suggests the adoption of Konrad, not knowing that the professor has already excluded him from his life by denying him friendship and advice.

Appearing at the beginning as the most depraved of the characters, Konrad is in reality a victim, rejected by the serious world of the professor and used by the world of Bianca. The film does not explain how he ended up on the "very different shores," but in the dramatic scene of the dinner, with one of the characteristic Visconti settings (a table sumptuously adorned with candles, flowers, and crystal), the repressed conflicts explode. We see how the pampered Konrad is in reality scorned and rejected by the people who are responsible for his elegant clothes, fast cars, and expensive apartments. Bianca, in fact, treats him like a nonentity, a person not to be taken seriously, an object which can be bought or replaced without second thoughts. "Do you know what my husband wanted to tell me?" she asks offhandedly. "He has nothing against a substitution . . . but he does not want to hear about Konrad anymore." Surprising everybody, Konrad asks Bianca to marry him, simply to prove to the woman that her refusal is based on hypocrisy. He is not a man that a woman of a "respectable society" would marry, but Konrad questions the respectability of society. "I know what I am worth. But I also know what you are worth. I am the little dog that an important lady can take into places where dogs are not allowed. His presence is endured when he steals from the kitchen, when he soils or when he bites. My methods, of which you are ashamed," he says to Bianca, "are the methods of your world."

Konrad's outburst provokes a strong reaction from Stefano, a secondary character who, up to this point, has simply appeared as a lazy scion of a rich society, a follower who enjoys his privileges and who is often rebuked in turn by Lietta and Bianca. The anger transforms his face, and for the first time we see another aspect of Stefano's personality. He becomes a man filled with cold hatred, and his usually inattentive mind is now totally focused on Bianca's words about the sudden departure of her husband for Spain. Suddenly and too late to give *Conversation Piece* a political relevance, Visconti introduces the news of an intended right wing coup d'état plotted by, among others, Stefano and Bianca's husband. The coup fails because of Konrad's warning to the police. "Your husband," Konrad says to Bianca, "ran away because they discovered that those belonging to his group were about to kill a dozen communist parliamentarians and some members of the Government. Ask Stefano about it. I am the one who denounced them."

With this political interpolation Visconti tried, as he often did in other films, to situate *Conversation Piece* in a wider context that would include not only individual problems but also socio-political implications.

An Attempt at Political Relevance

But Konrad's nebulous past as a member of the student movement and the sudden news of the departure of Bianca's husband for Madrid are not enough to widen the significance of the film, which remains totally concerned with individual lives, even if Konrad's death leaves the spectator with an unanswered question about the possibility of a political murder. Konrad is, in fact, found dead with Stefano's scarf in his hand. This somewhat silly detail (how could Stefano, if he committed the murder, be so stupid as to leave his showy and fashionable scarf which, in the first scenes of the film, he unnecessarily wears as a trademark, in the hand of the victim?) appears to be the extent of the director's attempt to give to his film a political meaning.

Several times in his career Visconti seemed to need to prove that his political orientations were more important than his attention to the individual and his problems. The fact that he was a nobleman, a count belonging to a rich and privileged class, and that he always proclaimed his communist faith are indeed two conflicting aspects of the life of the director, who often reacted with irritation when this sore spot was uncovered during an interview. To Lina Coletti who said to him: "Visconti the red nobleman. This was your label, wasn't it?," Visconti quickly answered: "What an idiocy! I never waved my nobility, never, never. I was not brought up to become a stupid aristocrat prostrated to the heritage of the family. I have always been a great liberal, a great rebel."[8] And certainly Visconti is not a useless aristocrat and certainly he is a rebel, but in several of his works it is not difficult to detect signs of sustained struggles to be "less count" and "more red." An example of Visconti's tendencies is *The Leopard*, in which his idea of transcending Lampedusa's views remains at the level of intention, while the director sympathizes almost completely with the noble Prince Salina. In *Conversation Piece*, along with the solitude and "an identical substratum of sensitivity," there is an autobiographical element contained in the professor's words after the dinner: "The intellectual of our generation looked for a balance between politics and morals. An impossible search."

In the final analysis, *Conversation Piece* is a film about impossibility—the impossibility of changing, the impossibility of balancing different life-styles, the impossibility of communicating. The two faces of Janus look in two different directions; while the war is going on, the song "La mia solitudine" [My solitude] plays in the background of the erotic party, expressing with its common words (but maybe they are so common because they are so true,) the main theme of the film: "My solitude, it's you—my real anger, it's you."

Konrad takes his leave of the solitary man whom he admired and with whom he would have liked to share his thoughts with these words, written right before the explosion which causes his death; "Dear Professor, I would like to be wrong, but I believe that we will never see each other again. Your son, Konrad." Konrad, whose personality is the most complex in the film, is a contemporary fallen angel, beautiful, corrupt, rebellious, ambivalent, and sad. No experience is too daring for the young man whose rebellion caused his fall from the world of arts and letters, where, judging from his acute observations, he would have excelled. Now pampered by a depraved and hypocritical world which he secretly abhors, he longs for a cleaner life, but he finds it impossible to execute the "clear cut" that the professor, moving away from him, suggests. "In the final analysis it is humiliating and ridiculous having been beaten. People laugh about it," says Konrad after seeing his bloody face. "If they kill you, you save your face. But like this, they laugh and that's all." Death for Konrad is, therefore, the only way out. He cannot go back to a past that has been lost forever, and it is too humiliating to be beaten again. Nobody will laugh at his bruises when he is dead.

The illustration of the fallen angel done by Doré for Milton's *Paradise Lost* (one of Visconti's favorite drawings) shows the striking beauty of an androgynous face looking back in sadness and anger, which contrasts sharply with the monstrous bat wings, a grotesque detail giving a beastly character to the beautiful body. A similar clashing of motives appears on the screen when the professor lays the handsome Konrad down on a gaudy circular bed, an obvious reminder of the young man's main occupation. But even for the professor, death is the only way out. Life, from which he isolated himself to seek the rarefied air of artistic and intellectual refinement, suddenly leaves him mortally wounded. "There is a writer . . . who tells of a lodger who takes the apartment above his. The writer hears him moving and walking. Then the lodger disappears, and for a long time there is only silence. But suddenly he comes back. After a while his absences become more unusual and his presence constant. It is death." After Konrad, Bianca, Lietta, and Stefano, death is the only lodger that the professor can accept in his attic.

Conversation Piece, launched in Rome on 8 April 1974 in an atmosphere of great excitement that brought to the set for the first scene several movie personalities and friends of Visconti, is the next to the last film in the director's brilliant career. "Dear friend, I embrace you with emotion and joy. Everything will go well, you'll see! Long live the cinema!" said a telegram from Federico Fellini, who was gallantly paying homage and respect to his rival, friend, and colleague.[9] Indomitable after the long illness, Visconti was back to work to bring to the screen another film successful in Italy but unfortunately almost unnoticed in the United States. *Conversation Piece* would have been a much more worthy conclusion of Visconti's professional life than the deficient *L'Innocente.* Visconti's direction in *Conversation Piece* is masterful, especially in his use of the "conversation pieces," which live in a purified stillness that contrasts sharply with the live action. The inconclusive politics do not detract from the psychological drama which proceeds with tautness and intensity, giving *Conversation Piece* its quality of inspired and inspiring film.

12

Unresolved Intentions: *The Innocent* and a Double Funeral Service

EVEN BEFORE THE BEGINNING of *Conversation Piece*, Visconti had wanted to film Mann's *The Magic Mountain*. This idea assumed more and more relevance each day because of Visconti's personal experience. "The mystery of illness is fascinating in *The Magic Mountain*. Today I understand that masterpiece more, because today I know the hospitals, which I did not before."[1] In the same interview, Visconti revealed a "singular coincidence": during his stay in the Zurich clinic where he was treated for the stroke that hit him after the filming of *Ludwig*, he found out that in that same place, in the same room where he was staying, Thomas Mann had died. The sad coincidence, far from disturbing Visconti, made him even more determined to bring to the screen Mann's novel about illness and its metaphorical meaning. Before initiating this complex labor, however, he decided to work on filming another novel, *L'Innocente*, by Gabriele D'Annunzio. But right before the beginning of the filming, another unfortunate incident complicated the state of his already frail health. Because of a fall while he was trying to regain his full ambulatory capability, he broke his hip and was confined to a wheel chair. At this point his great courage became tainted with bitterness and anger against infirmity, but he found in his work a saving grace. "The day when I am not able to work anymore, I will shoot myself. What could I do in the world? I cannot move, I cannot walk, I cannot travel anymore."[2] He continued to work, and in September 1975 he began *L'Innocente*.

The Innocent (1975): The Plot

Tullio Hermil, a sophisticated man who spends his life among the pleasures of the idle rich, openly betrays his beautiful wife Giuliana

Giuliana (Laura Antonelli) in a tense moment with Filippo Arborio (Marc Porel) in The Innocent. *(Credit of Museum of Modern Art/Film Stills Archive)*

with another beautiful woman, Teresa Raffo. Giuliana, hurt by her husband's unrepented infidelities, finds an admirer in Filippo Arborio, a writer and a friend of Federico, Tullio's brother.

When his passion for Teresa subsides, Tullio returns to his wife with renewed ardor, which, unfortunately for him, comes too late: Giuliana is now pregnant with the child of Filippo Arborio. Tullio, after the initial shock, tries to persuade Giuliana to have an abortion, but she refuses, saying that it is a crime. In the meantime Arborio, whom Tullio wanted to challenge to a duel, dies prematurely because of a tropical disease contracted in Africa.

Giuliana gives birth to a healthy boy, named Raimondo, who brings delight to Tullio's mother. She, like everybody else, is unaware of the child's paternity. Tullio, unable to accept the situation, takes advantage of the fact that the other members of the family and the servants are all attending the Christmas Mass, and exposes the child to frigid cold causing his death. Giuliana's hatred for her husband is now extreme, and Tullio, having also been rejected by his mistress Teresa Raffo, kills himself.

"It was time to come back to Gabriele D'Annunzio"[3]

With his last film, Visconti did come back to D'Annunzio, but in a baffling manner. Interviewed on the set of *The Innocent*, the director, confined to a wheelchair, expressed his will to reevaluate D'Annunzio and to vindicate his greatness after fifty years of neglect and mockery. For this reason he decided to bring to the screen D'Annunzio's novel, *L'Innocente* [The innocent], written in 1892.

A sensational poet at the age of twenty, a writer, a war hero, and a style-setter, D'Annunzio was one of the dominant characters in Italian cultural life at the beginning of the twentieth century. D'Annunzio's fame, however, is a good example to substantiate the observation that the glory of the world is elusive and unstable. In fact, because of his dedication to the search for exceptional linguistic expression and to descriptions of decadent characters inspired by the philosophy of Nietzsche, D'Annunzio, who also considered himself a superman, has often been scorned and ridiculed in the past forty years. His myth has been deflated, and the accusation of insincerity has been leveled against his work again and again.

Luchino Visconti, a man who led a nonconformist life and who often found himself involved in controversies, tried, with *The Inno-*

al voice, accompanied by intense glances, is soothing to
s sorrow. Tullio's insensitivity and depravity give the in-
t between Arborio and Giuliana a significance that cannot
ered a single moment of weakness. Giuliana loves Arborio
equently she loves her son Raimondo, even if her expression
hange when she learns from a newspaper, purposely placed
on the breakfast tray, of the premature death of Arborio.
nzio never mentions any thoughts of abortion in his novel,
isconti's film Tullio's insistence and Giuliana's refusal on the
hat she considers it a crime produce a crucial conflict. In
or's interpretation, Tullio's solution to the problem is an-
warranted modernization of a literary work that resists
rization.

nzio has Giuliana and Tullio think of suicide as the only way
ana reconsiders, thinking of her two little girls (absent in the
of the fact that her suicide would reveal the unhappiness of
age to Tullio's mother and brother, but she hopes that her
h will bring her to a natural death. When this does not
sadly and sarcastically comments on the tenacity of her
tries to put an end to his life by spurring his horse along the
ravine at the bottom of which the river Assoro, with its
s and somber water, issues a mortiferous call. Tullio stops
alloping only because Federico, who is trying to catch up
could also die.

rooding reflections after this incident provide a prelude
der. Tullio sees life as a "far away vision, confused and
onstrous." What Eugenio Montale calls "the pain of living"
in Tullio's thoughts, in every aspect of his life. Even
t manifestations of the spirit and the most noble enter-
ear to him irrevocably contaminated by selfishness, futil-
nsitoriness. "How can we live? How can we love?" he asks,
gnized in himself an "ideologist and an analyst of a deca-
n line with his pessimistic cosmic vision he sees in himself
ulses of "primitive unrulable natures." His clear self-
surprises him when he recognizes "spontaneous insur-
cruel instincts." While on one hand he takes pleasure in
ive development" of his intelligence, on the other hand he
mpossibility to coordinate a normal life of the spirit on the
hy of some cerebral centers." Decadent pessimism, the
set values and rules, and a hypersensitivity bordering on
ow the way to a heinous crime. No such self-tormented

cent, to make a personal statement in support of a now unpopular
writer. Unfortunately the film falls very short of its mark.

When he used literary sources, Visconti usually kept the author's
ideas and his own interpretation in perspective, at times taking
liberties, but never merging the two lines of thinking in a disconcerting course. Such a confusion, however, not only occurs with *The
Innocent* but the intended praise of D'Annunzio backfires, because
Visconti attempted the impossible task of giving contemporary relevance to the works of this writer. The reason it is impossible to
transplant D'Annunzio in contemporary times is that very few writers
have been more representative of an era and have so influenced it to
the point of being forever tied to it.

Visconti gambled and lost with a daring probably stemming from
his personal state of mind and body. "I don't give a damn about my
health any more," he said on the set of *The Innocent,* asking the
interviewer, Costanzo Costantini, to light him a cigarette against
strict doctors' orders.[5] The expression, more vulgar in Italian than in
the English translation here given, betrays bitterness channeled into
defiance.

D'Annunzio was a leader of a decadent current characterized by
antihumanism and always born, as Giulio Marzot says, from the
disintegration of spiritual synthesis.[6] We are still living in a decadent
time, but what makes D'Annunzio anachronistic is his answer to the
absurdity of the decadent reality. D'Annunzio's pseudosolution to
the conflicts of life is his adaptation of the philosophy of Nietzsche,
which, in D'Annunzio's works, becomes the justification for some
characters to place themselves above morality.

From the very beginning of *The Innocent,* which opens with a shot
of Visconti's hand turning the yellowing pages of the original edition
of *L'Innocente,* we see that the myth of the superman has lost all
credibility in contemporary times and cannot be given more fashionable clothes.

Tullio Hermil, who in the book considers himself not an elect spirit
but a "rare" one and therefore feels justified in experiencing every
unusual sensation, appears in the film as a well-dressed clown. "After
a while," he matter-of-factly tells Giuliana, "love goes away and is
substituted by esteem and affection. I would suffer if you left me." In
almost the same breath he adds, "Teresa is a sensuous woman, she is
beautiful, and I desire her."

It is no wonder that the audience, at the first showing of the film in
Boston, burst into laughter at this point and again several times

during the projection, specifically at what are moments of real tragedy in the book. In the novel Tullio is a spoiled member of a useless class, but he at least has the decency to feel guilty. In the film he is a vain butterfly glad to collect on his wings the colors of every flower that he can touch. Visconti could not re–create D'Annunzio's complex character, whose excessive sensitivity makes him constantly struggle against his own dissipation. For this reason the ordeal of Tullio and Giuliana, a veritable tragedy in the novel, appears shallow and ridiculous through much of the film.

The English subtitles do not help. When melodrama is written and read rather than spoken, its pomposity, not absorbed by voice inflections that are capable of toning it down, is too overt and graphic. The cleavage between two societies, the one described by *The Innocent* and the contemporary, to whom the film is presented, remains open, notwithstanding Visconti's effort to connect D'Annunzio to a contemporary sensitivity.

Probably for this reason, some reviews of *The Innocent* in the United States have addressed the acting rather than the cinematic value of the film. It is, in fact, much easier to inform the viewers about Giancarlo Giannini's performance in a new role, quite different from the ones played by the actor under the direction of Lina Wertmuller, and to praise Laura Antonelli's beautiful nudity, rather than to try to make some sense out of a perplexing work. Other reviews concentrate on the color of *The Innocent*, indulging in technical descriptions of its chromatic composition but constantly avoiding the relation between D'Annunzio and Visconti, which is the crux of *The Innocent*.

The departures that Visconti took from the text of D'Annunzio, moreover, involve not only the personality of the protagonist but also several episodes, some minor, some important.

In the film, Federico, Tullio's brother, is an elegant officer who enjoys the company of women and friends during vivacious evenings enhanced by good wine, food, and carefree, trivial conversation. Federico is also indirectly responsible for Giuliana's affair because he is the one who introduces Arborio to his sister–in–law. Probably for this reason, and especially because Federico reminds him of Arborio, Tullio gets carried away during fencing practice and seems on the verge of killing his brother. Sometimes a veiled hostility lingers between Tullio and Federico, who both appear to be mostly dedicated to a hedonistic enjoyment of life.

Unresolved Intentions

Federico is a completely different (
brother's definition he is an exemp
clever. His life is dedicated to work v
the family's property. Under his direc
of the earth, the land has a pastoral
contrast with Tullio's tormented and
kissing him on his beautiful and sere
him son," says Tullio, referring to his
gladly given the right of the first bo

One episode particularly emphasi
nature of the two brothers. Tullio
branches from an apple tree in bloom
the incident with a shadow of sorrow
the branch already dying in the trem
tries to soften the damage by saying
The incident is symbolic of Tullio's
beautiful woman whom he breaks
whom he starts to love again when

In the novel, Federico, in his sin
piness of Giuliana and Tullio, and s
nunzio presents as a veritable sain
about the gloomy atmosphere of t
the hostility of Tullio toward the cl
to understand why but feeling de

Another difference between nov
of Arborio, Giuliana's lover. D'A
through the hatred that Tullio lavis
acquires the negative characteris
seduces Giuliana not out of love bu
In Tullio's memory, Arborio is an
body as repulsive as the vulgari
naked men in the locker room
mentions his name, and she tells
tion, that she is now suffering to
weakness."

Visconti has a different view
romantic and intense young mar
fear when he observes it under
club. Arborio appears to be move
he meets her during the evenin

his musi
Giuliana
volveme
be consi
and cons
does not
by Tullio

D'Ann
while in \
grounds
the direc
other un
contempo

D'Annu
out. Giuli
film) and
her marri
frail healt
occur, she
life. Tullio
edge of a
tumultuou
the mad g
with him,

Tullio's
for the mu
vaguely m
is seething
the highes
prises app
ity, and tra
having rec
dent era."
all the im
observation
rections of
"the excess
blames his
"hypertrop
inability to
madness sh

reflections upset Visconti's Tullio, whose main preoccupation seems to be the restoration of his wounded male pride, and who, after the crime, talks about it quite matter–of–factly to his lover, Teresa Raffo.

Another main discrepancy between novel and film concerns the ending. D'Annunzio's Tullio lives on with the terrible remorse, and at one year's distance from the crime he writes about it in a first–person denunciatory confession, which constitutes the structure of *L'Innocente*. Visconti's Tullio, after an evening with Teresa Raffo, walks calmly toward a window and shoots himself through the heart.

Why did Visconti, who in his own words wanted to return to Gabriele D'Annunzio, change the novel so drastically? Why the modifications in the characters' personalities? Why the abortion? Why the absence of the two daughters?

During the filming of *The Innocent*, Visconti talked about the modifications of the character of Tullio Hermil. "Today nobody tolerates a Nietzschian superman," said Visconti, "and nobody tolerates a man that kills a child. So we present him differently in the film." The director continues by saying that Tullio's self-punishment is just, and he can thus be easily accepted by the public.[7] But Tullio's self-punishment is less than evident. In fact, he shoots himself after having said to Teresa Raffo, "The day I no longer find any pleasure in life, I will end it." End of pleasure, therefore, and not remorse, is the motive of Tullio's suicide. *The Innocent* also fails to achieve any contemporaneity and remains in an ideological limbo, since its themes relegate it to the era in which the book was written without even a remote possibility of modernization.

D'Annunzio should or should not be accepted by what he is and represents, and any regarbing of his dramas in more contemporary clothes is doomed to failure since a normalization of D'Annunzian characters and situations is an impossible task. In fact, we are not dealing with normal people caught in difficult situations; we are confronted rather by the anomalies of a society in which there is a fragmentation of values that are reorganized by some individuals using irrational principles.

Either this characteristic of these period pieces is accepted, so that they are presented in their original form to a contemporary public that should have the ability to understand them for what they are, or D'Annunzio should not be adapted for film.

Viewing *The Innocent* left people familiar with the works of D'Annunzio with the baffling feeling of having seen something terribly anachronistic, like Roman gladiators wearing wristwatches or

medieval knights carrying transistor radios. Those unfamiliar with
D'Annunzio remained unenlightened about the nature of his work.

A Chromatic Symphony

Nothing, however, is totally negative and, if the main purpose of
the film was not achieved, at least the decor of the interiors and the
voluptuousness of the color are positive aspects of *The Innocent,*
aspects that well represent the D'Annunzian world.

The elegance of the society portrayed gives *The Innocent* the
characteristic of a continuous fashion show, with handsome, slim,
and perfectly attired men and sumptuously dressed women swaying
and chatting in their red, flashy pink, and orange gowns. Beautiful
hats crowned with daisies, sparkling shoes with bows and pearls,
mink capes, fur blankets, blue brocades, and purple velvets are the
ornaments of a society in which style of attire and choice of exotic
lamps and fiery purebred horses were extremely important
occupations.

Like a symphony whose main theme is not agreeable, but whose
color is partly redeeming, Visconti's film re-creates, in its decorative
details, the environment so often described by D'Annunzio. The
styles of attire presented in the film recall an article written by
D'Annunzio and published by *Tribuna* in 1884, in which the writer
describes the passing of languid Roman ladies in their carriages on via
del Corso. The article, entitled "The Little Chronicle of the Fur
Coats," indulges in detailed descriptions of ostentatious elegance:
"Oh the beautiful otter cape decorated with blonde beaver! . . . The
most beautiful cape is the one belonging to the Princess of Venosa."
Countess Santafiora owns a "celebrated coat," while Countess
Taverna, whose face has the divine pallor so fashionable at the time,
also wears an otter cape. "Nothing excites the desire of the intimacy
of love more than an otter coat," concludes D'Annunzio.

Careful attention given to furniture, paintings, and clothing has
always been a quality of films directed by Visconti. In *The Innocent*
he continues his personal tradition of cinematic opulence. The elegance of the aristocratic class is depicted in a continuous display of
wealth that has the function of separating the privileged class from
the rest of the people. "Farmers love to see their masters well
dressed," says Tullio to Giuliana, helping her to put on her majestic

cent, to make a personal statement in support of a now unpopular writer. Unfortunately the film falls very short of its mark.

When he used literary sources, Visconti usually kept the author's ideas and his own interpretation in perspective, at times taking liberties, but never merging the two lines of thinking in a disconcerting course. Such a confusion, however, not only occurs with *The Innocent* but the intended praise of D'Annunzio backfires, because Visconti attempted the impossible task of giving contemporary relevance to the works of this writer. The reason it is impossible to transplant D'Annunzio in contemporary times is that very few writers have been more representative of an era and have so influenced it to the point of being forever tied to it.

Visconti gambled and lost with a daring probably stemming from his personal state of mind and body. "I don't give a damn about my health any more," he said on the set of *The Innocent,* asking the interviewer, Costanzo Costantini, to light him a cigarette against strict doctors' orders.[5] The expression, more vulgar in Italian than in the English translation here given, betrays bitterness channeled into defiance.

D'Annunzio was a leader of a decadent current characterized by antihumanism and always born, as Giulio Marzot says, from the disintegration of spiritual synthesis.[6] We are still living in a decadent time, but what makes D'Annunzio anachronistic is his answer to the absurdity of the decadent reality. D'Annunzio's pseudosolution to the conflicts of life is his adaptation of the philosophy of Nietzsche, which, in D'Annunzio's works, becomes the justification for some characters to place themselves above morality.

From the very beginning of *The Innocent,* which opens with a shot of Visconti's hand turning the yellowing pages of the original edition of *L'Innocente,* we see that the myth of the superman has lost all credibility in contemporary times and cannot be given more fashionable clothes.

Tullio Hermil, who in the book considers himself not an elect spirit but a "rare" one and therefore feels justified in experiencing every unusual sensation, appears in the film as a well-dressed clown. "After a while," he matter-of-factly tells Giuliana, "love goes away and is substituted by esteem and affection. I would suffer if you left me." In almost the same breath he adds, "Teresa is a sensuous woman, she is beautiful, and I desire her."

It is no wonder that the audience, at the first showing of the film in Boston, burst into laughter at this point and again several times

during the projection, specifically at what are moments of real
tragedy in the book. In the novel Tullio is a spoiled member of a
useless class, but he at least has the decency to feel guilty. In the film
he is a vain butterfly glad to collect on his wings the colors of every
flower that he can touch. Visconti could not re–create D'Annunzio's
complex character, whose excessive sensitivity makes him constantly
struggle against his own dissipation. For this reason the ordeal of
Tullio and Giuliana, a veritable tragedy in the novel, appears shallow
and ridiculous through much of the film.

The English subtitles do not help. When melodrama is written and
read rather than spoken, its pomposity, not absorbed by voice inflections that are capable of toning it down, is too overt and graphic. The
cleavage between two societies, the one described by *The Innocent*
and the contemporary, to whom the film is presented, remains open,
notwithstanding Visconti's effort to connect D'Annunzio to a contemporary sensitivity.

Probably for this reason, some reviews of *The Innocent* in the
United States have addressed the acting rather than the cinematic
value of the film. It is, in fact, much easier to inform the viewers
about Giancarlo Giannini's performance in a new role, quite different
from the ones played by the actor under the direction of Lina
Wertmuller, and to praise Laura Antonelli's beautiful nudity, rather
than to try to make some sense out of a perplexing work. Other
reviews concentrate on the color of *The Innocent*, indulging in technical descriptions of its chromatic composition but constantly avoiding the relation between D'Annunzio and Visconti, which is the crux
of *The Innocent*.

The departures that Visconti took from the text of D'Annunzio,
moreover, involve not only the personality of the protagonist but also
several episodes, some minor, some important.

In the film, Federico, Tullio's brother, is an elegant officer who
enjoys the company of women and friends during vivacious evenings
enhanced by good wine, food, and carefree, trivial conversation.
Federico is also indirectly responsible for Giuliana's affair because he
is the one who introduces Arborio to his sister–in–law. Probably for
this reason, and especially because Federico reminds him of Arborio,
Tullio gets carried away during fencing practice and seems on the
verge of killing his brother. Sometimes a veiled hostility lingers
between Tullio and Federico, who both appear to be mostly dedicated to a hedonistic enjoyment of life.

Federico is a completely different character in the novel. By his brother's definition he is an exemplary man, good, strong, and clever. His life is dedicated to work with his farmers, who cultivate the family's property. Under his direction, full of love for the fertility of the earth, the land has a pastoral beauty and serenity in direct contrast with Tullio's tormented and disorderly life. "Leo Tolstoi, kissing him on his beautiful and serene forehead, would have called him son," says Tullio, referring to his brother to whom he would have gladly given the right of the first born.

One episode particularly emphasizes the difference between the nature of the two brothers. Tullio absentmindedly breaks some branches from an apple tree in bloom, and Federico silently observes the incident with a shadow of sorrow in his eyes. Unable to reattach the branch already dying in the trembling of the small flowers, Tullio tries to soften the damage by saying that the branch is for Giuliana. The incident is symbolic of Tullio's behavior toward Giuliana, a frail beautiful woman whom he breaks with repeated infidelities and whom he starts to love again when it is too late.

In the novel, Federico, in his simplicity, is unaware of the unhappiness of Giuliana and Tullio, and so is Tullio's mother, whom D'Annunzio presents as a veritable saint. In the film Federico is uneasy about the gloomy atmosphere of the house, and the mother senses the hostility of Tullio toward the child Raimondo without being able to understand why but feeling desperate about it.

Another difference between novel and film concerns the character of Arborio, Giuliana's lover. D'Annunzio presents him indirectly through the hatred that Tullio lavishes on him, and therefore Arborio acquires the negative characteristics of an unscrupulous man who seduces Giuliana not out of love but simply out of selfishness and lust. In Tullio's memory, Arborio is an inadequate fencer with a skinny body as repulsive as the vulgarity of the conversation among the naked men in the locker room. After the affair, Giuliana never mentions his name, and she tells Tullio, during a dramatic confrontation, that she is now suffering terribly because of "one moment of weakness."

Visconti has a different view of Arborio. He presents him as a romantic and intense young man whose young body Tullio seems to fear when he observes it under the steaming shower at the fencing club. Arborio appears to be moved by sincere pity for Giuliana when he meets her during the evening spent with Federico's friends, and his musical voice, accompanied by intense glances, is soothing to Giuliana's sorrow. Tullio's insensitivity and depravity give the involvement between Arborio and Giuliana a significance that cannot be considered a single moment of weakness. Giuliana loves Arborio and consequently she loves her son Raimondo, even if her expression does not change when she learns from a newspaper, purposely placed by Tullio on the breakfast tray, of the premature death of Arborio.

D'Annunzio never mentions any thoughts of abortion in his novel, while in Visconti's film Tullio's insistence and Giuliana's refusal on the grounds that she considers it a crime produce a crucial conflict. In the director's interpretation, Tullio's solution to the problem is another unwarranted modernization of a literary work that resists contemporization.

D'Annunzio has Giuliana and Tullio think of suicide as the only way out. Giuliana reconsiders, thinking of her two little girls (absent in the film) and of the fact that her suicide would reveal the unhappiness of her marriage to Tullio's mother and brother, but she hopes that her frail health will bring her to a natural death. When this does not occur, she sadly and sarcastically comments on the tenacity of her life. Tullio tries to put an end to his life by spurring his horse along the edge of a ravine at the bottom of which the river Assoro, with its tumultuous and somber water, issues a mortiferous call. Tullio stops the mad galloping only because Federico, who is trying to catch up with him, could also die.

Tullio's brooding reflections after this incident provide a prelude for the murder. Tullio sees life as a "far away vision, confused and vaguely monstrous." What Eugenio Montale calls "the pain of living" is seething in Tullio's thoughts, in every aspect of his life. Even the highest manifestations of the spirit and the most noble enterprises appear to him irrevocably contaminated by selfishness, futility, and transitoriness. "How can we live? How can we love?" he asks, having recognized in himself an "ideologist and an analyst of a decadent era." In line with his pessimistic cosmic vision he sees in himself all the impulses of "primitive unrulable natures." His clear self-observation surprises him when he recognizes "spontaneous insurrections of cruel instincts." While on one hand he takes pleasure in "the excessive development" of his intelligence, on the other hand he blames his impossibility to coordinate a normal life of the spirit on the "hypertrophy of some cerebral centers." Decadent pessimism, the inability to set values and rules, and a hypersensitivity bordering on madness show the way to a heinous crime. No such self-tormented reflections upset Visconti's Tullio, whose main preoccupation seems to be the restoration of his wounded male pride, and who, after the crime, talks about it quite matter–of–factly to his lover, Teresa Raffo. Another main discrepancy between novel and film concerns the ending. D'Annunzio's Tullio lives on with the terrible remorse, and at one year's distance from the crime he writes about it in a first–person denunciatory confession, which constitutes the structure of *L'Innocente*. Visconti's Tullio, after an evening with Teresa Raffo, walks calmly toward a window and shoots himself through the heart.

Why did Visconti, who in his own words wanted to return to Gabriele D'Annunzio, change the novel so drastically? Why the modifications in the characters' personalities? Why the abortion? Why the absence of the two daughters?

During the filming of *The Innocent*, Visconti talked about the modifications of the character of Tullio Hermil. "Today nobody tolerates a Nietzschian superman," said Visconti, "and nobody tolerates a man that kills a child. So we present him differently in the film." The director continues by saying that Tullio's self-punishment is just, and he can thus be easily accepted by the public.[7] But Tullio's self-punishment is less than evident. In fact, he shoots himself after having said to Teresa Raffo, "The day I no longer find any pleasure in life, I will end it." End of pleasure, therefore, and not remorse, is the motive of Tullio's suicide. *The Innocent* also fails to achieve any contemporaneity and remains in an ideological limbo, since its themes relegate it to the era in which the book was written without even a remote possibility of modernization.

D'Annunzio should or should not be accepted by what he is and represents, and any regarbing of his dramas in more contemporary clothes is doomed to failure since a normalization of D'Annunzian characters and situations is an impossible task. In fact, we are not dealing with normal people caught in difficult situations; we are confronted rather by the anomalies of a society in which there is a fragmentation of values that are reorganized by some individuals using irrational principles.

Either this characteristic of these period pieces is accepted, so that they are presented in their original form to a contemporary public that should have the ability to understand them for what they are, or D'Annunzio should not be adapted for film.

Viewing *The Innocent* left people familiar with the works of D'Annunzio with the baffling feeling of having seen something terribly anachronistic, like Roman gladiators wearing wristwatches or

medieval knights carrying transistor radios. Those unfamiliar with
D'Annunzio remained unenlightened about the nature of his work.

A Chromatic Symphony

Nothing, however, is totally negative and, if the main purpose of
the film was not achieved, at least the decor of the interiors and the
voluptuousness of the color are positive aspects of *The Innocent,*
aspects that well represent the D'Annunzian world.

The elegance of the society portrayed gives *The Innocent* the
characteristic of a continuous fashion show, with handsome, slim,
and perfectly attired men and sumptuously dressed women swaying
and chatting in their red, flashy pink, and orange gowns. Beautiful
hats crowned with daisies, sparkling shoes with bows and pearls,
mink capes, fur blankets, blue brocades, and purple velvets are the
ornaments of a society in which style of attire and choice of exotic
lamps and fiery purebred horses were extremely important
occupations.

Like a symphony whose main theme is not agreeable, but whose
color is partly redeeming, Visconti's film re-creates, in its decorative
details, the environment so often described by D'Annunzio. The
styles of attire presented in the film recall an article written by
D'Annunzio and published by *Tribuna* in 1884, in which the writer
describes the passing of languid Roman ladies in their carriages on via
del Corso. The article, entitled "The Little Chronicle of the Fur
Coats," indulges in detailed descriptions of ostentatious elegance:
"Oh the beautiful otter cape decorated with blonde beaver! . . . The
most beautiful cape is the one belonging to the Princess of Venosa."
Countess Santafiora owns a "celebrated coat," while Countess
Taverna, whose face has the divine pallor so fashionable at the time,
also wears an otter cape. "Nothing excites the desire of the intimacy
of love more than an otter coat," concludes D'Annunzio.

Careful attention given to furniture, paintings, and clothing has
always been a quality of films directed by Visconti. In *The Innocent*
he continues his personal tradition of cinematic opulence. The elegance of the aristocratic class is depicted in a continuous display of
wealth that has the function of separating the privileged class from
the rest of the people. "Farmers love to see their masters well
dressed," says Tullio to Giuliana, helping her to put on her majestic

fur coat, which she wears at the Christmas midnight Mass while Tullio, who has remained at home with the child, perpetrates his crime. This scene is the only one that reaches a high level of pathos. The innocent child, sleeping in his white cradle adorned with lace, is exposed to the coldness of the winter while the wind blows snow from the open window, and the voices singing in the church carry words to which the crime that is being committed adds a particularly mournful meaning. "Oh my divine child, I see you trembling," the farmers sing in a wailing tone that shocks Giuliana with a sudden presentiment.

The opulence of the interiors finds its counterpart in the lushness of the gardens, especially the one on Villalilla, the "villa of the lilacs." Here, in the shadows of the willows, yellow roses bloom near blue iris, and the climbing convolvulus insinuates its white flowers between the leaves of the trees.

The garden presented by Visconti is faithful to the description given by D'Annunzio, who, to convey the sensuousness of the place, writes pages and pages full of color and sound (he dedicates two pages to the description of the singing of a nightingale). The villa itself, however, is quite different from the one described in the novel. D'Annunzio's description of the villa is one of the most spectacular pages of *L'Innocente*. Under the windowsills, on the gables, along the gutters, and in every indentation of the rustic facade, the swallows have built innumerable nests of clay, clustered together like the cells of a beehive. The uninhabited villa lives with the restless tender life of the storms of swallows shining in the sun and creating a stunning display of vitality.

Visconti's representation of the villa is quite different. We are shown a large white habitation, deserted and clean; in effect, what we see is just another summer home waiting to be occupied again as soon as the servants uncover the furniture. Visconti's representation lacks the secretive aspect of a place taken over by a swarming of nonhuman life, but it is nevertheless effective. The director wisely distributes shadows and light in a rhythmical sequence of brightness and darkness that symbolizes the love game played by Tullio and Giuliana, he falling in love again with the woman he so often betrayed, she discovering, for the first time it seems, some delights of love-making but at the same time hiding the "sin" of her own unfaithfulness. The sudden darkness of an empty room, the blinding brightness of an open window, and the shadows playing on the white walls are very effective symbols of the conflicting feelings of the two lovers.

Unfortunately, in his last film, edited after his death, Luchino Visconti could not enlarge upon the positive qualities, which are too scarce to balance the insolvency of the main themes that are left hanging in the obscurity of unfulfilled intentions and counterproductive interpretations.

13

Epilogue

AFTER VISCONTI FINISHED SHOOTING *The Innocent*, but before its editing, an attack of influenza further threatened the director's frail health. Only a few months before, on the set of his last film, he had said, "I am not afraid to die. I am not afraid at all. It's better to go and see what's on the other side. It's like going to the movies." To the very end, his iconoclastic spirit sustained the life of his intellect in spite of the infirmities that were plaguing his once so vigorous physique. On 17 March 1976, while listening to Brahms, Luchino Visconti peacefully died.

The funeral, attended by innumerable personalities of the artistic and political world, was held in the Church of Sant'Ignazio in Rome. Along with the Catholic ritual inside, a commemoration outside the church was held by communist friends. The dual observance stressed once more the complexity of a man who had, since his youth, professed communist beliefs, but who at the same time said, "I always believed in God. I have been educated as a Catholic. I am not an observing Catholic, but I believe in God. I believe in an entity, in something outside of us or maybe inside us. I believe in a mysterious force, greater than the individual."

Faithful to the end to his right to be himself, even if that meant opening the contrasting sides of his personality to criticism, Visconti appears as a man who, in a pure existential key, created his life, unafraid of the tremors provoked by his fascinating personality. Nobility, communist faith, agnosticism, catholicism, devotion to traditional values, unconventional lifestyle, realism, social involvement, aesthetism, decadence—these are the building blocks of Visconti's life and of an artistic production shaped in total nonconformity.

Notes and References

Preface

1. Guido Aristarco, "Esperienza culturale ed esperienza originale in Luchino Visconti," *"Rocco e i suoi fratelli" di Luchino Visconti* (Bologna: Cappelli Editore, 1978), p. 18.

Chapter One

1. Aurelio di Sovico, "Io Luchino Visconti," *Il Mondo* [found with no date in the archives of *La Stampa* in Turin, Italy], p. 62.
2. Lina Coletti, "Luchino Visconti," *L'Europeo*, 21 November 1974, p. 63.
3. Ibid.
4. Ibid., p. 65.
5. Ibid.
6. Di Sovico, "Io Luchino Visconti," p. 62.
7. Costanzo Costantini, *L'ultimo Visconti* (Milano: Sugar Co Edizioni, 1976), p. 89.
8. Coletti, "Luchino Visconti," p. 66.
9. Ibid., p. 63.
10. Costantini, *L'ultimo Visconti*, p. 39.
11. Lina Coletti, "Luchino Visconti," pp. 65–66.
12. Ibid., p. 66.
13. Jean Slavik, "Rencontre avec Visconti," *Cahiers du Cinéma*, April 1960, p. 38.
14. Ibid., pp. 37–38.
15. Ibid., p. 38.
16. Cesare Pavese, *Lavorare stanca* (Torino: Giulio Einaudi Editore, 1961) p. 122.
17. Ibid., p. 115.
18. Costantini, *L'ultimo Visconti*, p. 40.

Chapter Two

1. Aurelio di Sovico, "Io Luchino Visconti," *Il Mondo* [found with no date in the archives of *La Stampa* in Turin, Italy], p. 64.
2. Ibid.
3. Guido Aristarco, "Esperienza culturale ed esperienza originale in Luchino Visconti," in *"Rocco e i suoi fratelli" di Luchino Visconti* (Bologna: Cappelli Editore, 1978), p. 17.
4. Pierre Leprohn, *The Italian Cinema*, trans. Roger Greaves and Oliver Stallybrass (New York: Praeger, 1972), p. 111.
5. Ibid.
6. Geoffrey Nowell–Smith, *Luchino Visconti* (Garden City, N.Y.: Doubleday, 1968), p. 33.
7. Leprohn, *Italian Cinema*, p. 89.
8. Renzo Renzi, "Mitologia e contemplazione in Visconti, Ford ed Eisenstein," *Bianco e Nero*, 1949, p. 66.
9. Leprohn, *Italian Cinema*, p. 111.
10. Ibid., p. 112.
11. Francesco Rosi, ed., *"La Terra Trema" di Luchino Visconti* (Bologna: Cappelli Editore, 1977), p. 9.
12. Lino Miccichè, "Visconti e le sue ragioni," in *"Morte a Venezia" di Luchino Visconti* (Bologna: Cappelli Editore, 1971), p. 23.
13. Renzi, "Mitologia e contemplazione," p. 66.
14. Rosi, ed., *"La terra trema,"* p. 14.
15. Ibid., p. 17.

Chapter Three

1. Lina Coletti, "Luchino Visconti," *L'Europeo*, 21 November 1974, p. 65.
2. Aurelio di Sovico, "Io, Luchino Visconti," *Il Mondo* [found with no date in the archives of *La Stampa* in Turin, Italy], p. 66.
3. Ibid., p. 67.
4. Coletti, "Luchino Visconti," p. 65.
5. Di Sovico, "Io, Luchino Visconti," p. 65.
6. Ibid.
7. Coletti, "Luchino Visconti," p. 65.

Chapter Four

1. Pierluigi Ronchetti, "Luchino Visconti: La ricerca della 'madre chioccia,'" *Tempo*, 10 January 1975, p. 43.
2. Aurelio di Sovico, "Io, Luchino Visconti," *Il Mondo*, n.d., p. 67.
3. Callegari-Lodato, "Leggere Visconti," Amministrazione Provinciale di Pavia, n.d., p. 67.
4. Camillo Boito, *"Senso, Luchino Visconti,"* (Bologna: Cappelli Editore, 1977), p. 14.

5. Pierre Leprohn, *The Italian Cinema*, (New York: Praeger, 1972), pp. 147–48.
6. Boito, "Senso," p. 25.
7. Callegari-Lodato, "Leggere Visconti," p. 68.
8. Ibid.
9. Mino Guerrini "Luchino Visconti il mostro," *Tempo*, 31 March 1972 [page number illegible].
10. Enrico Roda, "39 domande a Luchino Visconti," *Tempo*, 20 October 1955, p. 6.
11. Ibid.
12. Di Sovico, "Io, Luchino Visconti," p. 68.
13. Leprohn, *The Italian Cinema*, p. 151.
14. Luchino Visconti, *Three Screenplays: White Nights, Rocco and his Brothers, The Job*, trans. Judith Green, (New York: Orion Press, 1970), p. 30.
15. *Great Short Works of Dostoyevsky*, trans. David Magarshack, (New York: Harper & Row, 1968), p. 177.
16. Visconti, *Three Screenplays*, p. 67.
17. Ibid., pp. 67–68.
18. Ibid., pp. 71–72.
19. *Great Short Works*, p. 161.
20. *Three Screenplays*, p. 56.
21. Ibid., p. 50.
22. Ibid., p. 80.
23. Ibid., p. 86.
24. Giovanni Grazzini *"Una carriera d'artigiano," Corriere della Sera* [found in the archives of *La Stampa* in Turin, Italy, with no date and illegible page number].

Chapter Five

1. Aurelio di Sovico, "Io, Luchino Visconti," *Il Mondo* [n.d.], p. 67.
2. Costanzo Costantini, *L'ultimo Visconti* (Milano: Sugar Co. Edizioni, 1976) p. 51.
3. Gaetano Carancini, "Cronaca del film," in *"Rocco e i suoi fratelli" di Luchino Visconti* (Bologna: Cappelli Editore, 1978), p. 209.
4. Ibid.
5. Guido Aristarco, interview with Luchino Visconti, *Cinema Nuovo*, September–October 1960, p. 406.
6. See reviews by G. R. Cavallaro, Paolo Valmarana, and Mario Verdone in *Bianco e Nero*, August–September 1960, p. 14.
7. Jean Slavik, interview with Luchino Visconti, *Cahiers du cinéma*, April 1960, pp. 38, 40.
8. Aristarco, interview with Visconti, p. 401.
9. Interview in *Schermi*, 28 December 1960, pp. 331–35.
10. Aristarco, interview with Visconti, p. 405.

11. Interview in *Schermi*, p. 334.
12. Jean Slavik, interview with Luchino Visconti, *Cahiers du Cinéma*, April 1960, p. 38.
13. Interview in *Schermi*, p. 335.
14. Ibid.
15. Carancini, "Cronaca del film," p. 211.
16. Ibid., p. 209.

Chapter Six

1. Quotation from the opening and closing of *The Leopard*.
2. Antonello Trombadori, "Dialogo con Visconti," in *Il film "Il Gattopardo" e la regia di Luchino Visconti* (Bologna: Cappelli Editore, 1963), p. 23.
3. Ibid., p. 28.
4. Tommaso M. Cimma, "La realizzazione," in *Il film "Il Gattopardo" e la regia di Luchino Visconti* (Bologna: Cappelli Editore, 1963), p. 159.
5. Ibid., p. 169.
6. An American star was expected to help boost the popularity of a dubbed version in the United States, where Lampedusa's novel, kind of a Sicilian *Gone With the Wind*, had been an unusually popular novel.
7. Trombadori, "Dialogo con Visconti," p. 29.

Chapter Seven

1. Franco Cristaldi, "Storia di una conciliazione, in *"Vaghe stelle dell'Orsa" di Luchino Visconti* (Bologna: Cappelli Editore, 1965), p. 39.
2. Luchino Visconti, "Un dramma del non essere," ibid., p. 32.
3. Ibid., p. 34.
4. Ibid., p. 31.
5. Mario Verdone, "Molti autori e 'mezzi' film," *Bianco e Nero*, October–November 1965, p. 1.
6. Rinaldo Ricci, "Giornale di bordo," in *Vaghe stelle dell'Orsa* (Bologna: Cappelli Editore, 1965), p. 127.
7. Franz Kafka, *The Metamorphosis*, trans. Stanley Corngold (New York: Bantam Books, 1972), p. 49.
8. Ibid., p. 52.
9. Visconti, "Un dramma del non essere," p. 32.
10. Stefano Roncoroni, "Dialogo con l'Autore," in *La caduta degli dei* (Bologna: Cappelli Editore, 1969), p. 16.
11. Lino Miccichè, "Visconti e le sue ragioni," in *"Morte a Venezia" di Luchino Visconti* (Bologna: Cappelli Editore, 1971), p. 47.
12. "An explication of *The Stranger*," in *Camus: A Collection of Critical Essays*, ed. Germaine Brée (Englewood Cliffs, N.J.: Prentice-Hall, 1962), p. 111.

13. All quotations are from Albert Camus, *The Stranger*, trans. Stuart Gilbert (New York: VintaBooks, 1954). Page numbers in the text refer to this edition.
14. Miccichè, "Visconti e le sue ragioni," p. 49.
15. Miccichè, "*Morte a Venezia*" *di Luchino Visconti*, p. 42.

Chapter Eight

1. Giovanni Grazzini, "Una carriera d'artigiano," *Corriere della Sera*. [This article was found with no date in the archives of *La Stampa*. The content, however, indicates that it was written between the release of *The Stranger* and *The Damned*.]
2. Stefano Roncoroni, "Dialogo con l'Autore," in "*La caduta degli dei*" *di Luchino Visconti* (Bologna: Cappelli Editore, 1969), p. 18.
3. Mark Shivas, "Visconti's Unbeautiful and Damned," *New York Times*, 9 March 1969.
4. Roncoroni, "Dialogo con l'Autore," p. 24.
5. Ibid.
6. Thomas Mann, *Buddenbrooks*, trans. H.T. Lowe-Porter (New York: Vintage Books, 1961), p. 20.
7. Roncoroni, "Dialogo con l'Autore," p. 14.
8. Ibid., p. 20.
9. Lino Miccichè, "Visconti e le sue ragioni," in "*Morte a Venezia*" *di Luchino Visconti* (Bologna: Cappelli Editore, 1971), p. 55.
10. Roncoroni, "Dialogo con l'Autore," pp. 27, 19.
11. Ibid., p. 34.
12. Ibid.
13. Ibid., p. 28.
14. Ibid.
15. Ibid., p. 18.
16. Peter Cowie, *International Film Guide* (London & New York, 1971), p. 181.
17. Brad Darrach, *Film 70–71* (New York: Simon & Schuster, 1971), p. 187.
18. Ibid., p. 184.
19. Richard Schickel, "Three Italians Obsessed with Decay," *Film 70–71*, p. 190.
20. Roncoroni, "Dialogo con l'Autore," p. 22.
21. Ibid.

Chapter Nine

1. Guido Aristarco, "Ciro e i suoi fratelli." *Cinema Nuovo*, September–October 1960, p. 404.
2. Lino Miccichè, "Un incontro al magnetofono con Luchino Visconti," in "*Morte a Venezia*" *di Luchino Visconti* (Bologna: Cappelli Editore, 1971), p. 111.

3. Mario Gallo, "Un incontro," p. 144.
4. Miccichè, "Un incontro," p. 127.
5. Lietta Tornabuoni, "Visconti tra Mann e Proust," *La Stampa*, 3 March 1970.
6. Ibid.
7. Ibid.
8. Miccichè, "Un incontro," pp. 114–15.
9. Ibid., p. 121.
10. Thomas Mann, *Death in Venice*, trans. H. T. Lowe-Porter (New York: Vintage Books, 1930), p. 12.
11. Ibid., p. 11.
12. Miccichè "Visconti e le sue ragioni," in *"Morte a Venezia" di Luchino Visconti*, p. 75.
13. Thomas Mann, letter to Carl Maria Weber, 4 July 1920, in *Letters*, ed. and trans. Richard and Clara Winston (New York: Knopf, 1937), pp. 103–4.
14. Mann, Letter to Elisabeth Zimmer, 6 September 1915, ibid., p. 76.
15. Mann, *Death in Venice*, p. 52.
16. Miccichè, "Visconti e le sue ragioni," p. 118.
17. Mann, *Death in Venice*, p. 29.
18. Miccichè, "Visconti e le sue ragioni," p. 122.

Chapter Ten

1. Lietta Tornabuoni, "Visconti fra Mann e Proust," *La Stampa*, 3 March 1970.
2. Aurelio di Sovico, "Io Luchino Visconti," *Il Mondo* [n.d.], p. 69.
3. Costanzo Costantini, *L'ultimo Visconti* (Milano: Sugar Co Edizioni, 1976), p. 19.
4. Ibid., p. 20.
5. Ibid., p. 21.
6. Ibid., p. 23.
7. Ibid., p. 27.
8. Ibid., pp. 27–28.
9. Giorgio Ferrara, "Giornale delle riprese," in *"Ludwig" di Luchino Visconti* (Bologna: Cappelli Editore, 1973), pp. 36, 40.
10. Guy de Pourtalès, *Louis II de Bavière ou Hamlet-Roi* (Paris: NRF Librerie Gallimard, 1928), p. 171.
11. Pietro Bianchi, "Trilogia Germanica," in *"Ludwig" di Luchino Visconti*, pp. 25–26.
12. Ibid., pp. 158–59.
13. Ibid., p. 192.
14. Ibid., pp. 192–93.
15. C. P. R., "Ludwig," *Films in Review*, April 1973, p. 242.

Chapter Eleven

1. Lina Coletti, "Luchino Visconti," *L'Europeo*, 21 November 1974, p. 62.
2. Ibid.
3. Costanzo Costantini, *L'ultimo Visconti* (Milano: Sugar Co Edizioni, 1976), p. 64.
4. Ibid., p. 73.
5. Mario Praz, *Conversation Pieces* (London: Methuen & Co., 1971), p. 33.
6. Coletti, "Luchino Visconti," p. 62.
7. Costantini, *L'ultimo Visconti*, p. 73.
8. Coletti, "Luchino Visconti," p. 65.
9. Giorgio Treves, "Un bel giorno d'aprile," in *"Gruppo di famiglia in un interno" di Luchino Visconti* (Bologna: Cappelli Editore, 1975), p. 124.

Chapter Twelve

1. Costanzo Costantini, *L'ultimo Visconti* (Milano: Sugar Co Edizioni, 1976), p. 52.
2. Ibid., p. 83.
3. Ibid., p. 78.
4. Ibid., p. 77.
5. Ibid., p. 78.
6. Giulio Marzot, *Il decadentismo italiano* (Bologna: Cappelli Editore, 1970), p. 9.
7. Costantini, *L'ultimo Visconti*, p. 79.

Selected Bibliography

Primary Sources

Cappelli Editore, of Bologna, Italy, has published almost all of the screen-plays of Visconti's films, often in editions with useful introductions as well as comments by and interviews with the director (all of the following are in Italian).

Bellissima (1978).

La caduta degli dei [The Damned, 1969].

Il Gattopardo [The Leopard, 1963]. Includes a dialogue between Visconti and Antonello Trombadori, in which the director clarifies his intentions.

Gruppo di famiglia in un interno [Conversation Piece, 1975]

Ludwig (1973)

Morte a Venezia [Death in Venice, 1971]. Particularly interesting because of a "book within a book" entitled *Visconti e le sue ragioni* [Visconti and his reasons], by Lino Miccichè, which examines the director's whole career. This edition also contains an interview with Visconti and letters by Thomas Mann referring to his famous novella.

Ossessione (1977)

Rocco e i suoi fratelli [Rocco and His Brothers, 1978]. Contains a long introduction by Guido Aristarco assessing Visconti's cultural and per-sonal experience.

Senso (1977). Contains also Camillo Boito's novel, which inspired the film.

La terra trema (1977). Includes an introduction by director Francesco Rosi, Visconti's assistant at the time of the shooting of the film.

English translations of screenplays:

Three Screenplays. Translated by Judith Green. New York: Orion Press, 1970. Includes *White Nights, Rocco and His Brothers*, and "The Job," from *Boccaccio '70*.

Two Screenplays. Translated by Judith Green. New York: Orion Press, 1970. Contains *La terra trema* and *Senso*.

Literary sources of Visconti's screenplays:

CAMUS, ALBERT. *The Stranger.* Translated by Stuart Gilbert. New York: Vintage Books, 1954.

D'ANNUNZIO, GABRIELE. *L'Innocente.* Milano: Arnoldo Mondadori Editore, 1968.

DOSTOYEVSKY, FYODOR. "White Nights," in *Great Short Works of Dostoyevsky,* translated by David Magarshack. New York: Harper & Row, 1968.

LAMPEDUSA, TOMASI DI. *Il Gattopardo.* Milano: Feltrinelli Editore, 1958. In English: *The Leopard.* Translated by Archibald Colquhoun. New York: Pantheon, 1960.

MANN, THOMAS. *Death in Venice.* Translated by H. T. Lowe-Porter. New York: Vintage Books, 1930.

TESTORI, GIOVANNI, *Il ponte della Ghisolfa.* Milano: Garzanti, 1958.

VERGA, GIOVANNI. *I Malavoglia.* Milano: Arnoldo Mondadori Editore, 1970. In English: *The House by the Medlar-Tree.* Translated by Mary A. Graig. New York: Harper's, 1890.

Secondary Sources

Books about Visconti:

BALDELLI, PIO. *Luchino Visconti.* Milano: Mazzotta, 1973.

CONSTANTINI, COSTANZO. *L'ultimo Visconti.* Milano: Sugar Co. Edizioni, 1976. This book discusses the last three years of Visconti's life and contains transcripts of the author's interviews with the director between 1973 and 1976. Obviously limited from a chronological point of view, it is helpful because of the interesting insights it provides into the director's personality (in Italian).

NOWELL-SMITH, GEOFFREY, *Luchino Visconti.* New York: Viking Press, 1973. Published before the release of *Ludwig,* this book ends with a chapter on *The Stranger, The Damned,* and *Death in Venice.* The earlier films are discussed chronologically, with special emphasis on *Sandra,* here called by its Italian title, *Vaghe Stelle dell'Orsa.*

SERVADIO, GAIA. *Luchino Visconti.* Milano: Mondadori, 1980. Most recent biography. Informative and anecdotical.

STIRLING, MONICA. *A Screen of Time.* New York & London: Harcourt, Brace, Jovanovich, 1979. Principally a biography about a friend, this voluminous book, more informative than interpretive, covers the entire life of Visconti.

Other books consulted:

CALDIRON, ORIO. *Il lungo viaggio del cinema italiano.* Venezia: Marsilio Editori, 1965. This book is an anthology of the review *Cinema* from 1936 to 1943. It surveys Italian cinematographical culture under the fascist regime until the appearance of *Ossessione*. It also contains two articles by Luchino Visconti, "I cadaveri al cimitero" [Corpses in the cemetery], in which the young director strongly affirms the need for a change, and "Cinema antropomorfico" [Anthropomorphic cinema], in which Visconti expresses his interest in the cinema as "work of a man alive among men."

GRAZZINI, GIOVANNI. *Gli anni sessanta in cento film.* Bari: Universale Laterza, 1977. As the title indicates, this book surveys one hundred films completed in the sixties, giving a quick but helpful panorama of a very important cinematographical decade.

LEPROHN, PIERRE. *The Italian Cinema.* Translated by Roger Greaves and Oliver Stallybrass. New York: Praeger, 1972. This book is a very orderly and informative survey of Italian cinema from its beginning in 1895 to 1979.

MARZOT, GIULIO. *Il decadentismo italiano.* Bologna: Universale Cappelli, 1970. This is a book of literary criticism examining the period of decadence in Italy and its many facets.

POURTALÈS, GUY DE. *Louis II de Bavière ou Hamlet-Roi.* Paris: Librerie Gallimard, 1928. Very informative on the life and times of Ludwig II.

PRAZ, MARIO. *Conversation Pieces.* London: Methuen & Co., 1971. Interesting collection that supplied Visconti with the inspiration for *Conversation Piece*.

PROCACCI, GIULIANO. *Storia degli italiani.* Vol. 2. Bari: Laterza, 1975. Knowledge of Italian history is particularly important for the understanding of films such as *Senso* and *The Leopard*. Giuliano Procacci's book is a terse but complete survey. Volume 2 covers the time between the period of Illuminism and the economic boom of the 1960s.

Filmography

OSSESSIONE (ICI, 1942)
Executive Producer: Liberto Salaroli
Assistant Directors: Giuseppe de Santis, Antonio Pietrangeli
Screenplay: Luchino Visconti, Mario Alicata, Giuseppe de Santis, Gianni
    Puccini, based without permission on James M. Cain's novel *The Postman
    Always Rings Twice.*
Photography: Aldo Tonti, Domenico Sala
Set Decoration: Gino Franzi
Costumes: Maria de Matteis
Music: Giuseppe Rosati
Editor: Mario Serandrei
Cast: Clara Calamai (Giovanna), Massimo Girotti (Gino), Elio Marcuzzo
    (Spagnolo), Vittorio Duse, Ghia Christiani, Michele Riccardini
Running time: 135 minutes
New York premiere: 2 October 1976, at the New York Film Festival.
16mm. Rental: MacMillan/Audio Brandon

LA TERRA TREMA (Salvo D'Angelo, 1948)
Assistant Directors: Franco Rosi, Franco Zeffirelli
Photography: G. R. Aldo
Music: Luchino Visconti, W. Ferrero
Cast: The people of Aci Trezza
Running Time: 162 minutes
New York premiere: 12 October 1965, at the New Yorker
16mm. Rental: MacMillan/Audio Brandon

BELLISSIMA (Film Bellissima AR.L., 1952)
Assistant Directors: Francesco Rosi, Franco Zeffirelli
Screenplay: Suso Cecchi D'Amico, Francesco Rosi, Luchino Visconti, from a
    story by Cesare Zavattini.

205

Photography: Piero Portalupi
Set decoration: Gianni Polidori
Costumes: Piero Tosi
Music: Franco Mannino, based on themes from Donizetti's "Elisir d'amore"
Cast: Anna Magnani (Maddalena), Walter Chiari (Annovazzi), Gastone Renzelli (Spartaco), Tina Apicella, (Maria), Tecla Scarano, Lola Braccini, Arturo Bragaglia. With the special participation of Alessandro Blasetti as the Director.
New York premiere: 15 May 1953, at the Trans-Lux East (the first commercial showing of a Visconti film in the city).
Not available for sale or rental in the United States.

SIAMO DONNE (released in the United States as **OF LIFE AND LOVE**, Tan Film, Ltd., 1953)
[Visconti contributed the final of four segments to this film. The other parts, based on stories by Luigi Pirandello, were directed by Giorgio Patina, Aldo Fabrizi and M. Soedd.]
Script of Visconti's segment from a personal reminiscence by Anna Magnani.
Cast: Anna Magnani, re-creating an early solo vaudeville act.
Running time: 103 minutes (entire film)
New York premiere: 6 October 1958, at the Baronet.
Not available for sale or rental in the United States.

SENSO (Lux, 1954)
Screenplay: Suso Cecchi D'Amico, Luchino Visconti, from a novel by Camillo Boito
Photography: G. R. Aldo, Robert Krasker
Music: Anton Bruckner. Orchestra Sinfonica della Radiotelevisione Italiana, directed by Franco Ferrara
Cast: Alida Valli (Livia Serpieri), Farley Granger (Franz Mahler), Massimo Girotti (Roberto Ussoni), Heinz Moog (Count Serpieri), Rina Morelli, Sergio Fantoni, Tino Bianchi, Christian Marquand.
Running Time: 125 minutes
New York premiere: 8 July 1968, at the Bleecker St. repertoire theater.
16mm. Rental: MacMillan/Audio Brandon

LE NOTTE BIANCHI (Franco Cristaldi, 1957)
Screenplay: Suso Cecchi D'Amico, Luchino Visconti, from the short story "White Nights," by Fyodor Dostoevsky.
Photography: Giuseppe Rotunno
Music: Nino Rota
Costumes: Piero Tosi
Choreography: Dick Sanders

Cast: Maria Schell (Natalia), Marcello Mastroianni (Mario), Jean Marais (the Lodger), Clara Calamai (the Prostitute)
Running time: 105 minutes
New York premiere: 28 May 1961, at the Carnegie Hall Cinema
Not for sale or rent in the United States.

ROCCO E I SUOI FRATELLI (Titanus Films, Rome, and Les Films Marceau, Paris, 1960)
Producer: Goffredo Lombardo
Assistant Directors: Rinaldo Ricci, Jerry Macc, Lucio Orlandini
Screenplay: Luchino Visconti, Vasco Pratolini, Suso Cecchi D'Amico, Pasquale Festa Campanile, Massimo Franciosa, Enrico Medioli
Photography: Giuseppe Rotunno
Setting: Mario Garbuglia
Costumes: Piero Tosi
Music: Nino Rota
Cast: Alain Delon (Rocco), Renato Salvatori (Simone), Annie Girardot (Nadia), Katina Paxinou (Rosaria), Spiros Focas (Vincenzo), Max Cartier (Ciro), Claudia Cardinale (Ginetta), Corrado Pani (Ivo), Paolo Stoppa (manager)
Running time: originally 175 minutes; American commercial release cut to 149 minutes.
New York premiere: 26 June 1961, at the Beekman
16mm. Rental: MacMillan/Audio Brandon (175 minute version)

BOCCACCIO 70 (Carlo Ponti, 1962)
[Visconti contributed the final of three segments, "The Job," to this film. The other parts were "The Temptation of Dr. Antonio," directed by Federico Fellini and starring Anita Ekberg, and "The Raffle," directed by Vittorio di Sica and starring Sophia Loren.]
Script of "The Job": Suso Cecchi D'Amico, Luchino Visconti
Cast of "The Job": Romy Schneider (Pupe), Thomas Milian (The Count)
Running time: 165 minutes (entire film)
New York premiere: 26 June 1962 at Cinema I and Cinema II.
16mm. Rental: MacMillan/Audio Brandon

IL GATTOPARDO (Titanus Films; American distribution by Twentieth Century-Fox, 1963)
Assistant Directors: Rinaldo Ricci, Albino Cocco
Screenplay: Suso Cecchi D'Amico, Enrico Medioli, Pasquale Festa Campanile, Massimo Franciosa, Luchino Visconti, from the novel of the same title by Giuseppe Tomasi di Lampedusa.
Photography: Giuseppe Rotunno

Set decoration: Giorgio Pes, Laudomia Hercolani
Costumes: Piero Tosi
Setting: Mario Garbuglia
Music: Nino Rota
Cast: Burt Lancaster (Fabrizio Salina), Claudia Cardinale (Angelica Sedara),
Alain Delon (Tancredi Falconeri), Paolo Stoppa (Don Calogero Sedara),
Rina Morelli (Maria Stella), Romolo Valli (Padre Pirrone), Mario Girotti,
Lucilla Morlacchi, Pierre Clementi, Giuliano Gemma.
Running time: 163 minutes
New York premiere: 15 July 1963, at the Plaza.
16mm. Rental: Films, Inc.

VAGHE STELLE DELL'ORSA (released in the United States as SANDRA,
Vides, 1965)
Assistant Directors: Rinaldo Ricci, Albino Cocco
Screenplay: Suso Cecchi D'Amico, Enrico Medioli, Luchino Visconti
Photography: Armando Nannuzzi
Set Decoration: Laudomia Hercolani
Costumes: Bice Brichetto
Setting: Mario Garbuglia
Music: From Cesar Franck, *Preludio, Corale e Fuga*, performed by Augusto
D'Ottavi
Cast: Claudia Cardinale (Sandra), Jean Sorel (Gianni), Michael Craig (An-
drew), Renzo Ricci, Fred Williams, Amalia Troiani, Marie Bell, Vittorio
Manfrino, Renato Moretti
Running time: 100 minutes
Premiere: 2 September 1965, at the Venice Film Festival.
New York premiere: 16 January 1966, at the Fine Arts.
16mm. Rental: Swank Films, St. Louis

LE STREGHE (Dino De Laurentiis, 1967)
["La strega bruciata viva" is the first episode of a composite film that has
apparently never been distributed in the United States. Visconti disowned
the work because De Laurentiis cut it without the director's consent.]

LO STRANIERO (Dino De Laurentiis, American distribution by Paramount, 1967)
Screenplay: Suso Cecchi D'Amico, Georges Conchon, Emmanuel Roble,
from Albert Camus's novel of the same title.
Photography: Giuseppe Rotunno

Cast: Marcello Mastroianni (Meursault), Anna Karina (Marie), Bernard Blier (Lawyer), Georges Wilson (Magistrate), Georges Genet
Running time: 104 minutes
New York premiere: 18 December 1967, at the Paris
16mm. Rental: Films, Inc.

LA CADUTA DEGLI DEI, also known as **GÖTTERDÄMMERUNG** (Warner Brothers, 1967)
Executive Producer: Pietro Notarianni
Producers: Alfredo Levy, Ever Haggiag
Screenplay: Nicola Badalucco, Enrico Medioli, Luchino Visconti
Photography: Armando Nannuzzi, Pasquale De Sanctis
Setting: Pasquale Romano
Costumes: Piero Tosi
Music: Maurice Jarre
Cast: Dirk Bogarde (Friederich Bruckmann), Ingrid Thulin (Sophie), Helmut Berger (Martin), Helmut Griem (Aschenbach), Umberto Orsini (Herbert), Renaud Verley (Günther), Albrecht Schoenhals (Joachim), Nora Ricci, Valentina Ricci, Florinda Bolkan
Running time: 155 minutes
New York premiere: 18 December 1969, at the Festival Theater
16mm. Rental: Warner Brothers Non-Theatrical Division, Hollywood

MORTE A VENEZIA (Warner Brothers, 1971)
Executive Producer: Mario Gallo
Associate Executive Producer: Robert Gordon Edwards
Assistant Director: Albino Cocco
Screenplay: Luchino Visconti, Nicola Badalucco, from the novella of the same title by Thomas Mann
Photography: Pasquale de Santis
Setting: Ferdiando Scarfiotti
Costumes: Piero Tosi
Music: From Gustav Mahler, Third and Fifth Symphonies, performed by the Orchestra Stabile dell'Accademia Nazionale di Santa Cecilia, directed by Franco Mannino.
Cast: Dirk Bogarde (Gustav von Aschenbach), Marisa Berenson (Aschenbach's wife), Björn Andresen (Tadzio), Silvana Mangano (Tadzio's mother), Romolo Valli (hotel manager), Mark Burns (Alfried), Leslie French (travel agent), Sergio Garfagnoli, Carole André, Franco Fabrizi, Luigi Battaglia.
Running time: 130 minutes
New York premiere: 17 June 1971, at the Little Carnegie
16mm. Rental: Warner Brothers Non-Theatrical Division, Hollywood

LUDWIG (MGM, 1973)
Producer: Ugo Santalucia
Executive Producer: Robert Gordon Edwards
Production Director: Lucio Trentini
Assistant Directors: Albino Cocco, Giorgio Ferrara, Fanny Wessling,
Luchino Gastel, Louise Vincent
Screenplay: Luchino Visconti, Enrico Medioli, Suso Cecchi D'Amico
Photography: Armando Nannuzzi
Setting: Mario Chiari, Mario Scisci
Set decoration: Enzo Eusepi, Corrado Ricercato, Gianfranco de Dominicis
Costumes: Piero Tosi, Gabriella Pescucci, Maria Fanetti
Music: Robert Schumann, Richard Wagner, Jacques Offenbach, performed
by the Orchestra Stabile dell'Accademia Nazionale di Santa Cecilia, di-
rected by Franco Mannino
Cast: Helmut Berger (Ludwig), Trevor Howard (Richard Wagner), Silvana
Mangano (Cosima von Bulow), Romy Schneider (Elizabeth), Gert Frobe
(Father Hoffman), Helmut Griem (Durckeim), Isabella Telezynska
(Queen), Umberto Orsini (Count von Holnstein), John Moulder Brown
(Otto), Sonia Petrova (Sophie), Folker Bohnet (Joseph Kainz), Marc Porel
(Richard Hornig)
Running time: 136 minutes
New York premiere: 8 March 1973, at the 59th. St. East.
16mm. Rental: Films, Inc.

GRUPPO DI FAMIGLIA IN UN INTERNO (Rusconi Films, Rome, and
Gaumont International, Paris, 1974)
Producer: Giovanni Bertolucci
Production Director: Lucio Trentini
Assistant Director: Albino Cocco
Screenplay: Enrico Medioli, Suso Cecchi D'Amico, Luchino Visconti
Photography: Pasqualino de Santis
Setting: Mario Garbuglia
Set decoration: Dario Simoni
Costumes: Vera Marzot
Music: Franco Mannino
Editor: Ruggero Mastroianni
Cast: Burt Lancaster (The Professor), Helmut Berger (Konrad), Silvana
Mangano (Bianca Brumonti), Claudia Marsani (Lietta), Stefano Patrizi
(Stefano), Romolo Valli, Elvira Cortese, Philippe Hersent
Running time: 122 minutes
New York premiere: 26 September 1975, at the New York Film Festival
Not available for sale or rent in the United States

L'INNOCENTE (Giovanni Bertolucci, 1976)
Screenplay: Suso Cecchi D'Amico, Enrico Medioli, Luchino Visconti, from
the novel of the same title by Gabriele D'Annunzio.
Photography: Pasqualino de Santis
Costumes: Piero Toki
Art Director: Mario Garbugia
Editor: Ruggiero Mastroianni
Music: Franco Mannino
Cast: Giancarlo Giannini (Tullio Hermil), Laura Antonelli (Giuliana), Jen-
nifer O'Neil (Teresa Raffo), Rina Morelli (Tullio's mother), Marc Porel
(Filippo Arborio), Didier Haudepin (Federico Hermil)
Running time: 115 minutes
New York premiere: 11 January 1979, at the United Artists Gemini II

Index

212